TELEVISION AND SOCIAL CONTROL

Television and
Social Control

Mallory Wober and Barrie Gunter

St. Martin's Press   New York

Scholarly and Reference Division
St. Martin's Press Inc
175 Fifth Avenue
New York
NY 10010
USA

Printed in Great Britain
First published in the United States of America in 1988

Library of Congress Cataloging-in-Publication Data

Wober, J.M. (J. Mallory)
   Television and social control/by Mallory
   Wober and Barrie Gunter.
   Bibliography: p.
   Includes index.
   1. Television broadcasting—Social aspects.
2. Television—Psychological aspects. I. Gunter,
Barrie. II. Title.
PN1992.6.W64   1988
302.2'345—dc19   87–18763

ISBN 0–312–01305–1

Contents

Preface

The seed of this book was sown in 1976, the year the International Association for Mass Communication Research held its biennial conference in Leicester. One of the sessions consisted of a seminar convened for those who were interested in cross-cultural research, by Professor George Gerbner of Philadelphia. Having spent some years as a psychologist in Africa and having only recently turned to research in the field of broadcasting, the first author was keen to combine the two concerns, and attended the seminar with great interest.

Professor Gerbner outlined the work he and his followers had been doing and asked for collaborators to come forward who would form a co-ordinated group of researchers. Three matters were discussed: first, the colleagues would analyse the contents of their television services following the lines laid down in the American work; secondly, surveys would explore the extent to which the matrix of television's contents had imprinted itself upon the minds and perhaps also thereby the behaviour patterns of the viewing publics; thirdly, it would be up to local researchers to raise their own funds, or somehow to organise their projects themselves.

Working within a fully defined job specification which left little room for major projects apparently answering questions raised elsewhere, it seemed more necessary and practical if anything was to be done along these lines, to start in a small way, to proceed by a process of adaptation and see where this led. This response was a clear example of the approach which many cross-cultural psychologists, especially those working in nations and societies very different from the ones in which research initiatives often arise, regard as practical. Even in two technically advanced and wealthy nations, the contexts in which social research can and does operate can be very different. This did not, however, preclude making a start.

Although the comparisons might begin, as in America, with content analyses, there were both practical and ideological restraints on this approach. Content analysis requires machinery and time; it also requires a set of definitions which can either be imported from an external source and which might not be valid or useful in a new context, or which would start afresh and produce results which were not comparable with the original examples, detail for detail. The practical as well as the conceptual problems linked with content analysis therefore prompted the first author to make a start in complementing Gerbner's work in a fresh way. As an example, while American television at that time consisted of three approximately equally significant networks, so that the contents on each could be given equal weights, the same was not the case in Britain. Here, there were two major channels and a small one; the functions of the minority channel (in terms of hours of broadcasting and average audience size) were almost certainly different in several ways from those of the two major channels. Should one weight the contents of the channel according to audience share? This had not been done in the American work, and the difference in procedures would make the results not comparable.

On the other hand, the survey aspect of the Annenberg work lent itself well to rapid redeployment in a new context. Many surveys were being done for the IBA and it would not be too complicated to carry some questions which could fulfil two functions. One purpose would be to inform the IBA, which has a responsibility under its Act of Parliament to establish the opinions of the public about the programmes (including advertisements) broadcast on independent Television; the second purpose would be to examine the validity of Professor Gerbner's theory in a new context.

Developed in America, the theory started with the finding that heavy viewers and light viewers tend to have different attitudes towards and perceptions of very many matters. The theory supposed that television's influence had brought about such differences. The reasoning was refreshing in that it worked in a different way from what was becoming commonplace and dully repetitive in so much other research.

For ten years or more, hundreds of studies had worked in a 'forward' direction of inference: seeing violence led (some) people to act violently. This new theory worked in a 'backward' and therefore new and more interesting way: seeing violence led (other) people to feel afraid. Unlike in Sweden there was violent drama on British television in action-adventure series and in films; people who saw more television were likely to see more violence, and without at this stage pursuing the finer pinpointing of what constituted violence for the individual viewer, the first thing to do was to look for a link between heavy viewing and greater fear of social danger amongst viewers.

Soon enough the survey questions were placed and the analyses made; the seemingly disappointing result was that the kind of pattern that Gerbner had described had failed to emerge. Some care had been taken in framing the questions so that we might avoid a 'yea-saying' effect (itself discovered in America) in which a phenomenon might be identified simply because some people tend to agree or over-estimate anything they are asked about; while others have a belittling tendency. Half the questions, therefore, were about security from burglary and attack, while the other half were about danger. The results were reported (Wober and Dannheisser, 1977) to a British Psychological Society conference, and were soon followed by reports in a similar vein from other researchers.

The situation was next reported in an American journal, asking whether, in fact, Gerbner's findings were as valid and the explanatory theory as convincing as had been claimed, after all. For the next two years some acrimonious debate went on in American journals, with academics re-analysing Gerbner's results and disputing his claims. All this was not about whether the British findings were valid in Britain, but about whether the American claim about a major, though previously unsuspected, direction of television's supposed effects was valid in America.

This was the nature of the controversy up to the point when, in early 1982, another conference took place, this time in Vienna. It was attended by Professor Gerbner, and by a number of European and American researchers all concerned with the topic of 'cultural indicators'. Under this heading several content analysts contributed studies of what might be defining the 'push' in cultural movement and development while others provided evidence of what might be called 'flow' in terms of attitude and other norms measured amongst their publics. As the book had been born in Leicester under the seminal influence of Professor Gerbner, we can now say that it had its confirmation in Vienna, this time in his priestly presence.

The first author had come to his session ready to take issue with the professor's case. Television was a new religion, Gerbner said. Being godless, he was challenged, it was not. Television taught the people their place on earth, he said, using his American data. Referring to our British results (now extended with the aid and initiative of the second author) and with other work newly met from Holland and Sweden in mind, his claims were doubted. But the skill and presentational force of the professor's case were enjoyable. Perhaps, like many effective religions, his message rested less on a scientifically provable truth than on the treatment of significant events as symbols in a system of belief that lay beyond the mundane details of evidence which trouble and concern unbelievers. Suddenly, a change of mind was put to the assembled company and the professor. There would no longer be a contest of the universal validity of his theories; it would be for us to secure and broaden the British evidence that had begun to emerge. For his part it remained for him to convince his compatriots more securely of his ideas.

The strategy of this truce was to underline the relevance of the possible reasons for the difference between the Annenberg claims of cultivation effects (mostly of an unpleasant kind) as a result of television, and the relative European 'failure' to report the same pattern of results. Staring us in the face was the difference between the means and intensity of controls exercised over television in America and in Europe. In America there is a largely market-regulated system in which, as Gerbner tells us, television comes to control society. On the other hand, in Europe, where there seem to be fewer or no such observable effects as in America, there are effective institutions through which society controls television.

This is what this book is about. The very broad question it explores is whether society can and does control television – by making it relatively scarce, by regulating the range and scheduling of its contents through various bureaucratic devices. In so doing, perhaps, any potentially harmful effects of television upon society may be nullified or replaced by benefits. On the other hand, society may relinquish, or never establish, such control over television; in which case, in spite of the methodological criticisms of his adversaries, Gerbner's claims may yet prove valid, not only in the United States, but in any other country which dismantles its machinery of social control and lets market forces take over instead.

Mallory Wober
Barrie Gunter

I   The first thesis of 'cultivation effects'

The theme of violence and its potentially harmful effects on viewers has dominated researchers' and society's assessment of television. Until fairly recent times, a 'hypodermic' model of the screen's impact has prevailed in much of the literature on the effects of television. Particular 'doses' of imagery have been thought to produce particular effects on behaviour: if children watch too much violence on television it will make them aggressive. For many years research has focused on the question of whether watching a certain amount or a certain type of television produces certain effects. Experiments have concentrated on observing and measuring behaviour in viewers after they have seen a single programme or isolated scenes from a programme.

Such laboratory experiments have implied a positive causal relationship between watching violent portrayals on television and levels of aggressiveness in individual viewers (Liebert and Baron, 1972) and more generally in society (Lefkowitz et al., 1972; Drabman and Thomas, 1974). Further evidence from field experiments has indicated that, at home too, a heavy diet of television violence may increase aggressive tendencies in adolescents and children (Leyens, et al., 1975; Parke et al., 1977).

The validity of the assumption that the major impact of televised violence is to instigate aggressiveness was challenged early on by some researchers (e.g. Feshbach, 1961; Feshbach and Singer, 1971). They explored the notion that viewing violence might have the cathartic effect of draining off violent impulses, but this theory did not become well established. Others tried to launch the idea that television can have pro-social imitational effects (Noble, 1975; Sprafkin, Liebert and Poulos, 1975; Baran, Chase and Cartwright, 1979; Sprafkin and Rubinstein, 1979), but this, too, has so far failed to win great support.

In America, major empirical investigations, such as those carried out under the auspices of the Surgeon General's Scientific Advisory Committee on Television and Social Behaviour (1972) focused concern on violent television portrayals and their contribution to aggression. During the first two decades of television's heavy infiltration into the nation's consciousness (1950–70), these investigations emphasised the ever-increasing portrayals of violence in a variety of programmes. Research suggested that, at least in some young viewers, such experiences would provoke anti-social behaviour, either through imitation or inhibition of internalised, socially-learned restraints on aggression.

During the years following the Surgeon General's report further projects sponsored by the major television networks in the United States produced conflicting evidence about the effects of television violence (Milgram and Shotland, 1974; Belson, 1978; Milavsky *et al.*, 1982). Belson's retrospective study of British teenage boys reported that viewing certain kinds of screened violence did contribute to aggressive behaviour. Longitudinal research by Milavsky *et al.* in America declared no effects, or at most a marginal link between viewing violence and enacting it. Milgram and Shotland's laboratory work failed to show imitational theft, although it was in a situation where some at least of the subjects may have seen through the experimenters' supposedly disguised plans. The paradigm of imitational effects left most researchers exhausted and ready to explore new approaches.

In the mid-1970s a new theory was raised to galvanise the energies of researchers as well as the concerns of policy-makers. George Gerbner with his colleagues at the Annenberg School of Communications, University of Pennsylvania, produced a new model for the analysis of television's impact on its audience. They argued that the earlier experimental perspective failed to give adequate representation to the complexity of the world of television drama with its integrated system of characters, events, actions and relationships, whose impact on the audience could not be measured with regard to any one programme or single scene from a programme viewed in isolation (Gerbner and Gross, 1976). In an important departure from traditional research perspectives, these writers argued that television is a powerful cultural force of considerable depth and penetration; it is an arm of the established social industrial order that serves to maintain, stabilise and reinforce, rather than to change, threaten or weaken conventional systems of beliefs, values and behaviours. The main effect of television is one of *enculturation*; that is, it cultivates stability and acceptance of the status quo. Television, they argued, does not minimise change in isolation, but does so in concert with other major cultural institutions. However, its pervasiveness in contemporary society, its ability to reach both illiterate and literate audiences, and its unique blend of auditory and visual impact, give television credibility and potency no other medium of communication can match.

According to Gerbner, television has effectively taken the place of tribal elders, of religion, and even of formal education in its role of myth-telling. Common rituals and mythologies are crucial for a society because they function as 'agencies of symbolic socialisation and control' and as such, 'demonstrate how society works by dramatizing its norms and values' (Gerbner and Gross, 1976, p. 173).

Another way in which this approach departs from other analytical frameworks is the emphasis it places on the victims rather than the protagonists of violence. In the complex world of television drama, lessons may be taught not only about how to behave violently (as claimed by the earlier wave of imitation theorists), but also about which social groups are most likely to suffer at the hands of an attacker. Recurring patterns of victimisation constitute symbolic demonstrations of the power structure of the television world; these patterns may be learned by viewers and affect their impressions about the real world. The effects of continually experiencing a symbolic world largely ruled by violence, where certain groups of individuals are considerably under-represented and harshly treated, are conceived by Gerbner to be much more far-reaching than mere tuition in occasional violent behaviour.

Gerbner reasoned that if the most consistent effect of viewing televised violence was to incite real acts of violence, elaborate empirical investigations would not be needed to illuminate the social repercussions – the public would probably be only too aware (perhaps from personal experience) of frequent overt displays of aggression (Gerbner *et al.*, 1979). Imitative aggression among children may occur fairly often but at a low level, while widely publicised cases of serious violence which seem to be influenced by portrayals on television or televised feature films are actually quite rare. In order to define and measure the impact of television on public consciousness and belief in a meaningful fashion, Gerbner and his colleagues (1979) argued that it was necessary to examine the 'total phenomenon of television' (p. 179) rather than isolated segments of it. In the service of this aim, they devised an analytical framework they called Cultural Indicators. This model begins with the premise that information is learned from dramatic television material and is incorporated into the individual's conceptions of social reality. Through analysis of relationships between individuals' reported television viewing habits, particularly the amount of time they spend watching, and their perceptions of their social and cultural environment, it is possible to reveal television's contribution to the attitudes, beliefs and values people hold with respect to the world in which they live.

Conceptually, the cultural indicators project involves two broad assumptions about the nature of television content, the audience, and the functional relations between them. First, television's images, regardless of whether these are offered as fact, fiction or even 'faction', are assumed to cultivate stereotyped notions about the social environment. Through its use of violence, for example, the major function of television is to teach the audience about the characteristics and station of different types of people and about the distribution of power in society: 'Television is the mainstream of [the] cultural process. It is an agency of the established order and as such serves primarily to maintain, stabilize and reinforce – not subvert – conventional values, beliefs, and behaviours...' (Gerbner *et al.*, 1979, p. 180).

A second assumption concerns the non-selective or ritualised nature of television viewing for the mass of the public. According to Gerbner *et al.*, (1979), 'television audiences (unlike those for other media) view largely non-selectively and by the clock rather than by the program. Television viewing is a ritual, almost like a religion, except that it is attended to more regularly' (p. 180). Consequently, the more time individuals spend watching television, the more they are assumed to be affected in their socio-cultural beliefs by its dramatic content. For people who spend large amounts of time viewing, television predominates over all other sources of information about the world. This phenomenon is embodied in the notion of the *heavy viewer*, defined for convenience as one who views for over four hours a day, thus 'living' in the world of television (Gerbner and Gross, 1976). In general, heavy viewers have been found to give different answers, compared with lighter viewers, to informational or opinion questions, biased in terms of the way people and events are portrayed on television. This has been interpreted as a function of the greater amount of television they watch.

Methodologically, the cultural indicators project consists of empirical analysis at two levels, designed to investigate first, the message structure of the symbolic world of television drama, and secondly, the impact it may have on the way individuals perceive the world around them.

Cultural indicators research begins with an assessment of the content of television drama. A coding technique called *message system analysis* has been developed by the Annenberg group to monitor the world of television drama in order to identify the symbolic messages conveyed by television portrayals. Such analysis has indicated significant and in some cases massive discrepancies between the proportions of people and events shown on television and their actual occurrence in real life. For example, women, ethnic minorities and older people tend to be under-represented in television drama programming relative to their respective proportions in the real world and yet at the same time are greatly over-represented as the victims of violent acts in television stories. Other social groups, such as law-enforcers, criminals and various professional or business institutions (e.g. doctors, lawyers, reporters, etc.) tend to be over-represented and glamourised.

Television's fictional world also emphasises certain personal attributes of individuals. Thus, women tend to be shown as young and attractive, and preoccupied by personal, romantic and family activities but are much less often caught up in professional occupational problems. Men, on the other hand, predominate in the professional sector, and also show more competence and assertiveness generally than do women. Observations of the portrayal of old people indicate that ageing is generally not depicted as an attractive process; the elderly are usually shown as highly dependent, and physically and intellectually inept. Examination of patterns of victimisation (i.e. being on the receiving end of a violent physical attack) indicate generalised tendencies for women and old people to be victims proportionately a great deal more often than young males (Gerbner *et al.*, 1977; 1978; 1979). (The characteristics of televised portrayals of women and the elderly will be examined in more detail in Chapters 4 and 5, respectively.)

Through its stereotyped portrayals of various groups and institutions, television presents a dramatic world with a clearly definable power structure in which the strong and the just dominate, whilst the weak and the strong but corrupt are suppressed or eliminated. An important question following on from this first stage of analysis is, to what extent are television's images assimilated by viewers into their conceptions of social reality?

The Gerbner group started by hypothesising that habitual viewing of television drama programming with its recurring themes of victimisation among various character-types will eventually impart information to a largely unwitting and heterogeneous public, cultivating a common system of knowledge concerning the power structure of society. Nothing was hypothesised about prior or alternative sources of learning that might make viewers absorb, filter or resist the message constructs of television drama. Certainly, television is a highly informative medium, not only in its news and current affairs programmes, and its documentary films, but also in its drama content, which provides a continuous stream of 'facts' or impressions about people, places and events with which viewers may not otherwise come into contact.

Evidence has been quoted to suggest that some people are taken in, even by programmes whose characters and settings are clearly fictional. Thus Gross and Jeffries-Fox (1978) noted that during the first five years of his appearance in the popular series, *Marcus Welby M.D.*, actor Robert Young received over a quarter of a million letters from viewers, mostly asking for medical advice. Did viewers assume that Robert Young, the actor, must have picked up a certain amount of medical knowledge whilst working on the series? Did they assume that the series probably employed a team of medical consultants who would be able to answer their queries? Or did they actually believe that the character Marcus Welby was a real doctor? Whilst anecdotes such as the above do not constitute empirically acceptable proof of television's influence, they do serve to illustrate an important point. Even the more sophisticated members of the public have many gaps in their knowledge about people, events or institutions in the real world which are not filled by direct experience, but about which something may be learned incidentally through watching fictional television portrayals. As Gross and Jeffries-Fox write:

> Most viewers have never been in an operating room, a criminal courtroom, a police station or a jail, a corporate boardroom, or movie studio. Much of what they 'know' about these diverse spheres of activity, about how these various kinds of people live and what they do in much of their 'real' world – has been learned from fictional worlds. (p. 248)

To investigate the consequences of viewing television drama's ongoing and pervasive system of cultural messages, Gerbner and his associates developed a second stage of assessment, of audience reactions, called *cultivation analysis*. Essentially, this technique set out to provide a quantitative measure of 'television biases' in public attitudes and opinions among people who watch a great deal of television – that is, the researchers wanted to find out whether viewers' social conceptions bore a closer relationship to the world of television drama than to the real world or some other perspective. Controlling for demographic factors, i.e. sex, age and educational level, responses of light viewers (i.e. people who watched television on average less than two hours a day) were compared to those of heavy viewers (i.e. people who watched television on average more than four hours a day). The differences in the percentages of heavy over light viewers giving 'television answers' provided the *cultivation differential*, indicating the extent to which misconceptions about social reality were attributed by the researchers to the influence of television. It was generally reported by Gerbner and his colleagues that, even when taking into account the effects of demographic factors, heavy viewing, both among adults and adolescents, is associated with a television-biased view of the world (Gerbner *et al.*, 1977; 1978; 1979).

Processes of cultivation

Psychologically, the consequences of viewing large amounts of television are assumed to occur at more than one level, and act through a number of social-psychological mechanisms. Several stages of influence can be distinguished.

1. Viewers see a 'television world' depicted in fictional drama programming that differs considerably in terms of the content of events (e.g. prevalence of crime and violence) and of roles (e.g. proportion of law enforcers, criminals, women, old people, ethnic minorities) from the real world.

2. Viewers experience a 'reality shift'; that is, they are influenced in their images of the real world by the content of what they see on television. This shift is more prominent among heavy viewers than among light viewers. Thus, as noted above, heavy viewers tend to endorse different beliefs about the world in which they live from individuals who experience a relatively light diet of television.

3. The imagery presented in drama programming is absorbed incidentally by viewers, and not only reflects their beliefs about equivalent aspects of the real world, but also produces *feelings* to correspond with these beliefs. For instance, heavier viewers not only overestimate the number of violent incidents in society, but also express a greater fear of being victims of crime and violence and greater interpersonal mistrust and alienation. Broader-based value systems may also be influenced in turn. Fear of crime may, for example, lead to calls for stricter law enforcement and harsher penalties for those who break the law. In relation to sex roles, frequent depiction of women in family settings may not simply influence perceptions that most women actually want to have families, but also that this is all that women *should* want out of life.

In the remaining sections of this chapter, we shall examine in turn each of these stages through which television's cultivation effects are hypothesised to act.

Profiles of television drama

The first premise of the cultivation hypothesis is that viewers see a television world that differs considerably from the one in which they live, both in terms of events and happenings, and in the roles of the people who populate it. A fundamental assumption here is that the influence of television programming can be traced back to the content of the portrayals it contains. To explore the profiles of television drama the cultural indicators team used a technique called *message system analysis* which functioned to identify those aspects of drama's content that may shape not simply the public's perceptions of the fictional TV world, but also, through generalisation, their conceptions of similar aspects of social reality.

From the time of its initial application in 1967, message system analysis has involved the annual monitoring of samples of prime-time, weekend and daytime television output on all three major American TV networks. Analysis has been limited to dramatic fictional content, which means that newscasts, documentaries, variety and quiz shows, and sports programmes have not been covered during coding – thus omitting a substantial proportion of popular television material. The purpose of this analysis was to provide a systematic, cumulative and reliable catalogue of events and roles occurring in programmes. Much of the coding has been concerned principally with the quantification of violence on television. For the purposes of monitoring television violence, a violent portrayal has been defined as 'the overt expression of physical force with or without a weapon, against self or other, compelling action against one's will or pain of being hurt or killed, or actually hurting or killing' (Gerbner and Gross, 1976, p. 176).

With this definition to guide them, trained coders are employed to catalogue such features as the frequency and nature of violent acts, the perpetrators and victims of violence, and the temporal and spatial settings in which the acts occur. Some of these coded features are combined to produce a Violence Profile, which purportedly represents an objective, quantitative and meaningful indicator of the amount of violence occurring in television drama programming.

The violence profile itself consists of two sets of indicators: the Violence Index and the Risk Ratios. The violence index is a direct measure of the amount of violence in television programmes, expressed in terms of the number of incidents occurring on average per programme or per hour. The risk ratios signify a character's chances of involvement in violence in the world of television drama, and, once involved, the likelihood that he or she is on the receiving end.

Since monitoring began in the late 1960s, message system analysis has revealed a particularly violent world of television drama in the United States in which an average of 80 per cent of all prime-time entertainment drama programmes analysed were found to contain some violence, and in which 60 per cent of major characters were involved in violence. During this time, the average rate of violent episodes over all programmes was $7\frac{1}{2}$ per hour and in weekend and daytime television fare aimed specifically at children, violent episodes averaged almost 18 per hour. Comparison of violence frequencies across programme types indicated that cartoons and feature films generally contained much more violence than made-for-television series or serials. Among television series, action-adventure or crime-detective shows and other programmes with a serious theme generally contained more violent incidents than situation comedies.

Gerbner believed, however, that merely counting the frequency of violent acts is not by itself very illuminating. The recital of violent themes in oral fiction or portrayal of violence on television serves a specific function and that is a demonstration of the power of certain individuals or groups to inflict violence and the tendency of others to fall victim to it. The effects of fable as an instrument of socialisation have been noted in many cultures. In western settings, the repetition of a limited pattern of social scenarios could teach lessons about the power structure of the world of television drama and for some viewers this lesson may be generalised to the real world. The risk ratios component of the violence profile was designed to provide a measure of this symbolic demonstration of power relationships in television drama.

Like the violence index, the risk ratios are a composite of more than one measure: the Violent-Victim Ratio, which denotes a character's chances of being an aggressor or perpetrator of violence or a victim; and the Killer-Killed Ratio which marks the risk of killing or being killed. Both ratios are calculated within each dramatic and demographic category for a broad spectrum of character types (see next paragraph). For those characters involved in violence, each of the ratios is derived by dividing the more numerous of the two crucial roles (i.e. violent or victim; killer or killed) by the less numerous over all characters or within specific character-types. A ratio preceded by a plus sign indicates that a particular character-type tends to appear more often as an aggressor than as a victim, while a minus sign shows that that type features more often as a victim than as a perpetrator of violence in the world of television drama.

In a series of reports, Gerbner and his colleagues (1977; 1978; 1979) have provided data to show that television drama demonstrates a pattern of unequal relative risks among characters of different age, sex and social class and ethnic groups, in which certain dramatic character types are victimised consistently more often than others. For example, Gerbner *et al.* (1979) reported that in general there were more victims than aggressors in American prime-time television between 1969 (when the violent–victim ratio was introduced) and 1978. The overall ratio was -1.20, meaning that for every aggressor on television entertainment drama programming there were 1.20 victims. Within demographic groups, men (-1.18) were less likely than women (-1.34) to be victimised. Risks of victimisation were high among children and adolescents (-1.60), unmarried women (-1.44) and especially high for elderly women (-3.33). Also, non-whites (-1.33) were generally more likely to be victimised than whites (-1.19). 'Good' characters (-1.29) were more likely than 'bad' characters (1.00) to be victimised, although the former ($+2.93$) were less likely than the latter ($+1.84$) to be killed. However, this killer–killed relationship was largely due to the fact that 'good' male characters ($+3.85$) who are frequently featured as heroic figures in prime-time action adventure shows were much more likely to be killers than to be killed. 'Good' female characters (-1.60), on the other hand, were much more likely to be slain than were 'bad' female characters ($+1.67$), even though less often involved in violence.

According to the cultural indicators team, the value of violent–victim ratios among various demographic sub-groups in fiction relates to the cultivation of concepts about chances of real personal involvement in violence. As they write in the Violence Profile No. 9:

> We may watch all kinds of characters to assess the general risk of involvement, but when we apply that generalized risk personally, we may be especially receptive to seeing how characters *like ourselves* (male or female, young or old, black or white, etc.) fare in the world of television. Regardless of how often they do get involved in violence, if they are usually hurt or killed, the lesson learned may well be one of high risk. (Gerbner *et al.*, 1978, p. 186)

Distorted images of reality

The second premise of the cultivation hypothesis is that television viewers may experience a 'reality shift', being influenced in their images of social reality by the content of what they see on television. In the previous section, we saw that viewers are presented with stereotyped dramatic and demographic characterisations on television drama programming which often differ fundamentally in nature and frequency of occurrence from corresponding aspects of social reality. Thus Gerbner *et al.* (1978) reported that while 30 per cent of *all* characters and over 64 per cent of *major* characters monitored in prime-time programming over a ten-year span were involved in violence as perpetrators, victims or both, United States census figures during this period indicated that in reality only one-third of one per cent of individuals tend to get involved in violence. The Gerbner group argue that viewers learn these content patterns, draw inferences from them and then generalise this information to their perceptions of the real world. Through their technique called cultivation analysis, Gerbner and his colleagues found that people who watch a great deal of television may exhibit a measurable 'television bias' in their perceptions of certain aspects of the real world corresponding to the way these aspects are portrayed in popular television output. Prime examples of this cultivation effect include public perceptions of the occurrence of crime and violence in society, the number of people working in law enforcement, and the chances of personal involvement in violence.

Gerbner *et al.* (1977) compared the answers of heavy and light viewers to questions about the occurrence of criminal violence and law enforcement agencies in society. Two response alternatives were derived; the first from the quantitative programme measures generated by message system analysis in the case of 'television answers', the second from official sources in the case of 'real world answers'. Table 1.1. shows the four questions posed in this study and in each case the 'television answer' is in capitals.

These four questions were presented to two samples of adults and two samples of adolescents and in every case responses indicated a significant tendency for heavy viewers to overestimate the incidence of violence in society by endorsing 'television answers', compared to light viewers. This association between amount of television viewing and perception of violence remained even after the major demographic variables of sex, age, education and, in the case of one sample of adolescents, IQ (Gerbner *et al.*, 1979) had been individually controlled.

As well as overestimating statistical probabilities of the number of people involved in criminally motivated violence, heavy viewers tended to give television-biased estimations on questions concerning the activities of the police. Among one sample of schoolchildren, for example, more heavy viewers than light viewers believed that the police often use force and violence at the scene of a crime and that police officers who shoot at running people generally hit them. Among another young sample, Gerbner and his colleagues found that heavy viewers tended to give higher estimates than light viewers of how many times a day a policeman pulls out his gun.

While the focus so far has been on cultivation effects deriving from portrayals of crime and violence on television, the same principles apply with respect to other television depictions. Thus, as well as influencing perceptions directly related to television violence, such as fear of crime, mistrust of others and alienation, further indications are that television may cultivate outlooks congruent with its own imagery in areas such as ageing, sex-role stereotyping, beliefs about family life, and health-related and political matters.

In one study, for example, Fox and Philliber (1978) dealt with perceptions of affluence, arguing that television over-represents middle- and upper-class characters and their lifestyle. If this is true,

Table 1.1.   Statements used by Gerbner to measure public perceptions of the occurrence of crime and violence in society

---

1.   *During any given week, what are your chances of being involved in some kind of violence? ABOUT ONE IN TEN About one in 100?*
     (Real world estimates obtained by Gerbner *et al.* from official police statistical records indicated 0.41 violent crimes per 100 people, while cultural indicators data for the world of television drama showed, at the time of this analysis, that over 64 per cent of fictional characters became involved in some form of violence.)

2.   *What per cent of all males who have jobs, work in law enforcement and crime detection? One per cent? FIVE PER CENT*
     (United States Census figures available at this time indicated that one per cent of the actual population were employed in these areas, while cultural indicators' research had shown that 12 per cent of all male characters of prime-time television between 1969 and 1976 were involved in law enforcement.

3.   *What per cent of all crimes are violent crimes like murders, rape, robbery and aggravated assault? Fifteen per cent TWENTY-FIVE PER CENT?*
     (According to Gerbner *et al.* official statistical sources had indicated a figure of 10 per cent, while television statistics derived from content analysis showed that 77 per cent of all major characters who committed crimes (as criminals) also used violence.)

4.   *Does most fatal violence occur between STRANGERS or between relatives or acquaintances?*
     (Official statistics for the United States from the National Commission on the Causes and Prevention of Violence indicated that 16 per cent of homicides occurred between strangers and 64 per cent occurred between relatives or friends. Television data collected by Gerbner for 1967–76 prime-time television drama on all leading networks indicated that 58 per cent of homicides were committed by strangers.)

Note 'Television answer' given in capitals.
Source: Gerbner *et al.* (1977).

and there is a television cultivation effect, heavy viewers should construct a social reality that overestimates the extent of affluence in American society. The affluence measure used by Fox and

Philliber was an average of answers given to seven questions, such as 'How many Americans out of 100 have homes that cost more than $40,000?' Their measure of television use was 'on the average, how many evenings a week do you watch TV at least one hour'. Their results showed a small but significant relationship between television viewing and perceptions of affluence. This relationship was reduced, however, when controls were applied separately for income, education or occupation of respondents, and was eliminated altogether by all three controlled at the same time. This highlights a major difficulty in interpreting message system analysis.

A major problem with this kind of analysis is that it assumes that the messages defined by the analysis are the same as those absorbed by the audience. The 'television answers' are presumed to represent meanings assimilated from programmes by viewers. The cultivation effects researchers use no direct assessment procedure to measure the kinds of 'messages' viewers *themselves* (rather than trained coders) perceive in programmes. Nor is there any consideration of the extent to which viewers' perceptions of certain social groups or social phenomena as depicted on television actually *differ* from their perceptions of these same entities as they exist in the real world.

With regard to television violence, for example, recent work by Gunter (1985b) has indicated that viewers are able to make complex, multidimensional judgements about violent television portrayals and assign different subjective weights of intensity or seriousness to portrayals which would be treated by the Gerbner model of content analysis as equally violent. Thus in objective terms if ten Americans or ten British die in each of two thrillers, both are said to be equally violent; but subjectively, British viewers consider the latter more violent than the former. Within the context of sex-role perceptions, recent British research has also shown that viewers make fine distinctions between the characteristics of women and men as they appear on television and as they appear or are in real life (Gunter, 1985a).

From perceptions to feelings

A third premise of the thesis of cultivation effects is that the imagery apparently learned from television's fictional world and subsequently incorporated into the individual's conceptions of social reality also affects the way that a person feels about such realities. In addition to obtaining responses to the questions referred to earlier about crime and violence, Gerbner and his colleagues examined data from large samples of adults and adolescents on their hopes and fears with respect to the way things are or are likely to be.

Misconceptions about the *occurrence* of violence in society might also give rise to a heightened sense of *fear* of violent crime in the world and the personal danger it holds. Gerbner reasoned that if perceptions of violence are associated with hours of television viewing, fear of violence might also be more prevalent among heavy viewers. To test this, Gerbner *et al.* (1978) related television viewing data to fears of walking alone at night either in the city or in the local neighbourhood for several adult and adolescent samples. A greater proportion of schoolchildren than adults expressed this fear, and there was a tendency throughout all samples for more heavy than light viewers to be afraid of walking alone at night. Thus, people who watch a lot of television were not simply more likely to overestimate the amount of danger that exists in the world than were less frequent viewers, but tended also to show greater fear of their environment. Gerbner and his colleagues were careful to control for several possibly confounding factors such as sex, age and educational level of television viewers but some writers have suggested that these may not be the only or the most crucial 'third variables' whose influence should be taken into account.

Doob and MacDonald (1979), for example, examined the possibility that fear of the environment may be due to the actual incidence of crime in a person's neighbourhood rather than to the frequency of watching television. In a survey conducted with people who lived in high- and low-crime areas of Toronto, they found the amount of television watched did not relate to the amount of fear a person felt about being a victim of crime, when controls for local neighbourhood crime rates were employed.

Doob and MacDonald obtained opinions on a large variety of questions to do with viewers' fears of specific situations. These items varied in their degree of relatedness to television viewing. Specific fears such as of walking alone at night for fear of being the victim of a violent crime, believing that the chances were high that a close friend would be the victim of burglary in the next year, or believing that an unaccompanied woman is likely to be attacked in a subway station late at night were only weakly related to total amount of television viewing when the effects of local crime rates were statistically controlled. But responses to more general (i.e. less personal) questions, such as 'Do you think that it is useful for people to keep firearms in their homes to protect themselves?', 'Should women carry a weapon such as a knife to protect themselves against sexual assault?' and estimation of the proportion of assaults or murders committed by or directed against minority groups, tended to be more powerfully related to reported television viewing behaviour, even in the presence of controls for levels of neighbourhood crime.

It is possible, then, that matters of a less personalised nature are affected by television portrayals more than are items concerning a person's own level of fear.

Another hypothesis is that television viewing is not an antecedent of fear of environmental changes at all, but is a consequence of it. People who are more afraid may stay indoors and watch more television (Zillman and Wakshlag, 1984), possibly sometimes to learn how to cope with crime (Mendelsohn, 1983), or simply to ease their fears (e.g. Boyanowsky, 1977). This selective-viewing hypothesis is pertinent not only in the context of fear of crime but also in connection with other areas of social perception. In subsequent chapters we shall discuss this hypothesis in greater detail and present evidence indicating that, although television may reinforce certain beliefs about the world, viewing behaviour may itself be influenced by existing constellations of attitudes and beliefs which viewers bring with them to the viewing situation.

The tendency of heavy viewers of television drama to perceive a lot of violence in the real world can give rise to the assumption that heavy viewers are more likely to have exaggerated feelings of mistrust, suspicion and anxiety. In a secondary analysis of national social survey data, three items from Rosenberg's (1957) 'faith in people' scale were related to data on the television viewing behaviour of the same national sample (Gerbner *et al.*, 1978). Gerbner called this assumed mistrust the 'mean world' syndrome and found that heavy and light viewers differed substantially in their beliefs that people 'would try to take advantage of you if they got a chance', that 'most people cannot be trusted' and that people 'mostly are just looking out for themselves'. Responses to these questions were significantly related to reported hours of television viewing even when other facts such as age, sex, education and income were controlled. However, there were differences between ethnic minorities. Blacks in general did not show this relationship between viewing behaviour and 'mean world' perceptions to the same extent as did whites, although better educated and wealthier blacks did. This result suggested that there may be certain subcultural differences in susceptibility to television's cultural messages. Middle-class blacks with better education and higher incomes may be attitudinally similar to whites in many respects, may live in similar social and physical surroundings, and may be affected by television similarly to whites.

Lower-class (poor) blacks, on the other hand, tend to live more often in run-down neighbourhoods where crime and violence abound, and their fears and feelings of mistrust and hopelessness may stem from more powerful roots than television portrayals. Research has shown that middle-class blacks and working-class blacks differ in their perceptions of television drama and in their beliefs about the reactions of other blacks to television portrayals. Howard, Rothbart and Sloan (1978) found that middle-class blacks tended to believe that the series '*Roots*' – a fictionalised account of the experiences of a black family originally brought to the United States during the era of slavery – would increase racial hatred and bigotry, hostility and anger, especially among lower-class blacks. However, the actual reactions of a sample of lower-class blacks to this television series was contrary to middle-class black expectancies – instead of increasing hostile attitudes, the series tended to encourage more deeply thought-out and humane views of race relations.

From feelings to behaviour
The social perceptions and emotional attitudes engendered by viewing large amounts of television are further assumed to be reflected in the actions or potential or intended actions of individuals some of which can be designated, either socially or psychologically, as unhealthy. One example of this kind of cultivation effect of television viewing given by Gerbner and his colleagues is that of the exaggerated need for self-protection. Individuals who are fearful of personal victimisation may be more likely than are less anxious people to take precautionary measures against criminal attack. If television viewing cultivates personal fearfulness, Gerbner reasoned that it might also influence the tendency to take extra steps towards improving personal security.

> Symbolic violence can ... achieve some of the repressive aims of real violence and do it much more profitably and, of course, entertainingly. Fearful people want-demand protection and will accept, if not virtually welcome, aggression in the name of safety. Our research shows that heavy viewing of television cultivates a sense of risk and danger in real life. Fear invites aggression that provokes still more fear and repression. The pattern of violence on TV may thus bolster a structure of social controls even as it appears to threaten it. (Gerbner *et al.*, 1979, p. 180)

In further secondary analyses of national survey data, they found that heavier viewers of television were more likely than lighter viewers to say they had recently taken various precautionary measures to protect themselves or their households against crime. These measures included keeping a dog, putting new locks on windows or doors, keeping a gun, or avoiding certain areas of their home town or city. All were significantly related to claimed amounts of television viewing, except for staying clear of 'dangerous' areas.

Whilst much of the cultivation analysis research has been concerned with fear or avoidance of aggression as a consequence of television viewing, the vast majority of studies on the influence of television have focused on the stimulation of aggression among viewers, particularly young people. When samples of schoolchildren were asked by the cultural indicators research team, 'How often is it all right to hit someone if you are mad at them? Is it almost always all right, or almost never all right?', the more they said they watched television, the more likely they were to choose the aggressive option.

Television viewing has also been found to be related to public opinion on international political issues. In yet another secondary analysis of national survey data, Gerbner *et al.* (1978) reported that heavy viewers were more likely than light viewers to say that it would be better for the United States to stay out of world affairs – another example, on a wider stage, of fear of attack. Although this effect is usually assumed to arise from fictional drama programming, another crucial source of influence at this time must undoubtedly have been television news coverage of events surrounding United States involvement in the Vietnam War. Opposition to the war was evident in news coverage on television from the early 1970s (Russo, 1971), and newsfilm showing atrocities committed by American soldiers against the civilian population as well as among military personnel in Vietnam shocked many Americans and brought to a peak already growing public opposition to the war. It probably had a major influence on the eventual decision by the administration to withdraw from Vietnam in the mid-1970s. It is perhaps noteworthy that Gerbner has little to say about or draw upon from this allegedly benevolent effect of television.

Reception of the Gerbner hypothesis
Like any others, researchers on the social effects of television have hoped that their findings would be believed, and the implications heeded. The climate of reception has, however, differed for different theories. The idea that television violence leads to imitative violence was the subject of a great deal of research, but positive findings (and there eventually were many) faced very stringent critical scrutiny and challenge, if not outright rejection, by analysts with a variety of viewpoints and motives. Some who realised that violence was a saleable commodity wanted to safeguard the market. 'First Amendment' free speech defenders assailed any research which might be the basis for censorial regulations. Eventually, however, a limited version of the theory can probably be said to be widely accepted – that some violence instigates violent actions among some viewers, on some occasions.

The Gerbner hypothesis was not received as true after a test of critical fire; instead, it was believed and reported in many quarters with considerable ease. A few examples may be quoted to illustrate this point. The London *New Standard* (28 January 1980) reported Gerbner's alleged dictum: 'The more TV you watch the more you acquire a mild paranoia about the world around you ... programmes ... cultivate a sense of insecurity ... TV is the ritual of a new religion ... and it constantly and unerringly feeds the fears of its captive flock.' More soberly, the *New York Times* (30 July 1981) summarised 'ways that TV affects children' and started with 'studies conducted by noted researchers such as Dr George Gerbner and his colleagues ... '. The article lists seven effects that 'have been established', including that 'television viewers often have a distorted view of how much violence there is in the world and thus are more likely to be anxious and insecure.'

In England again, a psychologist (Yaffe, 1979) mentioned in passing in a research assessment with quasi-official status that 'Gerber and Griss [sic] ... examined viewers' identifications with the *victims* of aggression attacks rather than with their aggressors and found a substantial number who fitted into this category'. This item had been taken from an article in the *Guardian* newspaper, noted for its typographical errors; their reproduction in this case had fortuitously shown that Yaffe's use of the material had been made without any direct knowledge or critical appraisal of the original source.

Not all readers, however, have accepted the implications which the Gerbner team attribute to their results. Comstock and others (1978), in a major review, point out that counting the number of physically violent acts may be meaningless without some assessment of their perceived significance. Gerbner and his colleagues believe that there is a definite relationship between the number of violent acts which people may see on television, and their feelings and attitudes. Comstock writes: 'there are many possible explanations for this relationship, and they must be explored before we accept television viewing as the cause of this phenomenon.' Nevertheless, he says the evidence is 'highly suggestive' (p. 69). In this passage and elsewhere, Comstock and his team of co-writers acknowledge that it would be curious if the Gerbner hypothesis were to be accepted on the basis of correlational evidence, when so many other alleged social processes have been doubted on the grounds that correlation does not, and indeed cannot, establish causality. Giving them credence would be odder, because Gerbner and Gross have themselves attacked the style of research which looks for causes and effects by establishing correlation between particular prior and subsequent measures. Nevertheless, Comstock gives cautious support to the Annenberg case, while expressing reservations.

A scholarly review of work on television violence from a legal perspective by Krattenmaker and Powe (1978) examined and found flaws in the Gerbner approach. They noted Gerbner's

> ability to write comprehensive English in popular journals...his is undoubtedly the most popularly known name associated with research into television and violence. But his methodology (until then) rarely received serious exploration and evaluation in scholarly journals... Behaviouralists may have disregarded Gerbner's rather idiosyncratic views but journals and legislators have not.

Krattenmaker and Powe realise that Gerbner has pronounced his conclusions in the manner of a prophet (especially in his claim that television is somehow a form of religion), but since he has supported his case on survey data he has to be judged on his treatment of these. The legal critics conclude that 'Gerbner's theories are best understood as abstract, aesthetic criticism . . . The most one can say is that Gerbner's ultimate conclusions simply are not subject to empirical testing despite his claims to the contrary.'

In the same year an English study was published that had set out to try to confirm the 'paranoigenetic' theory of television violence. This study (Wober, 1978) noted first that Gerbner's hypothesis was not substantiated in the US amongst black viewers, and that the correlations upon which Gerbner's conclusions rested were very small. Neither had they been subject to partialling out mutually related variables, at least in the work reported in papers up to 1977. British survey data failed to find the associations reported in American work which, if the effects being claimed were robust, should have been observable in a similar society. Further, a contemporary British study (Piepe, Crouch and Emerson, 1977), which had not sought overtly to confirm or disconfirm the thesis, did contain questions appropriate for doing so and showed no support for Gerbner's position. Wober surmised that 'what may be true in America is not true in Britain' and that 'the Gerbner thesis has still not been demonstrated convincingly in America, and the effect exists neither there nor in Britain'. With this challenge, the research bottleneck seemed to have been loosened, and several studies severely criticising Gerbner's methods, as well as some spirited replies, soon followed. These will be reviewed in the next chapter.

2 Television viewing and the cultivation of fear and mistrust

In a series of published reports over the past ten years, research data on American samples have been assembled which show that people who watch a great deal of television, especially dramatic, violence-oriented, action-adventure programmes, tend to endorse different beliefs about the world in which they live from individuals who experience a relatively light diet of television (Gerbner and Gross, 1976; Gerbner et al., 1978; 1979). This research particularly noted that heavy television viewers tended to indicate a greater fear of being victims of crime and violence, greater mistrust of authority, and less hope for the future than did light television viewers. Heavy users of television appeared to experience a 'reality shift', their images of the real world being influenced by what they saw portrayed in television drama.

The United States is the biggest exporter of television programming and its productions are prominent in prime-time schedules on television networks the world over. This fact, coupled with concern about the consistent demonstration of disturbed social imagery among heavy television viewers in the United States, has led in recent years to the analysis of cultivation effects among television publics in other countries. Does the influence of television as revealed by a cultural indicators approach have any substance beyond the boundaries of the United States? With the growth of television viewing as a leisure-time pursuit in developing countries, and with the prospect of an increased international flow of television carried by satellite which will tend to make use of inexpensive programming available from the dominant sources in the United States and Great Britain, policymakers in other countries will also be concerned to know what effects wider exposure to television may have on their own publics.

Television and social power structures
In his earliest writings on the topic, Gerbner advanced the premise that televised criminal and violent behaviour conveyed a dramatic cultural lesson concerning the power structures of society. Since violence on television is so pervasive and the numbers of victims

of violence outnumber perpetrators, cumulative, long-term exposure to this content could cultivate a sense of danger and mistrust, and an exaggerated fear of personal victimisation. This theme has been maintained over a decade of research and writing.

> Violence plays a key role in television's portrayal of the social order. It is the simplest and cheapest dramatic means to demonstrate who wins in the game of life and the rules by which the game is played. It tells us who are the aggressors and who are the victims. It demonstrates who has the power and who must acquiesce to that power . . . In the portrayal of violence there is a relationship between the roles of the violent and the victim. Both roles are there to be learned by the viewers. In generating among the many a fear of the power of the few, television violence may achieve its greatest effect. (Gerbner *et al.*, 1980, p. 180)

Annenberg research in the 1970s

During the second half of the 1970s, the Annenberg group published a series of papers in which they reported significant relationships among US samples between television viewing and degrees of personal fearfulness, sense of danger in the world, and mistrust of other people and authorities. Gerbner *et al.*, (1978) examined fear of walking in the city or their own neighbourhood at night among a sample of New Jersey schoolchildren and individuals sampled in the 1976 American National Election study and the 1977 National Opinion Research Centre's (NORC) General Social Survey. Comparing the responses of those individuals who claimed to watch television for four hours or more each day and those who claimed to view for less than two hours, Gerbner and his colleagues found that heavy viewers in all samples were consistently more fearful than were light viewers (see Table 2.1.)

In a subsequent paper, Gerbner *et al.* (1979) reported data on television viewing and personal fearfulness from two samples of adolescents, one from a suburban/rural school in New Jersey and the other from a New York City school. Once again, on relating personal estimates of amount of viewing to a variety of social perceptions, it emerged that heavy viewers were more likely than light viewers to express fear of walking alone in a city at night.

Drawing further upon various regional and national surveys of public opinion in the United States, Gerbner and colleagues reported that heavier viewers of television exhibited a stronger sense of mistrust and suspicion of other people than did lighter viewers (Gerbner and Gross, 1976; Gerbner *et al.* 1977; 1978; 1979). In the NORC's 1975 General Social Survey, for example, respondents were asked the question: 'Can most people be trusted?' Comparing the answers of heavy and light television viewers, Gerbner and Gross (1976)

Table 2.1   *Percentages of American adults and schoolchildren afraid to walk alone at night by level of TV viewing*

	TV Viewing		
	Light %	Medium %	Heavy %
NORC 1977 General Social Survey	43 (766)	44 (311)	49 (448)
CPS 1976 American National Election Study	41 (881)	39 (887)	44 (629)
New Jersey Schoolchildren	72 (141)	76 (339)	81 (161)

Base sizes given in parentheses.
Source: Gerbner *et al.* (1978).

reported that a significantly larger proportion of the former (65 per cent) than of the latter (48 per cent) chose to reply that you 'can't be too careful' in your dealings with others. This reply was designated as the 'television answer'.

Gerbner *et al.* (1977) expanded on the previous year's study and analysed responses to three mistrust items which had appeared in the 1976 NORC General Social Survey. The authors also added the same items to a survey of their own with children. As the findings summarised in Table 2.2 show, once again heavy viewers, both child and adult, were consistently more likely than light viewers to choose an answer which reflected a sense of mistrust and suspicion. These results were reinforced by secondary analyses of national social survey data and by primary analyses of the Annenberg group's own more localised surveys with children and adolescent samples (Gerbner *et al.* 1978; 1979).

British findings
Efforts to replicate Gerbner's findings among British samples in the late 1970s failed. Two studies, conducted by Piepe, Crouch and Emerson (1977) and by Wober (1978), tested relationships between levels of television viewing and personal fearfulness and interpersonal

Table 2.2. Per cent of adults and children giving 'TV answers' to three mistrust questions

	Adults TV Viewing			Children TV Viewing	
Light	Medium	Heavy		Light	Medium
%	%	%		%	%
A 26	31	38		46	71
B 48	61	65		41	76
C 32	37	44		68	75

Source: Gerbner *et al.* (1977).

Key: A Do you think most people *would try to take advantage* of you if they got a chance or would they try to be fair?

B Generally speaking, would you say that most people can be trusted or that *you can't be too careful* in dealing with people?

C Would you say that most of the time people try to be helpful, or that *they are mostly just looking out for themselves?*

'TV answers' are italicised.

mistrust in the same manner as had been done previously by the cultural indicators research team at Philadelphia.

Piepe *et al.* carried out 842 interviews in and around the Portsmouth area and related claimed amounts of television viewing to answers given to two questions: 'These days a person doesn't know whom he can depend on', and 'How often do you think that violent incidents happen around here?' For neither question did any substantial relationship emerge between claims of viewing hours and types of answers given.

The second survey, reported by Wober (1978), was commissioned for the Independent Broadcasting Authority and sampled over 1000 adults over the age of 16 years throughout the United Kingdom. Again, respondents were posed two questions based on original items used by Gerbner and his colleagues, but worded in a slightly different way deemed to be more meaningful to British people. One of these items concerned perceptions of how trustworthy people are and the other queried the perceived likelihood of being a victim of robbery. Together these items were combined to form a 'security scale'. Results indicated no systematic tendency for heavy viewers to have lower feelings of security scores than did light viewers. Several

American writers subsequently challenged Wober's early findings on methodological grounds. Neville (1980) argued that Gerbner's cultural indicators items and the re-worded items from Gerbner forming Wober's 'security scale' measure different attitude dimensions. However, this argument is countered by the results of a third British study which employed both re-worded items and others from Gerbner's scales in their original form and found that all these items loaded together on the same factor-analytic dimension (Wober and Gunter, 1982) which means that they do all belong to the same domain. The latter study will be examined in greater detail a little further on (see p. 30)

Another comment on the early British findings from across the Atlantic, designed to explain away the differences in American and British cultivation effects, was put forward by Hawkins and Pingree (1980). They argued that heavy viewers in Britain, at least based on the evidence of Wober (1978), probably see fewer violence-containing programmes per week than do viewers who watch equivalent amounts of television in the United States. Wober estimated that heavy viewers in Britain at the time of his 1978 study saw on average about $10\frac{1}{2}$ one-hour-long violence-containing programmes a week. Hawkins and Pingree estimate, on the other hand, from data provided in Gerbner's 1978 violence profile for US network prime-time television, that similar viewers in their own country would on average be likely to see more than twice that number of violent programmes each week. In fact, on these estimates, the British *heavy* viewer may see less television violence than many American *light* viewers whose two hours or so of daily viewing may yield approximately 12 hours per week of programmes containing violence.

There are two questionable assumptions in this criticism however which throw doubt on its validity. First, in their cultivation analysis research in the late 1970s, Gerbner *et al.* assumed a linear relationship between amount of viewing and levels of social anxiety and interpersonal mistrust – an assumption which has since been challenged following re-analysis of the same data base (Hirsch, 1980). Many of the survey samples studied by Gerbner were divided up into light, medium and heavy viewers according to different criteria of viewing (see Gerbner *et al.*, 1977; 1978). This is a point which we shall return to in more detail further on in this chapter. Thus, relative differences in levels of viewing of British and American television audiences should not preclude the occurrence of similar patterns of differences in levels of anxiety and mistrust between lighter and heavier viewers in both societies.

Secondly, there is an erroneous comparison on which Hawkins and Pingree's criticism of this early British research was based; this comparison concerns relative levels of violence-viewing among British and American TV audiences. These writers claim that British viewers probably see less TV violence than many American viewers. However, this assumption is based on measures of the relative occurrence of violence obtained by Gerbner's content analyses of prime-time TV programming only, whilst measures of levels of viewing amongst the UK public are based on *all* programmes, both within and outside peak-viewing times. The occurrence of violence in non-prime-time programming may be much less than that observed during prime-time, although Gerbner and his associates have obtained no data on this. Hence, American viewing figures cannot provide accurate indications of how much violent content the average American viewer normally sees over the course of a week's viewing.

Wober's study, however, based its viewing figures not on amounts of TV watching in hours per day estimated by respondents themselves, but on actual programmes watched (obtained from diaries covering one whole week's TV output on all networks) which in turn are classifiable separately as violent or non-violent. Therefore, a much closer match can be expected here between the amount of time respondents spent watching television and the quantity of violent content they were exposed to during this time.

How else then might the discrepancies in British and American findings in the late 1970s be explained? One possible explanation could be that the cultivation effects of television interpreted by Gerbner *et al.* in their secondary analysis of national public opinion survey data are specific to American audiences. If much prime-time programming in the two countries is of a similar range of types, this specificity of effect may be a function of US society itself or perhaps of the way television fits into that society rather than just of the nature of what is shown on television.

Another drawback implied in the American surveys is that most of the questions measuring quantities (of viewing, of risks and dangers) were worded in the same direction, so that people with an underlying tendency to generous markings would differ from those who tend to parsimony on all matters, and produce spuriously significant correlations. This danger was avoided in Wober's (1978) survey which failed to replicate American data for British viewers. Here Wober framed each of his questions in two sections, one a positive format put to half the sample, the other a negative format put to the other half, thus dispelling any possible influence of a positive or negative response set influencing the relations between self-reported amounts of television viewing and estimates of social dangers.

Secondly, cultural indicators studies (e.g. Gerbner and Gross,

1976; Gerbner *et al.* 1977; 1978) have not generally taken into account the *real* levels of violence in different localities which might jointly determine views of the reality of social threat *and* the amount of viewing done if people decided to stay indoors to escape what they perceive as a frightening world outside. For example, in their Canadian study, Doob and Macdonald (1979) reported that while people who watch a lot of television are more likely to indicate fear of their environment, this relationship disappears when the actual incidence of crime in the neighbourhood is taken into account. Their results implied that television viewing and people's fear of being victims of violence or crime may not be directly causally related.

Doob and Macdonald tested beliefs about the incidence of crime and violence in society among adult respondents in Toronto, Canada. They attempted to replicate the previous finding by the cultural indicators group that television causes people to overestimate the amount of danger that exists in their own neighbourhood, while controlling for the actual incidence of crime in the neighbourhood – a factor which was quite reasonably thought to contribute towards the social anxieties of individuals too. The sample consisted of residents from four areas: high-crime city, low-crime city, high-crime suburb and low-crime suburb. All respondents were asked to fill out the same 37-item fixed-alternative questionnaire which included views and beliefs about personal fear of victimisation, the likelihood of victimisation among other social groups, the need to take precautionary measures against crime, and estimates of the incidence of crime in Toronto.

Questionnaire responses were factor analysed givng rise to four factors, the first of which consisted of a nine-item fear-of-crime dimension. This index was related to total amount of TV viewing and amount of viewing of violent progamming. Across the four sampled areas it was found that those who watched most television (or violent television) tended to be those who were the most afraid. However, within areas this relationship was not quite so straightforward. Whilst it held up in the high-crime area of the city, it tended to be much less marked in the other areas.

Further analysis using canonical correlations (a procedure which sets up hypothetical new entities in such a way that groups of measured variables can be shown to relate to each new entity) showed interesting combinations of beliefs among certain kinds of people. Those people who did not see much local neighbourhood crime, who did not believe that it is unsafe for children to play alone in a park, and who were not afraid of personal attack, but were afraid of being burgled, tended to be females living in low-crime city areas.

However, people who were afraid to walk alone at night but who did not feel they would be victims of a violent crime tended to be females living in high-crime city areas. Presumably, their fears reflected their local environment and resulted perhaps in their taking extra precautionary measures to protect themselves from attack such as avoiding certain areas at certain times. The fact that they had taken such measures could, in turn, contribute to the belief that these actions reduced the likelihood of personal victimisation.

Finally, people who believed that unaccompanied female subway passengers and children playing alone in parks were vulnerable to attacks, but who felt safe themselves and believed their neighbourhood to be safe were suburban dwellers who watched a lot of TV violence. Clearly, personal safety here reflects the relative security of their comfortable suburban environment, but fears about attacks on lone females (perhaps something of which they had less direct experience) may reflect images shown on television or by other means.

A USA – Australia comparison of cultivation effects

Pingree and Hawkins (1980) replicated and extended the Gerbner approach to show relationships between television viewing levels and perceptions of the occurrence of violence in society and feelings of interpersonal mistrust ('mean world') among over 1200 schoolchildren in Perth, Australia.

Four violence in society items were the same as those analysed by Gerbner *et al.* (1977), tapping beliefs about chances of involvement in some kind of violence, the percentage of Australian men who have jobs as police officers or detectives, whether most murders are committed by strangers or relatives or acquaintances of the victim, and the percentage of all crimes involving violence, such as murder, rape, robbery and assault. The 'mean world' index consisted of three items: if they got the chance, most people would try to cheat me; you can never be too careful in dealing with people; and mostly, people are just looking out for themselves. Responses of children on all of these aspects of social reality indicated statistically significant biases towards 'the mean world' view among heavy viewers.

The relationship between total amount of viewing and the number of TV-biased responses about the incidence of violence in Australia was very strong. For measures of Australia as a mean world, television viewing was less strongly related, although statistically significant. Even when single and multiple controls for demographics and the perceived reality of TV were employed, relationships between TV viewing and violence in society and mean world remained.

Effects of programme type

Hawkins and Pingree also examined relationships between viewing certain types of programme and social perceptions. They found that perceptions of violence in society related strongly with viewing crime-adventure shows, cartoons and game shows, while mean world perceptions showed relatively weak relationships with all these. Viewing crime-adventure shows was related to both sets of beliefs.

One further interesting finding to emerge was the fact that respondents' perceptions of the way society appears in Australia (as against corresponding perceptions of the United States) related more closely to viewing imported American programmes than to viewing other foreign imports or programmes produced by local television networks.

The examination of the relative contributions to social beliefs of specific-content types adds some strength to Gerbner *et al.*'s argument that television messages are a causal agent in producing the world of television-biased responses observed in heavy viewers. If cultivation effects result from learning specific symbolic messages heavily repeated in programming, then those content types where the messages are clearest and most common should be the best indicators of television bias.

Pingree and Hawkins' results suggest that the effects of television programming on conceptions of social reality may extend beyond the culture in which that content is produced, although it is possible that Australian society is sufficiently similar to American society for TV content from the latter culture to have effects on the former. This, however, should have produced TV-related perceptions of American culture, which did not appear. Thus Pingree and Hawkins' results remain problematic. Whether US-produced TV programming, especially of the popular crime-adventure genre, exerts similar effects on the social conceptions of people in other countries needs to be further investigated. Research in Canada (Tate, 1976; Suedfeld *et al.*, 1985) – another society which has much in common with the United States – has indicated that TV has no independent effects on social conceptions such as those studied by the Gerbner group, when other 'third variables' such as personality characteristics are partialled out. Further studies in Great Britain have indicated that television has at most only weak effects on social beliefs and that these relate to viewing of particular programme types rather than to overall amounts of television seen. Also, controlling for differences in certain personality characteristics of viewers reduced the influence of television to insignificance in these British studies.

Swedish and Dutch studies of cultivation effects

In the Netherlands, following their initial contact with Gerbner in 1974, Dutch researchers were able to establish as comparable a collection of analyses to the American ones as conditions permitted (Bouwman and Stappers, 1984). There are ten Dutch broadcasting organisations (many of them religious foundations) which share space on two channels and Bouwman and Stappers did not expect there to be as much violence on Dutch as on American television; nor was there. As might be expected, the religious organisations were shown to programme less violence than others. But in explaining some of the unexpectedly high levels of simple 'objective violence' found on a few occasions the authors point out that anti-violence ideologies are not catered for in Gerbner's objectivist system of content analysis. Including incidents of violence portrayed in a pacifist programme does not properly represent the messages that might influence the audience in its attitudes to violence in society.

Proceeding from this, Bouwman (1984) reports a survey in which items from the mean world index, as well as others from Hawkins and Pingree, and Doob and MacDonald, were included. The outcome was that when statistical controls for level of education, age, sex and degree of urbanisation applied, only six out of 19 possible relations between TV viewing and the mean world and other items were significant. The published table shows only five such correlations among 19 items; four of these items concerned perceptions of reality (like whether most killing take place between strangers or friends) and only one dealt with feelings (you can never be too careful in dealing with people). Bouwman states 'that cultivation of fear by television drama does not seem to be a real phenomenon in the Netherlands'. In trying to explain what they feel is essentially a null result, Bouwman lists several possible causes including the fact that the role of television is smaller in Holland than in America; it broadcasts fewer hours per day, on fewer channels and comes under a system of social control. This final factor means that, when violence is featured, it is often featured for a deliberately anti-violent purpose, with the result that the meanings acquired by viewers are unlikely to be similar to those in most American programming.

Swedish television shows very little violence, so it is not likely that this should be a significant source of induced fear for viewers. Nevertheless, Hedinsson (1981) reports a study amongst schoolchildren which measured not only their amount of television viewing, but also their involvement as expressed through items such as; 'When I watch a TV programme that I like I sometimes wish I was part of the action.' Answers on these items were related to a number of other social perceptions.

Hedinsson found that the time spent watching TV was only weakly related to some of the social peceptions and was not related at all to the violence index of perceived amount of serious crime. On the other hand, TV involvement *was* related to the violence index, but only in the ninth grade. This relationship was not found in younger children. The strongest relationship was between a retribution index (the size of prescribed penalty for seven different kinds of crime added together) and amount of viewing. This more reasonably suggests that it is people with a stronger sense of punitive justice who seek to watch more television, rather than that television violence (of which there is significantly little) induces fear and suspicion. Another part of the study, dealing with perceptions of numbers of people working in various jobs in Sweden, does indicate that incidental learning from television occurred, and was linked both to the amount and the degree of involvement in viewing.

As in the Dutch case, the Swedish work with the more impressionable material of child subjects does not deny that cultivation or direct learning from televised materials is possible. But there is little or no evidence of learning inappropriate lessons about violence. The general outcome of these studies is not to deny that in the United States viewers may learn about violence and poor relations between groups from television. But these studies do suggest that, in the differing television ecologies of the Netherlands and Sweden, the same effects as those reported in the US do not occur.

Television and personal threat in Britain: Later evidence
Wober and Gunter (1982) explored the possibility that relationships observed by previous authors between amount and type of television viewing and social anxiety, mistrust and alienation might be explained in terms of characteristics which relate to individuals' personalities. The findings of Doob and MacDonald (1979) indicated that fear of environmental crime was related more closely to actual levels of such crime than to television watching. It is also possible that among this Toronto population, high local crime rates encourage individuals to stay indoors and watch more television, as well as making them more fearful.

This introduces another problem of how exactly the television viewing–social anxiety relationship is to be interpreted. The findings of all the major studies are essentially correlational and hence they cannot be used to infer direct causation. Therefore, whilst television viewing may indeed cultivate social fearfulness, it is equally reasonable to explain this relationship in terms of a reverse hypothesis, that it is those individuals who are already more anxious who watch more television.

There is evidence from experimental studies conducted in the mid-1970s which indicates that mood states can affect tendency to watch, and may also influence the specific type of content a person prefers to watch. Boyanowsky, Newtson and Walster (1974) found that threatened individuals under safe conditions exhibited a distinct preference for viewing potentially fear-inducing events. Thus, following a campus murder, a greater proportion of girl students who had shared a dormitory with the victim went to a movie depicting a cold-blooded murder than went to a non-violent romantic film; girls from another dormitory, who were presumably less directly affected by the murder, showed no such preference. In a later experiment, Boyanowsky (1977) replicated and expanded his initial demonstration of this effect.

If transient mood states such as those studied by Boyanowsky can produce short-term film preferences, we argued (Wober and Gunter, 1982) that it is not unlikely nor unreasonable to assume that long-term viewing patterns may be influenced by permanent dispositions of individuals which relate not just to isolated environmental conditions or stimuli but to the prevailing social structure as a whole (see Srole, 1956; Merton, 1957). Rotter (1965) developed an instrument designed to measure an enduring personality characteristic called *locus of control* which was supposedly shaped by the general, and especially the early, social experiences of individuals. The items used by Rotter were not dissimilar to those related to television viewing by Gerbner and his associates. We reasoned therefore that, rather than being a reaction simply to viewing large amounts of television drama as suggested by Gerbner *et al.*, perception of social threat and danger may represent one aspect of a general system of beliefs associated with the underlying social reinforcement history of the individual. If this hypothesis were correct, then it was further reasoned that Rotter's measures of locus of control should correlate significantly with other measures of social anxiety and mistrust.

Whether or not it can be inferred that locus of control rather than television viewing underlies social anxiety depends on the demonstration of independent relationships of Rotter-type items and Gerbner-type items with viewing behaviour. A survey was therefore carried out amongst a sample of British viewers in London in which items (some re-worded) from those used by Gerbner *et al.*, (1978; 1979) and others derived from Rotter (1965) were used to test for variations in the degree of relatedness between amount of television viewing and perceptions of threat to personal security and of general mistrust and alienation.

Questionnaire item responses were factor analysed and yielded four main factors which together accounted for 32 per cent of the common variance. Table 2.3 shows the factor loadings for each questionnaire item on these factors. Factor 1 was qualified by four items, including two Gerbner-type items on fear of victimisation and thus was labelled *fear*. Factor 2 was characterised by five items, including the three items from Rotter's locus of control scale and was termed *fate*. Factor 3 was defined by two items expressing feelings of selfishness or *cynicism*, and factor 4 also consisted of two items which represented feelings of *satisfaction*.

Correlations were computed between these factors and viewing behaviour. These showed that amount of fiction viewing correlated significantly with the *fate* factor only, whilst amount of information viewing correlated significantly with all factors. At the same time, correlations between factors themselves indicated that the Gerbner 'fear' factor and Rotter 'fate' factor were significantly correlated.

Viewing diaries which listed all programmes broadcast on the three major television channels during the week of the survey were used to measure amount of television viewing. Viewing was defined separately for two broad categories of programming – fiction and information. An initial series of correlations yielded a number of significant relationships between demographic variables (age and socio-economic class), and both opinions and television viewing. This left open the possibility that relationships between television viewing and social opinions were a function of third variables and had no independent association. Therefore, a series of partial correlations was computed to find out if the questionnaire factors had any residual relationship with viewing behaviours when the contribution of demographic variables was controlled. Analyses also looked at the effects of partialling out one factor on the strength of association between television viewing and the other factors. The results of these partial correlations are shown in Table 2.4.

While the relationship between the fate (Rotter) factor and viewing behaviour survived the partialling out, one at a time, of the fear (Gerbner) factor, age or class, none of the remaining factors, including fear, survived such partialling out of other related measures. Relationships between class and fiction viewing (but not information viewing), and age and information viewing remained largely intact when controls for additional variables were applied separately.

We concluded that since the Rotter measure related significantly to the Gerbner factor, while only the former was reliably associated with viewing behaviour in the presence of statistical controls for third variables, it could be that any relationships observed between fearfulness and television viewing may be little more than epiphenomena of deeper-seated personal dispositions or more general social

Table 2.3   *Factor loadings for opinion questionnaire items*[a]

Factor Name	Factors			
	1 Fear	2 Fate	3 Cynicism	4 Satisfaction
I am afraid to walk alone in my own neighbourhood at night (14)	0.79	0.15	0.11	−0.02
We live in a frightening world (15)	0.62	0.25	0.26	0.09
I worry about having my home burgled and property damaged (8)	0.42	0.21	0.20	−0.17
Most programmes are unsuitable for children (13)	0.39	0.18	0.33	−0.13
The pace of life is too much for me these days (3)	0.37	0.60	0.18	−0.08
Getting a good job depends mainly on being in the right place at the right time (11)	0.04	0.48	0.09	0.08
I feel that I have little influence over the things that happen to me (9)	0.27	0.46	0.21	−0.23
People's lives are controlled by accidental happenings (6)	0.07	0.45	0.12	0.04
Television news is the most reliable way to find out what is happening in the world (4)	0.14	0.41	−0.05	0.25
People are just out for what they can get these days (8)	0.14	0.07	0.66	−0.11
You've got to be pretty selfish these days (7)	0.14	0.07	0.66	−0.11
I am perfectly satisfied with my present standard of living (5)	0.05	−0.07	−0.01	0.58
Most people want to help you if you are in trouble (1)	0.00	0.09	−0.27	0.50
People are getting used to putting up with violence (2)	0.02	0.14	0.20	0.02
Family life is generally happier these days than it used to be (10)	0.02	−0.03	−0.08	0.13

[a]. Varimax rotated factor matrix.
Note: Questionnaire item number given in parentheses.
Source: Wober and Gunter (1982).

conceptions, such as locus of control, which underlie both amount of viewing and the relatively superficial social perceptions tapped by fear of victimisation items.

Table 2.4   Partial correlations between social attitudes, demographic variables and TV viewing (n = 322)

Partial correlation between	Fear	Fate	Age	Class
Fate–fiction viewing	−0.23**	—	−0.25**	−0.22**
Fate–information viewing	−0.23**	—	−0.16*	−0.26**
Fear–fiction viewing	—	0.01	0.10	−0.08
Fear–information viewing	—	0.05	−0.06	−0.16*
Cynicism–fiction viewing	0.09	0.02	−0.11	−0.10
Cynicism–information viewing	0.10	0.04	−0.12	−0.14**
Satisfaction–fiction viewing	0.06	0.06	−0.11	0.05
Satisfaction–information viewing	−0.12	−0.12	0.06	−0.12
Age–fiction viewing	0.00	0.05	—	0.01
Age–information viewing	0.47**	0.45**	—	0.49**
Class-fiction viewing	0.14	0.10	0.16*	—
Class–information viewing	0.10	0.05	0.07	—

* P<0.01.
** P<0.001.
Source: Wober and Gunter (1982).

As these findings are correlational, they can only be used to argue against the alleged source of distorted social perceptions (that is, excessive television viewing) but not to establish another implied source of causation. This British evidence suggests, however, that whatever is measured by Gerbner's item is less robustly related to viewing behaviour than the factor measured by items derived from Rotter's scale (at least for viewers in Britain). It may not be television which makes viewers wary of the environment; it may be that people who are more fateful in their outlook on life generally stay in more to watch television and they also express cautious attitudes. We shall return to this alternative hypothesis later. But first let us turn to refutations of Gerbner's analyses and conclusions that emerge from American researchers.

American challenges to Gerbner's work
In 1980 two important papers were published, one by Hughes (1980) and the other by Hirsch (1980) which were notable not only for their scientific analysis but also for the vehemence of their attack on the case made by the Philadelphian cultural analysts. Hughes

criticised the Gerbner group's work of the late 1970s on two important counts: first, for having omitted controls for available variables
which might reasonably be expected to produce relationships
between television viewing and social perceptions; and second, for
failing to control for extraneous variables simultaneously instead of
one at a time.

Hughes re-analysed the same data as those used by Gerbner *et
al.* (1978) from the 1975 and 1977 General Social Surveys and included controls for interrelated variables ignored by the Gerbner
group. Amongst the control variables were age, sex, race, income,
education, hours worked (per week), church attendance and size
of home town. Some of these variables were significantly related
to amount of television watched even in the presence of statistical
controls for the others, while some were not. For example, an initially
strong relationship between sex of viewer and television viewing
disappeared when controls were employed for hours worked per
week. This indicated that women watch more television than men,
perhaps because they are likely to work fewer hours outside the
home than men. Further such analyses led Hughes to conclude that
the exclusion by Gerbner *et al.* of race, hours worked and church
attendance from their 1978 analysis may have been quite a serious
one.

On relating five of Gerbner *et al*'s dependent variables with
amount of television watched whilst controlling simultaneously for
a range of demographic factors, Hughes found that only one of
the five relationships claimed by Gerbner *et al.* (1978) still held
up. Fear of walking alone at night was found to reverse the direction
of its relationship with amount of viewing, indicating that those
individuals who watch television heavily are *less* likely to be afraid
of walking alone at night in their neighbourhood.

Hughes discovered a number of items included in the NORC's
General Social Survey not reported by Gerbner *et al.* which provided
response patterns counter to the cultivation hypothesis. With one
such item ('Are there any situations you can imagine in which you
would approve of a man punching an adult male stranger') Hughes
found that, when controlling for sex, age and education, there was
not one instance, overall or within each demographic division, when
'heavy' viewers were more favourable towards physical violence than
'medium' or 'light' viewers. Within many demographic groups, the
proportion of 'heavy' viewers who expressed a distaste for violence
was significantly *higher* than among lighter viewers. In Hughes' own
words, such findings raise 'the possibility that in failing to ensure
cross-sample comparability, introduce multiple controls and report
items where the data do not support the argument for television's

'cultivation' of beliefs and attitudes, the Annenberg group has itself contributed to distorting scientific reality' (1980, p. 18).

Hirsch (1980) challenged the work of the Annenberg group mainly on three counts. First, he argued that Gerbner's categorisation of viewing behaviour is arbitrary and selective; secondly, there are unreported attitude responses on the original data bases which do not support the model Gerbner presents; and thirdly, there are ambiguities in Gerbner's reported data and in the way these data are presented.

Analysing the Annenberg group's violence profiles 9 and 10 (Gerbner *et al.*, 1978; 1979), Hirsch points out that although these reports read as though there is consistency across samples in the way viewers were categorised (i.e. as 'heavy' or 'light' viewers), reanalyses revealed six different definitions of these concepts employed across samples and used interchangeably. In violence profile 10, for example, if a child from their New Jersey school sample reported viewing three hours of television, he or she was coded as a 'light' viewer. An equivalent child from a comparable New York school sample was coded as a 'heavy' viewer. Hirsch argued that it was highly problematical to make the same assumptions about 'heavy' and 'light' viewers from different samples when the fact that each sample is divided at the median of its television hours distribution means that the definitions of 'light' or 'heavy' viewing may be idiosyncratic to that particular sample.

In a comprehensive exercise of re-analysis including re-categorisation of the original NORC sample used by Gerbner and his colleagues, Hirsch included two new categories: non-viewers (zero hours viewing) and extreme viewers (8 + hours). Whilst a principal assertion of the Gerbner group in their late 1970s papers had been that heavier viewers, in response to the lessons they have learnt from television, are likely to have higher scores on items tapping fear of victimisation, anomie and alienation, Hirsch found that on many of these items *non-viewers* had higher scores than light, medium-heavy or extreme viewers. The few people who watch no television at all generally turn out to be more fearful or alienated than television watchers. This finding, according to Hirsch, is clearly counter to the cultivation hypothesis, in which it is the responses of those least exposed to television messages which should be closest to the real world.

Turning next to the other end of the viewing spectrum, Hirsch compared the responses of 'heavy' (4–7 hours viewing daily) and 'extreme' viewers (8 + hours daily) on a series of NORC items also used by Gerbner. Hirsch found that the demographic composition of these heavy viewing divisions were different. Markedly higher proportions of 'extreme' viewers than 'heavy' viewers were women, housewives, retired workers or black, lower-class and less well educated. The 'cultivation' hypothesis proposes that people who watch the most television will provide 'television answers' to survey items more often than those who watch for fewer hours per day. By dividing the Annenberg group's 'heavy viewers' into two sub-groups of heavy and extreme viewers, Hirsch was able to test this hypothesis and also the logic of collapsing both of these types into a single category. Hirsch found that extreme viewers provided 'TV answers' *less often* than heavy viewers on 11 (61 per cent) of the 18 NORC/Gerbner items he re-analysed. Extreme viewers provided 'TV answers' most often on three anomie items ('the lot of the average man', 'bringing children into the world', and 'public officials being different'), on one Gerbner 'mean world' item ('people try to be fair'), and also on a suicide item and an alienation item.

Hirsch further criticised the Annenberg group for ambiguity and contradiction with regard to their position on cultivation analysis as causation. He argued that while they seemed to reject the relevance of 'causal analysis' (the old-fashioned 'hypodermic model' of effects) at the same time they have ignored the common conceptual ground which exists between causal analysis and cultivation analysis as they have defined it. Cultivation analysis has consistently employed the logic of introducing single controls for age, sex and education on the relationship between TV viewing and selected dependent variables. But since relationships of this sort are indeed complex, this is clearly an instance for which multiple controls are needed for reliable tests of hypotheses. Therefore, Hirsch employed multiple controls on the NORC data to examine the Gerbner contention that television viewing exerts a 'separate and independent contribution to conceptions of social reality within most age, sex, educational and other groupings'.

Following Gerbner *et al.*'s (1978) example of combining 'mean world' items into an index, Hirsch clustered these and the multiple questions on anomie, alienation and suicide onto four indexes. Two remaining questions on fear of walking alone within one mile of home and attitude towards physical violence comprised two further indexes. In five of the six indexes, there was no pattern of evidence to show that the average percentage of respondents providing 'TV answers increases automatically with hours viewed. Light viewers yielded 'mean' or 'scary' world responses the least, and both non-viewers and medium viewers generally provided higher percentages for these responses. But, after adjustment for the other variables, the percentage of heavy and extreme viewers giving the 'television answer' followed no pattern at all. There was a general non-linearity in the responses of all categories of television viewing. Where in one case the cultivation differential was linear, it moved in the opposite direction to that proposed by the cultivation hypothesis; that is, heavier viewers exhibited smaller supposed cultivation effects. Only in the case of one of six indexes ('mean world') was the high–low differential in the direction proposed by the cultivation hypothesis.

Some writers have raised objections to Hirsch's analyses and conclusions. Hawkins and Pingree (1982), for example, discuss Hirsch's work in their review chapter for the National Institute of Mental Health's update on research progress in the field of television and behaviour. One point they raised was that non-viewers and extreme viewers may be highly unusual individuals who can probably be distinguished in terms of numerous specific attitudes other than their out-of-the-ordinary television viewing patterns. Consequently, the fact that their beliefs did not exhibit the customary television cultivation influence identified by Gerbner and his colleagues does not preclude the possibility of such an influence occurring among the remaining 90 + per cent of the population falling within the light, medium and heavy viewing categories. However, if one is prepared to invoke peculiar patterns or kinds of beliefs for these extreme categories of viewer, could it not also be the case that variations in beliefs (albeit milder ones) exist also across the central three categories, which might influence social perceptions and probably also amount of television viewing?

Hawkins and Pingree offered another challenge to the criticisms of Hughes (1980) and Hirsch (1980). They suggest that Hirsch's procedure for controlling third variables may still leave open the possibility for a relationship between television viewing and social reality that is indepenent of such interrelated demographic variables. Even if a positive correlation between viewing and belief is reduced to zero because of education's relation to one or the other, sub-groups identified by their levels of education can still differ in the associations they exhibit between viewing and beliefs. Indeed Gerbner *et al.* (1980), in response to Hirsch and Hughes, reported that different kinds of relationship between television viewing and social beliefs exist within different demographic sub-groups that run counter to one another. They thus cancel each other out when the demographic variable in question is statistically partialled out, and consequently severely weakens television cultivation effects in the population as a whole. (More will be said on this later in the chapter).

Hawkins and Pingree also questioned the rationale for applying the cultivation hypothesis to education and suicide items, which is what Hirsch did. But if one is prepared to dismiss the relevance of these dependent variables because they are subjective, then logically one should also be dismissive of the alienation, 'mean world' and fear of victimisation items analysed by Gerbner *et al.* which also relate to subjective feelings.

More recently, Zillman and Wakshlag (1984) made the important point that perceptions and emotional states are distinct psychological entities and need not necessarily be linked. Thus, one could be aware of high levels of crime in society without necessarily also being highly fearful of becoming a victim of crime itself. The supposed cultivation of a *fear* of crime as a consequence of heavy television viewing is based on an assumption that because the world of television contains numerous criminal and violent incidents, the individual will *perceive* this feature of television and generalise from it to the real world. This, in turn, is presumed to lead to a personal apprehension about crime.

Several steps are required to prove empirically that this set of relationships exists. First, do individuals perceive television to be violent? Secondly, do viewers generalise television percepts to the real world? Thirdly, do individuals who perceive the real world as violent also have greater fear of crime? Gerbner and his colleagues provide no evidence on these questions, but nevertheless presume that one kind of response concerning fear of crime is the 'television answer'. Even if perception and feelings about the same entities do not necessarily run in parallel, it is difficult to see how one can be inferred meaningfully from the other unless an empirical demonstration is provided that such a relationship actually exists.

Mainstreaming and resonance

The Annenberg group have argued that cultivation analysis has demonstrated *amount* of television viewing to be an important indicator of the strength of its contribution to ways of thinking and acting. For heavy viewers, television is the dominant source of information about the world, over-riding all other sources. The main implications of this analysis are derived from an underlying assumption that heavy viewers will be more likely than light viewers to give 'TV answers' to questions concerning their opinions about social objects or events. However, substantially different patterns of association between viewing and social beliefs can emerge for different social groups. As we have seen already, Doob and MacDonald (1979) and Hughes (1980) found, for example, that when controlling for demographic or environmental factors which the cultural indicators team had previously not taken into consideration, such as local crime levels, number of hours worked per week and size of town of residence, relationships between viewing behaviour and social beliefs were considerably weakened. Furthermore, Hughes showed that when controls for these and other demographics previously included by Gerbner and his colleagues, such as age, sex, socio-economic class, race and education were implemented simultaneously, no overall cultivation effects emerged. In reply, Gerbner *et al.*, (1980a) argued that no *overall relationship* does not mean *no relationship at all.*

More detailed analyses of data from a more recent survey gave rise to the introduction of two new labels to apply to the differences in cultivation effects between social groups: (1) *mainstreaming,* which indicates a diminution in cultural differences among heavy viewers; and (2) *resonance,* which refers to special cases in which television's depictions of reality are congruent with a typical segment of the general population's actual or perceived reality, which purportedly leads to a marked enhancement in cultivation effects (Gerbner *et al.,* 1980b).

To elaborate, more educated or higher-income groups, for instance, have the most diversified patterns of social and cultural opportunities and activities, and they also tend, as a whole, to be relatively light viewers. Consequently, they are less likely to endorse television-biased answers to opinion items. But there are some heavy viewers *within* the higher education/high-income groups who respond differently. Their responses are more like those of other heavy viewers, most of whom have less education and income. According to the mainstreaming hypothesis, it is the college-educated, high-income, *light* viewers who diverge from the mainstream, i.e. the relative 'commonality of outlook' that television tends to cultivate; heavy viewers across all social strata tend to share a relatively homogeneous outlook.

However, television's influence on public beliefs about social reality does not only consist of the cultivation of a generalised commonality of world views, it also functions to enhance the salience of specific issues, objects or events. This effect is called *resonance.* In Gerbner *et al.*'s own words, 'When what people see on television is most congruent with everyday reality (or even *perceived* reality), the combination may result in a coherent and powerful 'double dose' of the television message and significantly boost cultivation' (1980b, p. 15). In other words, where patterns of events depicted on television are consonant with patterns of similar events in reality, the two message systems 'resonate' so as to amplify their salience to an observer. In response to criticism of their earlier analysis and interpretations by Hughes (1980), Gerbner *et al.* (1980b) re-analysed some of their data to illustrate the two phenomena of mainstreaming and resonance.

Mainstreaming

The phenomenon of mainstreaming was examined in relation to

the cultivation of fear of victimisation, interpersonal mistrust and anomie. Using a question concerning one's chances of being involved in violence in any given week, once again heavy viewers were found to be significantly more likely to give the television-biased answers. But there were also important differences between certain social groups. A large majority (80 per cent) of both light and heavy viewers with low incomes gave the higher-risk response, and showed no evidence of a relationship between viewing behaviour and response to this item. Examination of middle- and upper-income groups, however, revealed that the proportion of light viewers giving the 'television answer' was much lower. Light viewers with middle- and upper-bracket incomes were considerably less likely to express a high expectation of encountering violence, while heavy viewers with middle- or high-incomes exhibited almost the same level of perceived risk as the low-income group (Gerbner *et al.*, 1980b).

In another analysis, three items were combined by these writers to form a 'mean world' index which measured the degree to which respondents agreed that people are just looking out for themselves, that you can't be too careful in dealing with people, and that most people would take advantage of you if they got the chance. Table 2.5 shows the results of this re-analysis, indicating the overall relationship between viewing behaviour and 'mean world' perceptions, and in the light of the single and multiple controls for other demographic factors.

Overall, television viewing was found to be significantly associated with the tendency to express mistrust. What is more interesting, however, is the relationship between television viewing and interpersonal mistrust for specific groups of the population. The relationship was strongest for respondents who had had some college education, even though these individuals were in general less likely to express interpersonal mistrust than non-college-educated people. The most striking contrasts emerged from the comparison between whites and non-whites. As a group, non-whites tended to have stronger 'mean world' beliefs than did whites. Yet when the relationship of these beliefs to viewing behaviour was considered there was a significant *negative* association among non-whites between television viewing and mistrust. In contrast, there was a significant positive association among whites. Thus, say Gerbner *et al.*, 'those groups who in general are *least* likely to hold a television-related attitude are *most* likely to be influenced toward the "mainstream" television view; and those who are most likely to hold a view *more* extreme than the TV view may be "coaxed back" to the "mainstream" position' (1980, pp. 18).

Similar patterns emerged for relationships between amount of viewing and feeling anomie. Combining into a single index three

Table 2.5   Within-group partial correlations between amount of
television viewing and the Mean World Index

	Overall	Education		Income			Race	
		No college	Some college	Low	Medium	High	White	Non-white
Simple correlation	.12***	.06**	.14***	.03	.16***	.08	.12***	−.08
Controlling for:								
Sex	.12***	.06**	.15***	.03	.17***	.09*	.12***	−.07
Age	.12***	.06**	.14***	.02	.16***	.08	.12***	−.08
Newspaper reading	.11***	.06**	.14***	.03	.16***	.08	.12***	−.08
Subjective social class	.10***	.05**	.13***	.02	.15***	.07	.10***	−.07
Education	.07***	.06**	.12***	.01	.12***	.04	.07***	−.08
Income	.09***	.04*	.12**	−	−	−	.09***	−.11*
Race	.09***	.04	.10**	−.01	.15***	.08	−	−
Occupational prestige	.08***	.04*	.13***	.01	.13***	.04	.08***	−.08
All controls	.04*	.02	.08**	−.02	.11***	.04	.06**	−.10*
Final d.f. (8th order)	(2727)	(1853)	(861)	(1090)	(1290)	(317)	(2431)	(288)

$*\ p < .05$
$**\ p < .01$
$***\ p < .001$
Source: NORC General Social Surveys, 1975 and 1978,
from Gerbner et al. (1980).

of Srole's (1956) anomie items (the lot of the average man is getting
worse; it is hardly fair to bring a child into the world; and most
public officials are not interested in the lot of the average man),
it was found that the best indicator of anomie is education; that
is, less well-educated respondents expressed stronger feelings of
anomie than the better educated. When the association between television viewing and endorsing statements of anomie was examined
within educational sub-groups, this relationship still persisted for
those (college-educated) respondents who, as a group, were far less
likely to express anomie in their general attitude to life. For those
individuals with less education who were relatively alienated to begin
with, televison viewing had no apparent relationship wtih anomie.
Again, these results implied that television cultivates a convergence
of outlooks towards its 'mainstream', because the Gerbner group
take television to express anomie as a central theme of its content.

Resonance

The second important refinement of the original cultivation theory was that television-biased beliefs will be most pronounced when aspects of the social environment are congruent and thereby 'resonant' with television drama profiles. As noted earlier, not all attempts to reproduce the cultivation findings of the Annenberg group have met with success. In their study with residents in Toronto, Doob and MacDonald (1979) attempted to replicate earlier findings indicating that television causes people to overestimate the amount of danger that exists in their own neighbourhoods, whilst controlling for a previously uncontrolled factor – the actual incidence of crime in the respondent's neighbourhood.

Respondents in a door-to-door survey indicated their media usage and estimated the likelihood of their being a victim of violence. Neighbourhoods were chosen so as to include a high- and low-crime area in central Toronto and two similar areas in the suburbs of the city. When actual incidence of crime was controlled, no overall relationship emerged between television viewing and fear of being a victim of crime. Across the four areas of the city, those individuals who watched the most television or violent programming tended to be those who were most afraid, but within each area this relationship did not always hold. Whilst it was present within the high-crime area of the city, it tended to disappear in the other areas.

Doob and MacDonald interpreted their data as evidence of the spuriousness of the relationship between television viewing and fear of crime in the real world. However, Gerbner and his colleagues (1980b) have suggested instead that for those urban-dwellers who live in high-crime centres, television's violent imagery may be most congruent with their real-life perceptions. People who thus receive a 'double dose' of messages that the world is violent consequently show the strongest associations between viewing and fear.

Perceptions of danger

Gerbner *et al.* analysed the responses of a large national sample to five questions which were combined together to form a perceptions of danger index. They also made a distinction similar to that of Doob and MacDonald between residents living in low- and high-crime neighbourhoods. It was assumed that respondents who lived in the larger cities and who had low incomes were likely to reside in areas with relatively high crime rates, while high-income urban and high and low-income suburban residents arguably lived in less dangerous areas.

It was found that a significant relationship between amount of television viewed and perceptions of danger emerged in the presence of controls for demographic factors for low-income and high-income residents of suburban areas and also for low-income urban-dwellers. No such relationship occurred for high-income urban-dwellers. The strongest cultivation effects emerged for the low-income city residents and this was interpreted as evidence for 'resonance' whereby people who already lived in areas where crime levels were presumably high had their fears of falling victim to such crime enhanced by watching a great deal of (violent) television drama.

A further example of this resonance effect was evidenced in beliefs about the victimisation of the elderly. Content analysis of television drama programming had previously shown that old people tend to be victims of crime more often than young people in TV fiction. But while a significant relationship between amount of television viewing and tendency to think that old people are most likely to be attacked was found among older respondents, no such association occurred among young or middle-aged respondents. Resonance is said to occur when a feature of the world of television drama had particular relevance or salience for a part of the television audience as it has in this case.

Selectivity, reinforcement, or what kind of effect?

In recent studies, members of the Annenberg group have carried out their most comprehensive and complex analyses yet of associations between television content profiles and public perceptions of the social environment. Morgan (1984) reported an analysis of relationships between risk ratios for different demographic subgroups as portrayed on television and correlations between perceptions of victimisation among those same sub-groups in the real world and the amount of their television viewing. Morgan divided his television character and survey populations according to five demographic categories: age, sex, race, social class and marital status. There were five demographic characteristics for which risk ratios had been computed and which also provided easily measurable real-world parallels. Interactively, these mainly dichotomised categories generated 323 analytically distinct sub-groups.

In the analysis, the dependent variable was the *relationship* expressed as a correlation coefficient, between amount of viewing and perceived chances of victimisation within each of these sub-groups. The independent variables were the percentages of television characters in a given sub-group who commit violence or suffer violence, and the risk ratio (percentage of perpetrators divided by percentage of victims of violence) within each sub-group. Morgan examined the degree of association between the independent and dependent variables for each demographic sub-group. Results showed in general that, in terms of perpetrators and victims, as the percentage of characters in a group who are shown on television as perpetrators goes up, the partial correlation between amount of viewing and perceived chances of involvement in violence goes down. Viewers whose television counterparts are more aggressive show smaller associations between how much they watch and their perceptions of real-world risk than do viewers such as old people or women whose television counterparts are less aggressive. At the same time, the more that viewers see characters like themselves as *victims*, the *greater* the cultivation of a heightened sense of danger. In terms of non-fatal violence, the real-world groups who show the strongest evidence of the cultivation of a sense of risk are both less violent and more victimised in their television portrayals. There was virtually no association between the degree of audience cultivation and the percentage of killers, but a completely different relationship appeared for the percentage who are killed, particularly among major characters. The more viewers see leading characters like themselves killed (not just hurt), the *weaker* the association between amount of viewing and their perception of danger.

Morgan says this may be an artefact of the relatively unusual and special status of major characters who are killed on television. Few leading characters are killed in most groups – indeed, in many none at all is killed. When those groups in which substantial numbers are killed are examined alone, however, positive correlations emerge between television killings and the cultivation effect. Morgan states that: 'From multidimensional clusters of demographic matchings, we see that television is most likely to cultivate exaggerated perceptions of the likelihood of victimization among those viewers who *see their fictional counterparts as least powerful*' (p. 376). But a crucial question here is, where is the evidence from this or any other cultivation effects study that viewers do actually 'see' their fictional counterparts or any other aspect of television in one way or another? At no stage does the cultural indicators model, as employed by the Annenberg group, ever test in a direct fashion how viewers perceive television content and interpret the social meanings it supposedly conveys.

Another problem with the model which persists even through such a complex analysis as Morgan's is the assumption that viewing is largely non-selective and therefore that the relationship between social attitudes and beliefs on the one hand, and television usage on the other, is unidirectional. Not all viewers fill their viewing time with the same programmes. One viewer, whether heavy or light, may not watch the same kinds of programme as another viewer. Thus the content seen, information absorbed and messages learnt from television may vary considerably between viewers, and this will depend on the tastes and attitudes within viewers which determine their *choice* of which programmes to watch.

Cause or effect?

Several writers have observed that a key problem with the cultivation hypothesis lies in its reliance on correlational evidence to make causal statements about the relationship of television viewing and its cultivation effects (Zillmann, 1980; Wober and Gunter, 1982). It is not just that the evidence presented by the cultural indicators research team frequently failed to take adequate account of third variables when interpreting their significant correlations between weight of viewing and social perceptions; but more crucially, in conceptual as well as methodological sense, their model has failed to determine in what direction the relationship lies.

In determining whether television violence causes fearfulness and anxiety in viewers, or whether anxiety fosters heavy viewing, Zillmann (1980) argues for the latter alternative. While acknowledging that the display of transgression is an essential part of drama, he notes that such fare also typically features the ultimate triumph of justice. The criminal is caught, and the forces of law and order prevail. Zillmann argues that suspenseful television drama may distort reality but proposes that the bias is more likely to be in the direction of presenting an overly just, overly safe world. If the portrayal of criminal acts adversely affects the viewer's perceptions of reality, the anxious viewer should find comfort and relief in drama that presents the triumph of the 'forces of good'. Anxious people may resort to watching such action-adventure drama because it ultimately *reduces* their anxieties by projecting a just world – an image that may occur on television far more frequently than in their real-life experiences.

Several studies, from Britain and from America, have offered some empirical support for Zillmann's argument. In a departure from the usual correlational survey method, Bryant, Carveth and Brown (1981) Wakshlag, Vial and Tamborini(1983), and Tamborini, Zillmann and Bryant (1984) examined relationships between television viewing and social anxiety in experimental settings. In a British study, Gunter and Wober (1983) reported a field survey in which respondents filled out a viewing diary to indicate not simply how much television they watched over a one-week period, but also the types of programme they watched. Viewing patterns were than related to questionnaire responses on a variety of social beliefs.

Bryant *et al.* (1981) presented groups of respondents with a controlled television viewing diet for a six-week period. At the outset of the experiment respondents were divided into low- and high-anxiety types on the basis of responses given to items from Taylor's *Manifest Anxiety Inventory*. Low-anxiety and high-anxiety individuals were randomly assigned to one of three viewing conditions: (1) light justice-depicting, (2) heavy justice-depicting, and (3) heavy injustice depicting action-adventure programming. Justice-depicting programmes concluded with a clear triumph of justice or good over evil, while in injustice-depicting programmes, order was never truly restored. The viewing diet was controlled inside the laboratory, but outside, at home, respondents were free to watch whatever and whenever they pleased.

After six weeks of controlled laboratory viewing, anxiety, fearfulness and other social belief measures were also taken. Respondents were also told that tapes of six action-adventure series were held in stock and they were invited to view these programmes as part of a study on television formats. The number of these programmes viewed during this subsequent stage provided a measure of voluntary selective exposure to action drama.

Results showed that both amount and type of viewing affected viewers' anxiety levels. Light viewing and heavy-justice viewing produced a slight increase in anxiety levels among low-anxiety individuals, but resulted in a *reduction* in anxiety in indivduals already highly anxious. For heavy viewers of programmes in which injustice was habitually depicted, both low- and high-anxiety individuals exhibited significant increases in anxiety, with the greatest increment occurring for those who were already highly anxious. Individuals high in anxiety at the outset also held stronger beliefs that they would at some time be victimised than did those initially low in anxiety. For both groups, however, a heavy diet of action-adventure material, with or without justice, resulted in increased perceptions of victimisation. As for *fear* of victimisation, as distinct from its *perceived likelihood*, Bryant *et al.* found that viewing television injustice produced significantly greater increase in fearfulness than did television justice. Heavy viewers of action-adventure programmes who saw repeated incidents of restoration of justice also rated their chances of vindication in the event of personal victimisation greater than did injustice viewers.

In a subsequent experiment, Tamborini *et al.*, (1984) extended the work of Bryant *et al.* and attempted to overcome certain methodological shortcomings of the earlier study. Whilst Bryant *et al.* measured the effects of a particular viewing diet immediately after the final programme, Tamborini and his colleages employed delayed, as well as immediate, testing to examine long-term effects of exposure to television crime content. Tamborini *et al.* also distinguished effects at a number of different judgemental levels, e.g. whether increased concern about violence related specifically to the individual at a personal level or more generally to society at large. These researchers also examined the possibility that enhanced fearfulness was not a generalised reaction but was specific to certain situations.

Experimental participants viewed one of four videotaped programmes: a non-violent episode of *The Love Boat* (control); a version of a TV movie *High Midnight* in which the bad guys were punished (justice-depicting); a version of the movie in which the bad guys go unpunished (injustice-depicting); or a 30 minute crime documentary on crime in Harlem, New York. Respondents' perceptions were assessed either immediately after viewing or three days later, along a series of items designed to distinguish several dimensions of apprehension. Results showed that watching different types of crime and violence had different effects on social perceptions at different levels, and that these effects usually dissipate over time. Only viewing of the crime documentary appeared to have a more lasting impact on perceptions. Tamborini *et al.* were also able to demonstrate that fear of crime or victimisation may be situation-specific. The researchers were able to distinguish fear in urban areas from fear in rural settings, and fear for personal safety from fear for someone else.

This research indicated that viewing a certain kind of television programme dealing with crime can influence certain social perceptions while leaving other associated judgements unaffected. For example, watching the crime documentary and the injustice-depicting crime drama led to more exaggerated 'perceptions of crime' and fear of assault in urban environments. Watching the injustice-depicting crime drama also increased anxiety, while viewing the crime documentary also elevated fear for one's spouse or close partner. However, no effects were found of watching these programmes, or any of the others, on personal fear or fear of assault in rural environments.

The above studies indicate that it is not only the amount of television viewing but also the type of content viewed that is important in relation to the moulding of social perceptions. Whilst Gerbner and his colleagues have categorised the cultivation, via heavy television viewing, of exaggerated fears about personal safety and of increased mistrust of others, some writers have suggested that another message may be transmitted by television drama which ought to condition a completely different kind of social perception.

Although dramatic story-lines in fictional television programmes often feature violent conflict between the good guys and the bad guys, giving the impression of a violent world infiltrated by criminal activity, nearly all such programmes finish on the note of good triumphing over evil, and with the ultimate bringing to justice of law-breakers. If television has a lesson to teach about the world, it is as likely to be that the world is a just place as that it is a dangerous one (Zillmann, 1980).

In a survey which both tested this hypothesis and examined the possibility that beliefs may determine viewing patterns and preferences rather than the other way around, Gunter and Wober (1983) posted viewing diaries and opinion questonnaires to a representative London panel from whom 500 usable replies were returned. The diaries indicated how much television and what types of programme respondents watched during the survey week. The questionnaire contained items of personal fearfulness, interpersonal mistrust, anomie and belief in a just world. (The latter were from a scale developed by Rubin and Peplau (1975) to measure the extent to which people believe the world is a just place.) This dimension is regarded, much as locus of control has been, as an enduring characteristic that can reliably discriminate between individuals.

Respondents' scores on each of the above social belief dimensions were related to the overall amount of television viewing and amount of viewing specific categories of programming such as action-adventure, soap operas, news and current affairs, and US television series. Results showed that in the presence of multiple statistical controls for sex, age and social class, just two significant relationships survived between viewing behaviour and social beliefs.

Respondents who had strong just-world beliefs tended to be heavy viewers of action-adventure programmes and US television series (which consisted mainly of action-adventure anyway). These relationships suggest a cultivation effect of television which runs in opposition to that proposed and observed by Gerbner and his colleagues. Among the British viewers sampled in this survey, the social message assimilated from action drama programmes related to the triumph of justice over evil rather than the harm that criminals are frequently shown to inflict on innocent or law-abiding others. It could also be said, however, that these results do not reflect a cultivation effect of television at all, but instead indicate that people who believe that the world is a just place turn selectively to dramatic content to obtain reinforcement and clarification of their beliefs.

Evidence for this selectivity of viewing hypothesis has emerged from two more recent studies. In an experimental investigation, Wakshlag *et al.* (1983) varied individuals' initial apprehension levels before giving them the opportunity to select films to be viewed from a list. Participants in this study were shown either a documentary about crime or an innocuous documentary about the Himalayas.

A series of items designed to measure degree of apprehension about crime or fear of victimisation were given after viewing and indicated that the crime documentary did produce significantly stronger apprehension reactions.

Participants were then shown a list of titles of films with accompanying synopses which varied in the degree to which they featured victimisation and restoration of justice. Results showed that individuals who saw the crime documentary chose fewer victimisation and more justice restoration films than did their counterparts who saw the nature film.

In a survey with a national sample in the USA, Mendelsohn (1983) reported a number of interesting relationships between the need to know about the prevention of crime and the extent to which people watched crime dramas or paid attention to crime news. This study provides evidence not only for a selectivity hypothesis but also for cultivation of a different kind of effect than the effect emphasised by the Annenberg group. Concerns about potential victimisation often associated with residing in a dangerous neighbourhood were positively related to attention to news about crime in all major media and extent of viewing crime drama programmes on television. Among frequent viewers of televised crime fiction, Mendelsohn found that such viewers are more likely than others to believe they have a great deal of control over things that affect their personal lives. They are also more apt to believe that individual citizens can act to reduce crime, and are more often highly confident about their own ability to protect themselves against crime.

Mendelsohn's findings indicate that individuals who say they have a need for information about protection from crime turn to certain kinds of media content (e.g. crime drama programmes) in order to learn, if at all possible, strategies for crime prevention. Mendelsohn concludes that these programmes may therefore serve a valuable instrumental function for certain kinds of people living in threatening environments and, if 'the media cultivate anything, they appear to cultivate crime prevention competence among such publics – not hysteria' (Mendelsohn, 1983, p. 7).

Concluding remarks

In this chapter we have considered the notion that heavy television viewing may cultivate a fear of crime and enhance feelings of mistrust. Support for this cultivation effect of television was generated during the second half of the 1970s primarily by George Gerbner and his colleagues following secondary analyses of data from large-scale nationwide US public opinion surveys. Their early findings were not replicated in Great Britain (Piepe *et al.*, 1977; Wober, 1978). Subsequently, questionmarks were raised about the validity of the findings even in the United States (Hirsch, 1980; Hughes, 1980). The latter criticisms were largely methodological. More recently, however, and leaving aside the validity of the data analysis on a methodological level, other writers have suggested that conceptually the cultivation analysis model is limited and fails to take into account other equally meaningful theoretical interpretations of its findings, (Zillmann, 1980; Gunter and Wober 1983; Zillmann and Wakshlag, 1984).

It seems highly likely that the original Gerbner picture of cultivation effects is an oversimplified one. Recent research has revealed, for instance, that cultivation effects may take the form of quite specific associations between viewing of certain types of programmes and perceptions of victimisation likelihood within particular contexts or settings (Weaver and Wakshlag, 1986). There is evidence also that while estimates of risks for others may be related to patterns of media use, estimates of risk to self are less likely to be. Instead, the latter appear to be determined primarily by direct, personal experience with crime (Tyler, 1980; Tyler and Cook, 1984).

Elsewhere, research has shown that the perceived reality of television content is an important mediating factor upon which the occurrence of television's cultivation effects may depend. Individuals who believe that television content provides an accurate representation of real life may exhibit significant degrees of association between amount of viewing and perceptions of or concern about crime. Those who do not hold such beliefs about television, however, tend not to show any such indications of a possible cultivation effect of television (Potter, 1986).

The messages purportedly absorbed by audiences from television drama as identified by Gerbner and his colleagues relating to enhanced fearfulness may not be the only salient messages for viewers. Increased public trust in the efficacy of law enforcement and social justice may also be related to heavy viewing of certain kinds of programme (Zillmann, 1980; Gunter and Wober, 1983). Furthermore, whilst evidence of a correlational relationship may suggest causality, the direction in which it operates has not been conclusively established. Zillmann and Wakshlag (1984), for example, suggest a reverse hypothesis: 'Instead of heavy exposure [to television] causing fear, fear might cause heavy exposure' (p. 3). The relationship may in fact be even more sophisticated than this since different types of people could exhibit different patterns of viewing and response to television (see Wakshlag *et al.*, 1983; Tamborini *et al.*, 1984). A model is required which takes into account not

simply how much television people watch but also the types of programmes they watch and the different interpretations viewers place
on the content they see.

3 Television and the democratic process

Introduction

In this chapter we look at some important studies on ways in which television is said to cast some influence on public beliefs about the political process. There are four overlapping compartments into which research into the relationships between television and political democracy can be placed. First, there is 'political socialisation', in particular as it applies to children who are still in the process of acquiring political ideas; secondly, a similar process in so far as it affects adults; thirdly, we look at political structures such as Parliaments and elections and at the ways in which these reach and serve their publics through the mass media; finally, as a reflection of political structures, we can examine the ways in which television itself 'looks at' the political centres and represents these to the more peripheral publics. Running through all these four compartments is a common theoretical concern as to whether television itself (and the way in which it is operated, by those who make it and those who watch it) has an influence, or whether it is simply a neutral conduit. If it has influence this can be in two directions; one is towards the politicians and their behaviour, and the other direction faces the public.

Political socialisation among children

A great deal of the early work on the political socialisation of young people emphasised the role of family and school influences (Langton and Jennings, 1968; 1969; Chaffee, McLeod and Wackman, 1973; Jennings and Niemi, 1973), but these social forces accounted for only a small part of the variance in political beliefs among children and adolescents. This suggested that there were other sources of influence, including the mass media.

When questioned about their major sources of political information, adolescent samples usually name the media, with television being pre-eminent. Chaffee, McLeod and Atkin (1971) reported that both junior and senior high school students rated television as a more important source of political information than parents, friends or teachers. Television becomes a particularly important source of public affairs information as the child approaches adolescence (Chaffee, 1977).

Chaffee, Ward and Tipton (1970) conducted a panel study with nearly 1300 junior and senior high school students with an initial survey wave nearly five months before and a second within two weeks after the 1968 US presidential election. They found that early media exposure predicted later political knowledge independently of initial knowledge levels. Newspapers were the most important source of information, but television also contributed.

A relatively simple view of the process of political socialisation implies that politicians and 'issues' are like objects on a stage in front of the populace, and that children have the task of getting to know these actors and of developing attitudes towards them and the principles which they pursue. Thus Dominick (1972) poses two questions: first, 'What kinds of children are likely to draw most of their political information from the media?', and secondly, 'Do children, most of whose political information comes from impersonal media, exhibit patterns of knowledge, attitudes and behaviour different from those of children who receive most of their information from non-media sources?'. Perhaps the most important implicit idea in these two questions is that 'political information' is a focus of enquiry. This is clearly important, but it is equally important to recognise that we do not need only to identify attitudes towards society and its whole structure and contents, as well as to the formal political arena; personality differences between members of one society and another may also have a profound bearing on the political potential of the new generation. Evidence of this kind is available in the cross-cultural literature, but has not often linked the study of television experience with personality formation.

Social class differences

Pursuing simpler questions first, Dominick supposed that 'low-income children' would receive less information about the formal political scene from their families and friends than would economically advantaged children, and that low-income children would depend more on television for their 'political information'. He further assumed that they would develop different attitudes towards the political scene and be less politically active and knowledgeable than would children from higher status families. More specifically, because 'the media confer an element of prestige upon the person or topic that media content emphasises' and because 'television, especially commercials' show politicians in their best light, Dominick hypothesised that children depending on television for their political information would support 'the government and political institutions' and show less political cynicism.

Before examining Dominick's results with the benefit of a decade's hindsight, it is important to point to something that has been as neglected as Cinderella in mass media research in most western countries, that is, intelligence. It has been demonstrated that intelligence, educational attainment and socio-economic status are all correlated. This is taken by some people to imply that low intelligence *justifies* low status, or that different goals and methods in education are suitable for different groups in society. None of these disturbing and contentious notions is advocated here; merely, that it should be recognised that intelligence does correlate with educational and economic status and the first is just as, or more, likely to help explain individuals' relation to the formal political system as are the latter two attributes (Freeman, 1983). There are two entrenched reasons why intelligence has been neglected, and these should be recognised.

First, the social survey which is the standard method of mass media research, is not a suitable vehicle for the assessment of internal attributes such as intelligence and personality. Secondly, the ideology of much mass media research has looked away from the realm of individual differences and towards situational elements; hence the term 'political *socialisation*' for a process which fails to indicate that innate intellectual potential may limit the grasp of political ideas (especially of implicit mechanisms) for some people. Concentrating on external social situations deflects attention from personality features such as locus of control and authoritarianism which are vital determinants of the ways in which individuals can and will relate to the political process.

Leaving aside the implicit features of Dominick's study, he found amongst over 300 sixth and seventh grade schoolchildren in New York that television was said more often than other media (including press, radio and personal sources) to be the source of most of their information about government, president and politicians (but not elections, where print was said to be the main source). One hypothesis was suggested, that low-income (male) children were more likely than others to cite television as their source of most information about politics; but the other, that children who 'depend a great deal on televison for their political information' would show different attitudes, knowledge and behaviour had no systematic support. One reason for this is that the method of analysis was very 'low-powered' – children were merely divided into two groups of high and low television use and compared on attitude measures. This is not just an insensitive procedure for assessing television consumption overall, it also neglects a profoundly important distinction. This is that television viewing may be (and is, as sources cited below show) selective, so that news and current affairs material may be more heavily viewed by some children who are not necessarily heavier viewers of everything else as well. In effect, Dominick's assumption is that television is a homogeneous 'message system' rather than a combination of different kinds of programme type. This assumption is made firmly explicit in the work of Gerbner and his colleagues; but our position is that such assumptions are not justified until they are empirically tested and justified. Such justication may be found in one television system, or in all or in none.

Media preferences
Following in Dominick's footsteps Conway and her colleagues (1975) hypothesised that 'children's orientations to the political system vary with the type and amount of media consumption . . . children who consume more of the mass media would be more aware of the political parties and differences in their policy orientations'. While the latter explanation has faith in the homogeneity of 'mass media' contents and in their effective and valid representation of the political system, the prior distinction as to 'type' led to what was Conway's most important finding; that was that measures of party identification among nearly 300 fourth to sixth graders related with amount of viewing of news and current affairs, but not with overall levels of viewing. This displays a difference in *function* between parts of the television output, and raises questions about the ways in which each strand (the factual and the fictional) may differently impinge on political sensibilities. A second important feature of Conway's results was that both children's interest and parental interest in politics interacted with use of television and measured knowledge and party identification.

Conway's work differed from Dominick's in yet another important way. Dominick asked children to account for an interaction– 'Where do you get your information about X?' Children can answer such questions, but they may or may not be correct in their understanding of themselves and what have really been the most formative influences on them. Conway's approach was to establish knowledge and attitudes among children and then, having separately assessed their patterns of use of mass media, to infer at the level of research analysis any demonstrable links between these measures. This is a preferable procedure for all groups, because the reasons and causes that people put forward for various phenomena are often influenced by aspects of what they are trying to interpet. For example, higher status people may feel television is a less valuable medium than the press, so they may claim that the latter is a more 'important' source of information, for them, about political or other matters. However, television may indeed be a most important source of 'information', even if this is not consciously acknowledged.

In Britain, studies have also been carried out to see how and whether teenagers' political knowledge is linked to their uses of television and the two other mass media. Stradling (1977) carried out a major study involving over 4000 children approaching school leaving age (approximately equivalent to US twelfth graders); his study was strong in its measures of five different kinds of political information derived from tests carried out in schools. The five areas covered political office-holders, local politics, national political institutions, policy issues and international affairs. The measure of television viewing was less elaborate, being a personal claim of how often the individual watched news each week; nevertheless, Stradling's own analysis did not examine the question of the role of mass media use in establishing political knowledge. The data were therefore sought out and re-analysed (Wober, 1980).

It was clear that there was a substantial relationship between watching TV news more often, and having better knowledge scores, both among boys and girls. There was a smaller but similar differential for claimed use of radio news and an intermediate one with newspaper reading. Cross-tabulations were next made for each 'media use' combination, showing average knowledge scores for those who saw TV news often and heard radio news often, heard radio seldom but saw TV often, TV seldom and radio often, and so on. The outcome of these comparisons was to suggest a 'TV effect' while controlling seperately for radio and for press use, and similarly radio and press 'effects' in terms of differences in measured knowledge. At the same time the percentage of those who intended to stay on at school, in excess of those who wanted to leave school at sixteen, was noted for each of the cross-tabulated cells defined, in terms of news media consumption. Table 3.1 shows the values for the two indices thus derived.

The interpretation placed upon these results was that greater reported use of mass media sources was indeed related to greater knowledge. However, there was clearly no great debt owed to television as an agent of its own potency; for the teenagers who used TV news more often, while they had better knowledge (by a modest margin) than those who used TV news less often were people whose intention to stay on at school revealed them as having greater interest in acquiring knowledge. In the case of newspaper use, a small knowledge differential was linked with no interest differential. One might therefore take newspaper reading to produce better knowledge for teenagers *regardless* of their interest levels, while by comparison tele-

Table 3.1   Political knowledge as a function of media use

	Political knowledge increments implying 'effects' of	Average percentage excess of those intending to stay in school
TV	6.3	15.9
Press	3.8	0.3
Radio	2.8	4.3

vision news viewing only produces a small knowledge increment when it takes place amongst interested viewers. The conclusion is broadly similar to that of Salomon (1979) who reported that information gain from television was established primarily when there was an applied interest.

The role of knowledge

Furnham and Gunter (1983) conducted a further study of adolescents' political knowledge which examined the influence of the mass media more directly. Political knowledge was tested among 238 16 to 18 year olds resident in London using 35 multiple-choice questions derived from the work of Stradling (1977). Questions focused on five areas: (1) the different political party policies; (2) who the prominent national political leaders are; (3) who the prominent local political leaders are; (4) knowledge of parliamentary and local political issues; and (5) knowledge of responsibility for the public services. Media questions asked about exposure to television in general, television news, radio, daily newspapers and Sunday newspapers. Respondents were also asked to say how interested they were in politics, economics and current affairs, and how much they talked about current affairs with adults or peers.

In terms of political knowledge, the results were strikingly similar to those of Stradling. The adolescents appeared to know most about responsibility for public services and party political leaders and least about party political or parliamentary procedure. The best predictor of political knowledge was degree of interest in politics. This was an especially good predictor of party leader knowledge and to a lesser extent of knowledge about party politics and parliamentary procedure. Only two media variables were weakly related to political knowledge. Claimed frequency of watching television news and of reading Sunday newspapers were positively related to political knowledge; overall amount of television viewing or radio listening were unrelated to knowledge about politics.

The findings just reported have to be viewed in the context that the knowledge scale used was a broad one, with a minimum of −37 and a maximum +43 (this stemmed from the multiple-choice questions that Stradling had devised, and the opportunity that candidates had to record negative scores if they had, for some reason, systematically picked wrong answers throughout); on this scale even the highest scoring sub-groups had scores no more than 12 and the samples as a whole displayed very limited political knowledge. Both exercises suggested most strongly that the problem which Stradling, for his sponsors the Hansard Society, felt should be tackled by political education in schools is to kindle interest in politics among young people.

Political interest

Several studies have shown that such interest is very limited. One survey (IBA, 1978) included 473 youngsters aged 12–15 years who were asked to recall what they saw the day before, and the greatest number cited comedy items; three-quarters of those citing comedy seen the day before said they liked the items they saw 'a lot'. Among the smaller group saying they had seen news or current affairs the day before only one third said they liked these items 'a lot'. The following year an annual survey (IBA, 1975) included questions on what people would like to see more of and less of on TV. The group aged 16 to 24 had the best *net* demand for comedy and light entertainment; but these people had a *negative* net demand for news and current affairs; that is, more people wanted less of it than those who wanted more of it. Such results are substantiated in separate studies of programme appreciation among both teenagers and adults, in the same region during one week. Comparison of the two samples shows not only that average appreciation among teenagers for all the news items they saw was substantially less than it was among adults; teenagers also saw many fewer items per person than did adults. Across the week teenagers recorded having seen 7.9 newscasts on average, amongst those who had seen any; for adults the figure was 11.0 newscasts.

It is not only children and teenagers who had only limited interest in news. The same is true for adults. Just after the Falklands War in 1982, British journalists wrote that the nation was unified and 'glued to' the television, watching large numbers of news broadcasts. The industry's measurement contractors provided data showing that, among those who had seen *any* of 20 newscasts listed on two channels on ten weekdays at the height of the conflict only 5 per cent had

Table 3.2   Appreciation for news, information and drama programmes made for children

| | Ages | | | |
Average appreciation index, for:*	4–6	7–9	10–12	All
12 episodes, children's news	40	51	69	51
All general interest programmes	65	71	74	69
All drama	81	85	82	83

* Scale from 0–100; aggregated across three separate surveys.

seen four or more of these items. Further analyses (Wober, 1982a) showed that this rate of cumulative news viewing was no different from what it had been at the same time in the previous year. An attitude survey showed that over one third of a representative sample in Eastern England felt there had been too much news coverage of the conflict. Half the sample felt the amount was right and only one in twenty wanted more information, saying the coverage had been insufficient. One year after the Falklands war there was a general election and an analysis (Gunter *et al.*, 1984) again examined cumulative news viewing during the broadcast campaign. On average, even amongst those who viewed any news, only a single news broadcast was being seen per evening at this supposedly particularly interesting time.

Children's news programmes
British television is adminstered as a public service and, in keeping with this philosophy, special time and programming are set aside for children's material. Within this category the BBC has for several years put out a newcast addressed to children, called *John Craven's Newsround*. This is a long-standing attempt to inculcate interest in politics, as well as information, into younger viewers. The IBA's bi-monthly measurement of appreciation amongst children has included assessment of this programme and results clearly show that it is one of the less well-liked children's programmes.

Newsround is not primarily concerned with the conduct of local and national politics; it is more similar in style and content to the early evening news magazines, which rely considerably on 'human interest' material for amusement. It remains possible that the limited political content of *Newsround* and the format of the programme, which resembles that of the adult bulletins, does prepare some child viewers to take more interest in news when they grow older. While the rising appreciation scores with age support this, it is a question which would be difficult to investigate in greater detail and on which there are no published studies. Instead, there is much unsupported conjecture about how children's interest in politics may be stimulated by television. Some programme-makers try to inject politically illustrative material into contemporary fiction. Thus a serial called *Number 73* made for Saturday morning children's television in Britain dealt with those who live in this house, one of whom stood as a candidate in a local election. Such material – in Britain at any rate – has to remain impartial in terms of seeming advocacy of party positions, so the scope for fiction related to active political topics is limited.

Implicit political messages
In much programme-making addressed to teenagers they are assumed not to have, or to want much interest in politics. Adolescents are involved in contemporary music, and this is a possible source of 'political socialisation'. British programmes like *Top of the Pops* and *The Tube* feature musical groups whose 'lyrics' (whose content and style stand opposite to an earlier meaning of the term lyric) are full of social comment. Further, it appears that adults who particularly like rock music are more attentive to the words involved than is the case within the field of classical music or jazz (Wober, 1984). Again, the question of whether or how musical styles and other forms of contemporary expression may or do dispose their followers to support or neglect various factions on the formal political scene is one that remains to be explored. However, the spectacular success of the televised Live Aid concert in July 1985 in raising money for famine relief demonstrates the political ability of rock musicians to mobilise youthful interests and to harness them for particular political actions.

The knowledge gap
In evaluating the uptake of information from the mass media, it is necessary to refer to the existing levels of information in viewers, which can and do vary. Researchers commonly refer to something known as 'the knowledge gap hypothesis' (e.g. Gaziano, 1983) which first of all points out that knowledge levels differ between different segments of the population; secondly, another fact is that possession of the kind of knowledge most researchers have considered politically important, and which they have measured, correlates with socio-economic status. The hypothetical feature of these two facts, set out in America (Tichenor *et al*, 1970) is that further knowledge

will be more efficiently ingested by people of higher status so that, even as television makes information more available to any who wish to use it, knowledge gaps will increase.

A few writers (e.g. Dervin, 1980) have taken a 'relativist' position, arguing that knowledge gaps and their proliferation exist in areas which are relatively unimportant to the 'ignorant' viewers. There is an implication that these people have some other fields of knowledge in which they are, in turn, at an advantage. However, it is 'mainstream' knowledge that is used in formal politics to determine the outcomes of democracy.

Gaziano (1983) reviewed mostly American studies (with some Swedish, Israeli, Indian and African samples) and found several which report a reduction of knowledge gaps; but many of these cases involve acquisition of vocational information (as for example among Indian peasants, Shingi and Mody, 1976) or where there is a very low 'ceiling' (as for example, knowledge of President Kennedy's assassination). A third condition where knowledge gaps may decrease is where publicity is intense, such as happens during an election campaign, or when a programme series has tackled a particular topic in depth.

One such series, *Ireland: A Television History*, was made by the BBC and dealt with Irish history over the last 300 years as a background to the present 'troubles' (a concurrent shorter ITV series was called *The Troubles*). The BBC's research (Rawcliffe-King and Dyer, 1983) focused on the second episode, which had set out to cover and inculcate eight distinct factual points; adult samples were studied in Great Britain, Northern Ireland and in Eire. In Great Britain it was clear that simple factual and 'knowledgeable' (i.e. as revealed by conceptually elaborated answers) information was gained more amongst those of a high than of a low economic status; in Ireland (both in the North and the Republic) larger increases overall were made among people of lower status (largely, it seems, because people of higher status already had this knowledge) but 'knowledgeable' viewers again increased more markedly among those of higher status. The researchers consider their findings broadly support the notion that as more information is given, so information gaps will increase; and they also conclude that 'there are limits to the amount that can be learned from a television programme'. This is perhaps a conservative conclusion, hence the study did not do anything experimentally to explore this possibility of upper limits. For instance, the design of the study overrode the operation of spontaneous interest, as the panels (who were representatively sampled) were specifically asked to watch the programme. Otherwise, some of them might not have viewed it. If interest was greater among

Table 3.3   Opinions about Northern Ireland among domestic and re-
           mote population samples

		Sample		Agree	Don't know	Disagree
Information	In real life Northern	N. Ireland	%	62	20	17
	Ireland is not as violent as TV suggests	Yorkshire	%	29	40	31
Attitude	The future of Northern	N. Ireland	%	56	22	22
	Ireland looks very bleak	Yorkshire	%	67	24	10

Source: Wober (1980c).

those of higher socio-economic status, this would have amplified the effective information gains still further in that sector, in the natural selective viewing situation.

An IBA study (Wober, 1980c) suggests that, among the domestic audience, people with lower education levels did tend to have viewed both the BBC and ITV series slightly less extensively than did more educated viewers. Adults in Yorkshire produced smaller audiences for both series than were measured in Northern Ireland and in the latter province those who also watched more of the regular local early evening news were more likely to have seen both these special series. Proximity to portrayed events therefore not only links with greater interest in following their portrayal; there is also evidence that it provides a way to corroborate (or to reject) impressions that are made available through the mass media. On this particular occasion two questions were asked that explored this issue and the results are shown in Table 3.3.

Adults in Yorkshire derive their information as well as their attitudes towards topics for which they have no independent source of evidence from the mass media. In Northern Ireland itself, perceptions of the conditions of living in the province are very different from perceptions recorded in Yorkshire; and attitudes differ significantly as well. If this kind of effect is demonstrable for adults, similar differences are likely to occur also with children. Cairns *et al.* (1980) showed five and six year olds pictures of derelict houses or train derailments and asked them for comments. Some children lived in London, others in a quiet town in Northern Ireland, and three groups came from Scotland; two of these could only receive news from a Northern Ireland transmitter while the other received Scottish services in Glasgow.

It was clear that children actually living in Northern Ireland were more likely to mention bombs and explosions, those in peaceful Scottish locations though receiving Northern Irish television were next most likely to associate bombs with the pictures of dereliction, while those in London and Glasgow were least likely to think of such associations. These results with young children are in an opposite direction to those with adults and suggest that children respond at a perceptual level, while adults interpret their perceptions within a context of other knowledge that they have.

More recently, McWhirter *et al.* (1983) explored this reaction more thoroughly and indirectly. Asking Northern Ireland children aged from 4 to 15 years their knowledge of death (pets, acquaintances, consequences, causes) they found that death was more often (and correctly) attributed to sickness than to accidents or to violence. After age 7, violence was decreasingly mentioned as a cause of death, the older the children were. This demonstrates the process by which the perceptions copiously supplied by television are gradually placed in a context of more detailed local knowledge.

In sum, children may receive political information from television but they may receive what some might consider disinformation as well. Young children have fewer resources than adults have to examine information available on television and to attempt to validate it. It may or may not be fortunate therefore that they have a low level of interest in politics; this means that they arrive at the threshold of voting age poorly equipped with information relevant to democratic participation. This does not mean that they are unequipped to inform themselves about the politics of their society; they have on the one side, what is provided on television (and newspapers and radio); and they bring to it their intellectual competence to learn (which, as intelligence is defined, means that about 20 per cent will not have the ability to grasp simple ideas and a limited array of facts), their interest and their personality structure.

There are many reasons for thinking (as has been indicated above) that interest will have a lot to do with what can and may be learned in early adulthood. There are also marked reasons for supposing, as will be shown below, that patterns of personality structure will also help to determine how people interact with the political scene. These personality patterns (see Himmelweit and Swift, 1976) have been influenced by the television viewing experiences young adults have encountered across the full range of programming, not just the overtly political material. Powerful theories also assert that general programming influences the political stance of adults and it is to this field of potential political socialisation that we shall now turn.

Political socialisation among adults

Much of the 'lead' news presented on television deals with political matters either on the home front or from abroad (Glasgow University Media Group, 1976). The influence of television news, however, depends on the kind of information it imparts to its audience. Research has indicated that television news broadcasts communicate more effectively on one level than on another. In particular, television can function as a powerful image-builder. It can cultivate beliefs about politicians' personalities more effectively than any other mass medium. It is less efficient, however, at enhancing comprehension of political issues (Patterson, 1980; Gunter, 1985).

There is some indication that people who depend on television for their political news exhibit less knowledge and understanding of national and local public affairs and have less trust in local government officials than do less television-dependent people (Becker and Whitney, 1980).

Michael Robinson (1980) has offered a theory of the cultivation of political malaise by television news. This theory suggests two stages through which viewers pass on their route to political alienation and mistrust. The constant emphasis on social and political conflict on television news, together with the high degree of trust which people place in the news, combine to cause susceptible viewers 'first to doubt their own understanding of their political system' (p. 316) and then to enter a second phase 'in which personal denigration continues and in which a new hostility toward politics and government also emerges' (p. 316). Once infected, a contagion-like process ensues in which these political cynics spread their ill-feelings toward government among others who had not been directly touched in this way by television.

Robinson reported an empirical test of his theory drawing upon survey data collected during a 1968 election study by the Michigan Survey Research Centre in Ann Arbor. He divided individuals into those who relied upon something other than television for political information, those who relied principally on television, and those who followed politics *only* through television. He then compared the percentages of each category of respondent who agreed with statements about politics ('Sometimes politics and government seem so complicated that a person like me can't really understand what's going on', and 'Generally speaking, those we elect to Congress in

Table 3.4   Beliefs about politicians and politics as a function of claimed reliance on television

	Those not relying on television %	Those relying on television %	Those relying only on television %
Percentage who cannot understand politics	63	71	91
Percentage believing 'quite a few' government leaders are crooked	21	27	34
Percentage believing Congressmen lose touch with constituents	47	57	68

Source: Robinson (1981).

Washington lose touch with the people fairly quickly') and about the perceived trustworthiness of people in government ('They are a little crooked, not very many are, or do you think that hardly any of them are at all?').

Comparing the responses of his three categories of people, Robinson found substantial differences between the television-dependent and those not reliant on television. Those who said they relied only on television for political information were 28 per cent more likely to say they could not understand politics, 13 per cent more likely to believe that 'quite a few' government leaders are crooked, and 21 per cent more likely to believe that congressmen quickly lose touch with constituents than were those individuals not reliant on television. Furthermore, these differences were still present after controls for education were introduced.

Gerbner's evidence (1982) that American viewers' political attitudes may have been affected by television viewing is perhaps the most persuasive of the series of assertions that have come from this group of researchers in Philadelphia. However, even these political effects claims must be viewed with caution as the paper in which the effects of television viewing on political orientations are put forward contains 17 references, of which eight deal with parallel papers by the same group. Only two of the other studies can be said to be independent efforts to demonstrate the same kind of process. These are by the DeFleurs (1967), who reported that children know more about unusual occupations frequently portrayed on television than about common jobs rarely seen on the screen; and by Volgy and Schwartz (1980), who related viewing to the confidence placed in doctors who are frequently seen on screen, in contrast to scientists who are less frequently portrayed. The 1982 Gerbner paper (unlike the next one by Gerbner *et al.* (1984) on political attitudes which is more guarded in its interpretations) has a prophetic tone of emphasis in which evidence that is essentially correlational is firmly interpreted as causal, and in a given direction.

The paper opens with the statement: 'Television is part and parcel of our daily life, investing it with particular meanings'. Thus the influence and potency of television are taken as already having been demonstrated. Television is, moreover, seen as an integrated and homogeneous 'message system'; 'its drama, commercials, news, and other programmes bring a relatively coherent world of common images and messages into every viewing home' (p. 102). 'Television provides . . . a shared daily ritual of highly compelling and informative content. . . .' These researchers do not resolve the claims of Kubey (1980) or the demonstration by Wober (1983) that viewing is for most an experience of little involvement or impact. The Philadelphia group are firm that television is powerful and consistent as an influential message source. They argue that 'competition for the largest possible audience . . . means striving for the broadest and most conventional appeals . . . no matter how skewed or off-centre a view might really be, it should "balanced" by more "extreme" manifestations, preferably on "both sides" to make its presentation . . . suitable for mass marketing' (p. 103). The market motive is given as the source, therefore, of a middle-of-the-road political ethos.

In Britain there is a potential parallel to this situation; for ITV is required, by its 1981 Act of Parliament, to provide news and current affairs that observe a political balance, and the BBC is bound likewise by its Charter; but this responsibility lies primarily within the field of fact rather than of fiction. In Britain, diversity rather than homogeneity has been an ever-present goal of scheduling and it has recently been further encouraged. In the same year that the Gerbner paper made claims about the systemic homogeneity of American television, in Britain a fourth channel was started which had as its main responsibility to be eclectic and diverse, to cater for interests and tastes as yet inadequately provided for by the three then existing channels and particularly to serve minority interest groups. Channel 4 was soon reaching 50 per cent of the population in any week and gradually improved its share of overall viewing times from under 5 to 6 or 7 per cent by its second year. Whatever the case for accepting Gerbner's interpretations of his team's findings for America, there are structural grounds for expecting the British situation to be different.

Cultivating a middle-class mentality

The American data amalgamate results across four years' national surveys (1975, 1977, 1978 and 1980) yielding in all over 6000 respondents. They estimated their average daily viewing time in hours, and answered many other questions in an hour-long interview. The first results on effects of viewing experience are that people of low socio-economic status are more likely to call themselves 'middle-class' the more they report viewing television; people of objectively higher status are more likely, when describing themselves as heavy viewers, to call themselves 'working-class'. Unless there are other processes at work, such as ceiling effects, regression towards a mean or personality correlates that weave together these particular patterns of response, it does seem as if television viewing experience in America may be cultivating a more widespread 'middle-class mentality', which is of fundamental importance in structuring a population's attitudes towards the political spectrum.

Using a seven-point self-assessment scale (from 'extremely liberal' to 'extremely conservative') from which responses were recoded into three categories, it was found that significantly more heavy than light viewers in all the demographic sub-groups (examined by age, sex, education, income, regional and actual political affiliation criteria) called themselves moderates; heavy viewers were less likely than light viewers to describe themselves as occupying 'extremes' of the political spectrum, as self-assessed liberals or conservatives. These broader aspects of self-identification (whether one claimed to be liberal or conservative) were exemplified in a number of specific political positions. On an item favouring a legal ban on inter-racial marriage, for example, the proportions of self-claimed liberals and conservatives affirming each proposition, who were light viewers were shown to differ by fifteen percentage points. But the views of liberals and conservatives who were heavy viewers differed by only five points (heavy viewers being less integrationist). Similarly, self-professed liberals who reported heavier viewing were more likely than those who reported lighter viewing to say that communism is the worst form of government and to be willing to curtail the freedom of speech of 'the left' (actually, atheists, communists and homosexuals) as well of as 'the right' (actually, racists and militarists). Similarly, self-professed liberals who were heavy viewers approached the conservatives' position in being likely to argue that homosexuality is always wrong, and to oppose abortion and the legalisation of marijuana.

Finally, results were analysed on a group of eleven items about which respondents were asked whether they felt the nation spent too much or too little. Here, the researchers believe that advertising-sponsored television's mission is mass-mobilisation for consumption, so it should foster populist and self-indulgent attitudes (i.e. the government should be encouraged to spend in areas which benefit oneself rather than others). On seven issues they labelled 'liberal' (spending on health, environment, cities, education, foreign aid, welfare and blacks) there was no relation between weight of viewing and attitudes towards government spending among self-professed liberals. Instead, self-professed conservatives, when heavier viewers, took more liberal opinions. The most remarkable of these is that heavy-viewing conservatives were notably less likely than their light-viewing counterparts to say that too much was spent on welfare.

On what the researchers term 'conservative issues' (spending on crime, drugs and arms) heavy-viewing liberals have opinions more like those of conservatives, namely, to feel that the government is spending too little. Noting implied contradictions, a table was constructed of those with cognitively dissonant views – people who at the same time feel their taxes are too high but also oppose spending cuts and reductions in services. Here, the largest proportion – 44 per cent – occurs amongst those who are heavy viewers but also describe themselves as liberals; this inconsistency is at a notably higher level even than amongst conservatives, whether of high or low viewing levels.

There is no need to dispute the facts of any of these findings. What is less convincing is the interpretation that is to be placed upon them. On the one hand, the Gerbner group insist that heavy viewing has had an effect in moving attitudes towards a 'mainstream'; for some issues this mainstream lies towards the right of the political spectrum, involving opposition to racial integration, tolerance of homosexuals, drugs and abortion. For other issues, however, the mainstream is more towards the left; in particular, heavier viewers (especially among conservatives, who it has been shown are more likely to have higher income and socio-economic status) are *less* likely to say 'we spend too much' on welfare, health and blacks. These are not areas in which spending is likely to benefit the respondents themselves.

It is disconcerting that, in interpreting the findings, the Gerbner group have given no consideration whatever to any explanations other than the ones offered. It is more normal for researchers to examine several possible explanations for the results found and then to discard the less likely mechanisms. In the present case we have results in which people who report that they are heavy viewers at the same time report authoritarian attitudes and describe themselves as liberal. Why do they do this? Has the content of their viewing, unknown to themselves, warped and changed the nature of their attitudes on specific policy matters on which they might originally have earned the title of liberals? Or (and this is what the researchers neglected to discuss) has heavy television viewing led people whose attitudes always were repressive, to identify themselves to interviewers as liberals for reasons of social desirability? Or, as a third possibility, is there some combination of personality characteristics, independent of television, that leads people to offer a mixture of inconsistent evidence about themselves? This is where the Gerbner group's results on logical (though apparently not cognitive) dissonance (their Table 8, p. 124) leave the largest uncertainty. As it stands, we have evidence and an interpretative claim that pass, relatively unquestioned, into the literature, that American television had a powerful acculturative effect. This effect is to mould attitudes towards a morally rightist though in some respects fiscally leftist direction, all of which is laid at the door of a system which is controlled, in its own interests, by 'big business'.

The Gerbnerist explanation may or may not be valid in America. To a considerable extent the resolution of this question must remain in the hands of other American researchers. They have to obtain the survey data and analyse it more fully, or use similar questions but add controls for personality measures or social desirability in responding. Or they need to devise their own ways to place the interpretations on a sounder footing. One simple step – as presaged in the work of Conway in comparison to that of Dominick – is to measure television viewing of different types of programmes separately to see if 'effects' are more attributable in specific directions. The Gerbnerist implication is that effects should be attributable to fictional and entertainment programmes more than to explicitly informational output, because in the latter the viewer is, to some extent at least, being invited to make up his or her own mind about what is being said. If the Gerbnerist interpretation is valid, however, one reason for the state of affairs that they report may well rest with the ways in which television is financed and controlled. As Gerbner describes it, the air-waves are not unlike the atmosphere of the Roman coliseum in which the public whim was crudely related to the way in which the fate of a gladiator might be sealed. The weight of majority feeling clearly crowded out the implications of minority sentiments, while majority feelings moved more often towards harsher than softer social action.

Research in Israel and Britain

One means of looking further into the ways in which people 'read' the messages of television was developed in Israel by Adoni, Cohen and Mane (1984). They asked over 400 twelfth grade students to answer questions about three purposely constructed two-minute television news items, as well as about the realms of life these items dealt with. The study was based on 'media dependency theory', which argues that, when people have no direct access to or experience of events, they have to depend on news media for their ideas about these events. If this theory is valid, television news and reality would seem more similar in fields of which the viewers had no personal experience and knowledge and more different where viewers had their own sources of corroboration. This is broadly what the adults' perceptions of Northern Ireland as reported above have demonstrated. It is also what the Israelis found. Concerning a school integration problem, closest to the experience of the respondents, perceptions of actuality and of television news treatment were more markedly different from those concerning remoter political conflicts. This not only supported the media dependency proposition; it also showed that people effectively distinguish between social and television reality when they have the opportunity. Further, unlike the Gerbner studies, in the Israeli case the amount of actual viewing of television news was unrelated to the extent to which people differentiated between the real and the television worlds of reality.

This finding was concerned with television news. The Gerbner case, for all its insistence on television's homogeneous character which blurs across programme types, needs more discrimination; it stands its best chance of establishing a valid contribution to the debate about the effects of television with regard to the possible effects of fiction and entertainment programming.

In London an opportunity to pursue such an analysis arose during the Falklands War of 1982. A one-week television appreciation diary was placed with members of a panel in the London region and they also received an additional questionnaire sheet for self-completion. When they had been recruited, which may have been up to several months previously, they had indicated their basic party identification (as Labour, Conservative or other). Now they received questions about how they thought the war should be covered on television, and on how it was being covered, as well as five questions from an established scale measuring authoritarianism, which have relevance to a broadcasting enquiry about the war ('Human nature being what it is, there will always be war and conflict; what young people need is strict discipline and the will to work for family and country', etc.). These items were reasonably good parallels to those used by Gerbner *et al.* on race integration, toleration of deviants, welfare spending, and so on. The London survey was particularly useful in that the diary of a week's viewing provided a reasonably reliable

Table 3.5.   Authoritarianism as a function of political allegiance and television viewing habits

Viewers' political identification	Scores amongst those who recorded:			
	Light	Medium	Heavy	Viewing of
Labour	14.2	14.2	16.7	Adventure/Action
Conservative	15.2	14.0	14.9	
Labour	13.4	14.6	17.1	Soap opera
Conservative	14.6	14.8	15.1	
Labour	14.9	13.8	16.3	News and current
Conservative	15.0	13.9	15.6	affairs, on ITV

Source: Wober (1982b):

record of overall amounts as well as proportions of viewing to various types of programmes.

One step was to set out a table in exactly the same form as the Gerbner group had done, only in this case the weight of viewing was separately assessed for different types of material. Table 3.5 shows the pattern of authoritarianism scores (on a scale with values extending from 4 to 20).

This kind of pattern is quite similar to the Gerbner group's findings. Amongst Conservative viewers authoritarianism varied little with increased amounts of viewing; but among Labour viewers (akin to Gerbner's American title of Liberal) authoritarianism was greater among heavy viewers. These differences occurred not only for one segment of informational material viewing but also for two fictional areas of programming. However, a causal inference was resisted, for several reasons; one was that the authoritarianism items can fairly be regarded as indexing a personality variable; personality structure is usually established by the time one is an adult and is not likely to be 'caused' by viewing patterns, or seeing more of various programme types. Indeed, it is more plausible to suppose that it is personality type that determines pattern of viewing. The inference of causation by television became even less plausible after the next step in the analysis. For each group whose political inclinations were known (and for those who did not say) authoritarianism scores were correlated with weight of viewing for each of five programming segments or types, controlling in each case for variation in age,

Table 3.6 *Partial correlations between authoritarianism and television viewing*

| | Partial correlation with authoritarianism score among: | | |
	Conservative	Labour	Unidentified
With N =	146	114	350
Amount of viewing for:			
Action-adventure	− ·16*	·11	− ·04
Soap opera	− ·05	− ·13	·01
Sport	− ·02	− ·09	·07
News and current affairs on ITV	− ·03	·08	·03
News and current affairs on BBC	− ·04	·03	·14**

* p < 0.05
** p < 0.01
Source: Wober (1982b).

socio-economic status and the amount of viewing to all remaining programme material apart from the one being considered (See Table 3.6).

Now, having introduced controls for other underlying features we see that among acknowledged Labour supporters there are no significant relationships between authoritarianism scores (whether these be considered as attitudes and open to influence, or as personality measures and less flexible) and amount of viewing to various programme types, taken one at a time. Amongst Conservative supporters those who watch more action adventure (which they did, perforce, on ITV as this is where most of it was shown) are less authoritarian; but this need not be interpreted as an effect of viewing this particular material. It could be a sign of pragmatic flexibility as Conservative identity usually links with a declared preference for viewing BBC. Further, it appears that, for the politically uncommitted or those who refuse to state their allegiance, those seeing more information on BBC are more authoritarian. Again, this is more plausibly a feature of selective viewing rather than an influence of the programmes themselves.

In all, this British material suggests that the processes of influence reported by the Gerbner group among American viewers are unlikely to be occurring as a result of watching British television. It would be useful to throw more light on this question if the same kind of analysis could be repeated at a less unusual time than during the Falklands campaign, in Britain; and if a wider range of items assessing television's supposed influence were used. What is also needed on the American side is an analysis along the lines adopted in Britain, of viewing taken for each programme type; although in America, the technical difficulties of measuring viewing patterns across a week, for a representative sample are a considerable deterrent. Until such comparisons are made it is clearly more parsimonious to interpret the available results by saying that neither in Britain nor in America is there convincing evidence that watching television has produced a measurable swing to the political right (the American data, indeed, were gathered at a time when that nation was rejecting Gerald Ford and voting for Jimmy Carter as President). On several attitude measures, the American evidence *may* indicate such a right-ward trend. If this is the case the reason is likely to be, as the Gerbner group state, that the American system is run for the primary users who are advertisers; those who are used are the viewers. On the other hand, the British system is still organised so that the primary users are the viewers and those who are (willingly) used in the deal are the advertisers. The latter system is, perhaps, more likely to conserve the autonomy of viewers and their ideas and attitudes than is the former.

Political structures that seek television as a channel of communication

Political parties are engaged in unceasing competition within western-style democracies to get in a position to put their ideals and principles into practice. This means that to communicate to whole populations and to do so clearly, the means of actually reaching the widest audiences are the popular television channels. No daily newspaper or radio station in most countries (see Tunstall, 1983) gets anywhere near reaching the 80 per cent of the population who see one of the two main British TV channels in any week, or one of the three main network channels in America, and their equivalents in most other western democracies. However, a means of reaching the populace is not, by itself, enough. Political parties might like the opportunity to use this tool to say what they like, by whatever means they find convincing, when they like. But with the experience of propaganda machines in the hands of dictatorships in the first half of the century the democracies have devised ways of limiting the access of parties to television. In America the channels are owned by corporations which run as businesses, and cannot for that reason become subservient exclusively to either one of the major opposing parties. In Holland there is an elaborate scheme of access built upon the proportions of support that parties (including religious bodies) have mustered. In Britain the two broadcasting organisations are run by public service agencies which are separated from the day to day machinery of government and thus from the hands of any party that happens to be in power. Most of the material that follows in this section deals with the British case; but this may serve as an example with which readers in other democratic countries can compare the functioning of their own systems.

In Britain, political parties cannot and do not seek to reach the voters (as viewers) by writing or sponsoring fiction or comedy. This leaves 'actuality' programming as the area in which they operate and they do this in three or four principal ways. One way is to get on with their own business in Parliament or in local government and let the news tell the story of speeches, votes and other political actions and gestures. This tends to give an advantage to the party in government as they can be seen in the actions of government as well as in party controversy. The British system requires television to maintain due impartiality in reporting political affairs and meticulous care is given to allowing opposition spokespeople equal time and a chance to respond to governing party statements and appearances on television.

A second medium is that of formal statements made for television by the parties themselves (rather than by the broadcasters) and these are allowed in Britain in agreement between the parties and broadcasters, taking place about a dozen times per year. These party political broadcasts have their origins in the Presidential and Prime Ministerial 'fireside chats' on radio and for a long time in Britain they followed a formal style of head-to-the-camera talk with limited pictorial or graphical illustration. During the three-week election campaigns preceding a national election, PPBs are stepped up in number and become party election broadcasts (PEBs). For several years PPBs and PEBs were shown on all channels at the same time, with the aim of achieving a kind of formal total communication with the population, as well as of minimising the chances of one party having a much larger audience at a particular time than other parties might get elsewhere. However, in 1979, PPBs and PEBs began to be shown non-simultaneously.

A third approach is for politicians to manufacture or make use of news events, which they do by issuing press statements, visiting countries abroad or joining in formalities and celebrations of their own or of other organisations. Overlapping with this category of the management of news is the government's opportunity to control the timing of announcements (typically, of changes in economic indicators of the nation's progress, or of announcements of investment schemes). In special circumstances there is an opportunity to control journalistic access to information and this occurs more frequently in foreign conflicts and only seldom domestically. Controversial examples occurred during the Falklands War, which example was followed by the American military expedition to Grenada; the Middle East too has provided several examples of this kind of behaviour. In 1967 the Israelis allowed much more access than did the Arab countries to the front line which was thought to add public relations esteem to their military success. Since then, Israel has become, after London, Washington and Paris, the fourth most well-staffed location in the world for foreign correspondents; these tend to look for and report conflict, which has not always worked to Israel's advantage.

During the 1982 invasion of Lebanon several television teams in Beirut had the opportunity to transmit daily pictures of shelling and Israeli air raids, followed by evening walks through the ruins led by Yassir Arafat. In 1984, the Syrians and later the Cubans allowed television coverage of the visits of Mr Jesse Jackson the Democratic Presidential candidate, who acheived the dramatic release of American prisoners and added momentum thereby to his campaign.

Overlapping with this sector of politicians' uses of television is an interaction with it that the cynical would call Machiavellian but which others might defend as outside the political process and hence not likely to influence voters. This includes the appearance of politicians' wives, husbands or other close family in semi-formal occasions such as opening new hospitals or launching ships; and the appearance of politicians or their close family in good-humoured 'chatshows' or other formats such as the radio programme, 'Desert Island Discs'. Here, the appearance is personal, and political matters are not discussed. But, because the opportunity is being taken to establish or reinforce parts of an identity that may not have developed to the politician's taste or advantage through political action, such 'non-political' appearances may well be highly political. If a politician's image is becoming tarnished or tough, it may help his or her standing as a leader, and through that the party's electoral chances, for the politician to reveal unsuspected but welcome characteristics such as keeping unusual pets, being devoted to mothers or supporting other causes that strike a chord of sympathy with viewers. In 1984, a case occurred in a negative sense in which the Prime Minister, Margaret Thatcher, put off a visit to South East Asia. In the words of the *Times*' lead story (30 August 1984): 'it is accepted [in Downing Street] that the public might have resented seeing television coverage of Mrs Thatcher against an exotic tropical background at a time of industrial and economic difficulty'.

Televising Parliament

In all these areas in which the political community addresses the public via television there are two questions that concern us. The first is whether there are obvious influences on the public, and the politicians clearly assume that this is so, as we can see by the care that they take in trying to manage their messages. The second is less obvious, and concerns whether there are indirect effects on society as a result of communication patterns that are set up.

One of the most important issues is whether or not Parliament (or Congress, or any country's legislature) should be televised. On the one hand, it is argued that there will be beneficial direct effects on society, making the public more aware of what goes on (for part of the time) in the legislature; on the other hand, it is also suspected that, just as television has changed other institutions which it has taken to portraying regularly (such as sports, and popular music) it may also change legislatures. Some people argue that such 'backward' effects would be beneficial – at least in the British case – others consider that the opposite would be true. Some countries have had considerable experience in televising their legislatures (Canada, Holland, Israel, Australia); but no systematic body of assessment has established what kinds of television portrayal would produce positive effects either 'forwards' (directly, upon the viewers, and their knowledge and attitudes) or 'backwards' (indirectly, by changing the functioning of the legislatures). One possible example of a positive forwards effect, with a new body such as the European Parliament, could be that the portrayal of its proceedings would make people more aware of the body's existence, its cross-party coalitions, the issues it deals with and the powers it develops.

Some of the issues surrounding the televising of Parliament have been discussed by Wober (1979a), after a survey canvassing public opinion on the matter. A clear 29 per cent more respondents favoured the idea of 'adding TV cameras to the radio microphones now in Parliament' over and above those who opposed the proposal. Yet, if public opinion is a leading reason for structural change, more attention might have been given by now to the 38 per cent net support for a system of proportional representation. The House of Lords was in 1985 the subject of a six-month television experiment. A survey amongst the peers themselves suggested that, apart from discomforts concerned with lighting, the Members accepted the exposure and considered that it had no untoward effects on the operation of the House of Lords' business. Two separate surveys amongst the public failed, however, to disclose any gains in interest or knowledge about the House of Lords or to show any improvement in attitudes concerning the service given by the work of the House of Lords or the House of Commons. While declared interest related to and probably helped generate knowledge there is no evidence from either wave of the public surveys that greater viewing of informational programming generated knowledge, when level of interest was statistically controlled (Wober, 1985). It is possible that when people believe they know more about the proceedings of Parliament, because they see extracts, they may be in a deeper state of misconception about it than they were in beforehand. If there is direct broadcasting, and secondary effects develop, such as altered times spent in the Chamber by its members (with less time available for other work), such ensuing changes will need to be monitored and introduced into broadcasting coverage analysis, so that it will be possible to evaluate the innovation effectively.

Evaluating party election broadcasts
Some years ago an effort was made (Wober, 1974) to analyse whether PEBs had functioned so as to increase voting turnout. Comparisons were made between audience size estimates for the PEBs in each region of the ITV system, and figures compiled to show voting turnout for the constituencies in each region. It was found that regions with heavier viewing of PEBs actually yielded lower voting turnouts. Although the study had not been able to introduce sophisticated controls for the age and class profiles of the regional populations, which interrelate both with voting and with viewing behaviour, the analysis discouraged any ideas that PEBs may help to increase voting turnout. This kind of conclusion was also implied in the work of Budge and Farlie (1983). Nevertheless, the existing parties have remained very keen to cling to their PEB facilities, while for a new party (such as the Social Democrats, or the Green Party) the allotment of PEBs affords a genuine opportunity to state a case, as well as a symbolic foothold in the political scene as a group which has to be reckoned with. Blumler *et al.* (1978) have argued from their evidence that party political broadcasts (not necessarily just at election time) have a genuine informative function; but two difficulties attach to this view. One is that the claim does not rest upon direct evidence in the form of an actual test of knowledge, in a properly controlled field study, but upon respondents' self-reports of knowledge; secondly, interest is clearly a contributory factor that can lead to increased information gaps. Blumler noted that 'a large minority of the electorate was taking definite steps to avoid' seeing PEBs.

This was true as well for PPBs. In an analysis of over a year's viewing figures (Wober and Svennevig, 1980) 'desertion rates' were calculated. These are the difference between the PPB audience, and the average audience size for the quarter-hour preceding and that immediately following the PPB, divided by the latter figure. Disertion rates were just under 50 per cent for eleven simultaneously scheduled PPBs; they were almost equal to this for eleven other PPBs, shown at the same time on BBC channels and at another time on ITV. This survey used a measure of knowledge about PPBs to correlate with a scale of claimed knowledge about politics. This claimed knowledge level was shown in a multiple classification analysis to have no significant link with the levels of active political involvement; but subjective knowledge level (i.e. how much individuals themselves thought they knew about the political scene) was related to claimed numbers of PPBs seen. This gives some support to the possibility that PPBs do convey some information effectively, but this may not be equally true for all parties. Following one general election, Wober (1979b) showed that viewers' actual knowledge of Conservative and Labour policy was positively related to their viewing of those parties' PEBs; but no such relationship existed for Liberal PEBs. This suggested that little knowledge of Liberal policy could be attributed to what these PEBs had tried to convey. Knowledge of Liberal policy was so low that it could also be inferred that the broadcasters' programmes had done very little to inform people effectively about this party.

In America, the party broadcasts take the form of paid-for commercials (the British equivalents do not involve payment to the networks). As Ranney (1983) points out, these short messages are expensive and production advice and strategy rests in the hands of a new profession of political publicists who have developed various techniques (such as walking across the state, or taking modest jobs for a day) that present the candidate as an ordinary being. Ranney also believes that leaks of information are quite widespread and constitute one way in which controversial material is given publicity. Ranney reports that 17 out of 21 democracies studied give time to parties for broadcasts of their own design and production, and three (India, Norway and Sri Lanka) are like the United States in not giving free access.

There is continuous journalistic sniping at PPB facilities (e.g. by Adrian Berry in *The Daily Telegraph*, 28 July 1980, who wrote: 'politicians are perhaps the most boring people to appear on our screens. Imagine . . . the glorious day when we will no longer have to watch those most boring of all TV programmes, party political broadcasts . . .); and this accords with modest measured appreciation for such items. On the 100-point appreciation index scale of the IBA, PPBs score usually between 45 and 55; this is certainly 15–20 points less than most comedy and light entertainment; but there are 'comedies' which score less (though they do not run for long), and plays and old films likewise. The scale is an asymmetric one with a mark of 40 corresponding to a label of 'neither one thing nor the other' whle 60 refers to 'fairly interesting or enjoyable'; so marks of 45–55 are in fact mildly positive.

The political managers of party broadcasts in Britain and elsewhere have realised that there is opposition to their opportunity to address voters directly in this way and they have tried to modify their stance by making their messages more personalised, containing dramatic vignettes with outdoor pictures and alluring camerawork. The 1979 British survey (Wober, 1979b) showed that viewers claimed to be against such approaches; yet the result of that election was that the side most conspicuously using such communication methods, won. The personalisation and theatricalisation of campaign messages may have played some part in the Conservatives' electoral success, but the case remains unproven.

Broadcaster's methods of reporting the political process

In addition to news, which is often presented as an intense conflict (whether of humanity against nature, or humanity against itself) broadcasters provide current affairs documentaries and coverage of special events such as election campaigns. Typically, these are presented as a cross between sport and war, and events and processes which do not lend themselves to dramatic presentation may be considered 'not news'. Thus, both by choice and by default, there is a process of 'agenda-setting' by which critics of broadcasting have said that television (and radio and the press) manipulate public opinion. The default case refers to those events and processes which do not enter, or which make only marginal appearance in the news; public awareness can only sketchily grasp such information, if at all, because it simply is not widely available: it is not on the 'agenda'.

As we mentioned earlier in this chapter, non-Irish viewers' opinions of the situation in Northern Ireland were considerably more pessimistic than those of the Northern Irish themselves. An example of how 'agenda-setting' might contribute to this occurred when, on one day, the main newscasts featured the killing of a politician in the province: that day, there had also been a soccer match in which Northern Ireland beat Israel to qualify for a place in the European Cup. The fact that some tens of thousands of spectators had gone without incident to the match, which was an important event for the pride of the province had passed unnoticed, while much smaller crowds were shown on television at the funeral of the politician. In August 1984 much attention was given to the death of a protester who was shot by a plastic bullet, while the killing and funeral of a member of the defence forces was largely ignored.

There is a potential paradox in trying to assess the effects of this kind of reporting. The implied broadcasting criterion is that unless the item is sufficiently dramatic and conflict-ridden, usually posing rather than solving a problem, it has less chance of being shown, and this, it is suggested, had adverse effects on viewers. Yet Gerbner's critique (and that by others such as Glasgow University Media Group, 1976) is that the presentation of conflict in a certain way serves to cement a feeling of cohesion in the mass viewing public, who are brought by the spectacle of threat to the social order, to wish for its preservation. Put another way, bland events which might be thought to lull a population into a sense of security tend not to be reported; news tends to prefer the worrisome events. The effect of such a diet, however, is said to be to make people seek security – and to do so by supporting policies conventionally described as conservative. An alternative possibility not considered by Gerbner is that calamitous news is sufficiently often perceived as the abnormal occurring to someone else, so that for most viewers reassurance about the status quo and hence a sence of security may be developed.

Selection for inclusion in the news has been entitled 'agenda-setting' (Becker *et al.*, 1975, Behr and Iyengar, 1982). We also need a term for the exclusion of material from the news. For this, we suggest 'agenda-cutting', referring to the cutting off from access to the stage of public attention events that are judged to be 'non-newsworthy' (by journalists, that is). Frequent complaints are made that large, peaceful demonstrations are afforded little or no coverage, while unrepresentative disturbances attract attention. In both these areas there are opportunities for effects on society in a 'backward' direction; that is, because of the known or judged behaviour of broadcasters in focusing on conflict, groups aiming for coverage try to stage events accordingly. Agenda-cutting cannot in itself produce effects in a 'forward' direction upon viewers, for, by definition, they do not see excluded material. Agenda-setting, on the other hand, *can* produce effects on the public consciousness and some critics (e.g. Curran and Seaton, 1981) allege that this does happen.

Political programme formats
Various broadcasting forms have been devised to put across political and electoral information. In America there are Presidential (and candidate) debates; there is the race to 'call' an election (that is, to disclose its results based on exit-poll data) before the winner is 'officially' recognised by the loser's acquiescence; and there are

numerous documentary and studio discussion formats. In Europe, debates have been experimented with in Holland (though rejected, so far, in Britain); but in all European countries a single time-zone operates so elections cannot be predicted as a result of exit-polls or other procedures before a major part of the population has had time to vote. Ranney (1983) gives evidence that in certain American elections turnout rates have been cut when voters have felt ther vote would no longer make a difference to the winning of an election. 'Running mates' have lost narrow contests which they might otherwise have won against the overall trend. Some researchers, however (e.g. Tuchman and Coffin, 1971), have reported that voting behaviour is unaffected by early declaration of forecast outcomes; and other researchers still maintain that in general no significant effects ensue from such hasty television journalism (see Tannenbaum and Kostrich, 1983).

Two comments are relevant to this American problem. One is that if there are indeed no effects on electoral behaviour of 'news' told in prospect before the 'real' news has actually come about, then there seems no point other than in gratifying journalistic enthusiasm and in entertaining some of the public (and irritating another part of it) in delivering pre-close of poll 'results'. The behaviour of American broadcasters in hastening after scoops seems to be more validly interpretable as a symbolic refusal to submit to a centralised and bureaucratised order; rather, there is a preference to demonstrate symbolically an initiative and independence that may spring from deep roots of the national political culture at the precise moment when its operation is most conspicuously on display. The second point is that it remains a task in political communication to persuade the electors that high turnout itself is a worthwhile target, serving to validate the communal decision being made. Against this is the minor tactical intention precisely to deny such validation by abstention; there is also the principle that the contest is more like a war than like the (British) view of sport. Thus winning is what is important, not just taking part. There seems to be little or no research readily available which explores the existence or prevalence of such underlying values, which may intervene in shaping any 'effects' of broadcasting on public behaviour.

Turnout is one of the main criteria by which the broadcasters' (as well as politicians') campaign for the first elected European Parliament has been evaluated (Blumler, 1983). Having shown that party election broadcasts had a limited role in the campaign (Kelly and Siune, in Blumler, 1983, p. 47), Thoveron (p. 156) shows survey evidence from eight countries (not including Britain and Ireland) demonstrating that, on average, negative statements about the television coverage attracted more affirmation than did positive judgements. Were there any effects on knowledge gain and or on voting participation as a result of watching election coverage? Results are divergent and inconclusive. On the one hand, Blumler (pp. 191–2) produces analyses showing that campaign exposure, aside from interest, related significantly to turnout and to awareness of issues. He also (p. 197) shows that in four out of seven countries voting turnout related positively to amount of 'channels of exposure', particularly in people with lower rather than higher levels of declared interest. This, Blumler points out, appears to run counter to knowledge-gap expectations, which would predict greater effects in people already possessing greater interest and knowledge. These analyses are, however, based on a single wave of interviews carried out very soon after close of polling; in such circumstances people's recall of their viewing and the expression of their interest are likely to be influenced by perceptions of themselves as active voters. Indeed, Blumler himself agrees that 'issue awareness itself did not emerge from the analyses as a necessary pre-condition of turnout': we are left with the absence of any explanatory mechanism to show why viewing of the coverage (or claims to have done so) related to claims to have voted.

To reinforce doubts in Blumler's interpretation of his data, his own colleague, Schoenbach (1983), studied two waves of interviews with panels, in Britain, Holland and Germany and summed up by saying that 'the contributions of television and newspaper exposure to changes in knowledge are rather disappointing' (p. 308). There were such relationships, but out of 41 comparisons between media use and knowledge measures, only twelve were significant, and only at a weak level. Quite a different search for processes that might mediate voting behaviour was described by Wober (1981b) who first demonstrated that attitudes towards Europe, in Britain, were composed of three separable factors. These were economic, cultural and political. While individuals' positions in the economic and political realms did not relate to voting behaviour, one's cultural orientation to Europe evidently did do so.

This research opened up a new direction of enquiry. It suggested that television coverage of material that may not be political, but rather which appears 'cultural' – for example, wine and holiday advertisements and holiday programmes – may affect 'European consciousness'. This may in turn have some or more effect on voting participation in a European election than may be achieved by direct or explicit political campaign coverage.

There is some superficial resemblance between the implications of this research and the claims made by the Gerbner group. Both involve suggestions that some television output, not explicitly political, may have effects of a political kind upon the mass audience. But while the British work suggests links between viewing, viewers' attitudes and voting turnout it does not focus on the partisan alignment of that voting. The American-based claim by Gerbner does relate viewing to a particular cast of political opinion. In Britain and in other European countries, however, well-defined administrative structures provide for the balanced expression not only in overtly political programmes, but also in the rest of broadcasting, of the varied kinds of outlook espoused by the major contending political groups in society.

Political satire
The overlap of politics with comedy was clearly illustrated in an episode in Britain during the 1960s (Briggs, 1979). Noting that 'sometimes, moral and political issues were inextricably intertwined, since "permissiveness" often came (wrongly) to be thought of as a left-wing manifestation' (p. 125), Briggs provides several case-studies of incidents where the BBC and the government of the day came into potential or actual conflict. Most of the examples related to explicitly political programmes and were concerned with safeguarding the independent role of broadcasters. One case, however, concerned a satirical review *That Was The Week That Was* (*TW3*, in short) which was not merely a political programme. *TW3* 'had its own jazz group . . . the studio became a club or cave . . . the tone of the new programme was iconoclastic, anti-establishment . . . To be anti-establishment tended to mean being anti-Government, which at that time meant being anti-Conservative' (pp. 218–19). The weekly series rapidly became much more popular than its planners had evidently expected, and generated a considerable amount of controversy in the press.

Briggs does not report any research that might associate this programme with changes in public political opinion. However, the Board of Governors was worried about the programme, and relieved when it came to an end at the close of 1963. If *TW3* had done anything to undermine confidence in a Conservative government, Briggs' next example, of a documentary called *Yesterday's Men*, was said to have incensed the Labour leadership.

This compilation of interviews appeared to rub the politicians' noses in their electoral defeat of 1970. Apart from the tactlessness of the title, there was the role of a pop group called The Scaffold 'which provided satirical and incidental music' (p. 222). The programme thus exemplified non-political atmospheric elements which may have served to provoke serious reaction. Again, Briggs provides no evidence of audience opinion on the programme, or of any subsequent reverberations in terms of political opinion; rather, any effects were 'backwards' upon the participants (that is, the Labour leadership) and Briggs concludes that when the Party returned to power 'some read into the ... White Paper, published after the Annan Report, evidence that it [i.e. the programme] had still not been lived down' (p. 226).

Viewers' perceptions

While Briggs is primarily a social historian offering a sociology of the production process, others have in recent years begun to record studies in which analyses of content have been aligned with measures of viewers' perceptions of the coverage. Thus Schulz (1982) integrated surveys of television contents and of viewers' characteristics and perceptions, showing first of all that demographic and personality measures correlated with attention to political information; these were then entered in multiple regression analyses focusing on information-holding as the dependent measure. This showed that television and radio are the most effective sources of 'event awareness'. One important anachronism was reported: 'reading the popular tabloid *Bild-Zeitung* ... makes people feel that they are well-informed on politics although they actually are not, according to objective measures. A reverse effect results from frequent viewing of public affairs programmes on television.' Accepting this stricture (which has been pointed out at the start of this chapter, in comparing the procedures of Dominick and of Conway) the point of Schulz's research was to go on to relate subject 'event awareness' to a variety of measures of news structure.[1] The two strongest correlations were with frequency of coverage and with maximum length of stories; the position of stories in the bulletins or newscasts also had a lesser, though significant relationship with awareness. Viewers 'were particularly aware of an image of politics structured by news factors like emotion and aggression, proximity and unexpectedness'.

Schulz's study like that of Behr and Iyengar (1982) who compared measures of news content, real-life indices of political and economic events, and public opinion regarding these topics in the United States, suggests that agenda-setting is a reasonably well-demonstrated phenomenon. These demonstrations, however, hinge upon the news and current affairs material that the broadcasters generate, not upon other entertainment programmes, or upon the smaller amount of communication that the politicians put together in commercials or party political broadcasts.

Summary

Researchers have explored whether children acquire information and attitudes of a political nature as a result of their watching television. Over two decades of work, some of the progress has had to concentrate on methodological refinement, coming to realise that asking people (especially children) to account for processes they may be experiencing can be a misleading procedure. It seems better to take measures at two or three stages of individuals' encounter with a cultural source and to infer any process of knowledge acquisition of attitude formation analytically. Given these refinements, it begins to appear that children do acquire some political information – though not a great deal – from their viewing of informational programmes. Less is known about the development of attitudes towards different political ideologies and doctrines in relation to their information viewing.

Little is known either about any effects that may exist from watching non-news and informational programming on children's attitudes towards politics. More is known about the kinds of children, in terms of their abilities, status and interests, in relation to their political interests, knowledge and attitudes. Basically, it seems that people of lower ability, status and interest have less knowledge (and hence less well-informed attitudes); they tend to watch less informational programming and achieve less information gain. The knowledge-gaps which research amongst adults observes have therefore come into being from a mixture of causes; and the dynamics which brought these gaps into existence for the most part remain in place and continue to exert their effects. Some studies do suggest that an element of closure of knowledge-gaps might occur in certain conditions; but these conditions are sometimes trite, as where the knowledge item is a single fact of which the whole society is aware, such as the assassination of President Kennedy. In other instances of knowledge-gap reduction there have been massive campaigns so that saturation of a 'lower' information stratum may be achieved some time after it has occurred in 'higher' strata and their members' attention turned elsewhere.

For us adults the claim has been made that the broad range of coverage generated in the television system of a free market economy will tend to intensify a coalescence of attitudes located towards the centre-right of the political spectrum. Two elements are important in the location of this coalescence. One is that there is an implied drive towards consensus, so that there is some reluctance to be seen as standing too close to the edge of the perceived spectrum; the other is that the direction of development is towards the right rather than the left, symbolising a need for stability and coherence rather than for change, which is seen as the desire of the left.

Not only is this claimed outcome something of a paradox in a society where the overt values are apparently those of change and in this sense dynamic instability; it is also reported that similar developments were not detected in an analogous piece of British research. However, British findings have concurred with American ones that where there is no direct access to knowledge of events and where people depend on the mass media for their impressions, perceptions and attitudes can develop which are very different from those among people with direct access to the events at issue. One of the reasons why media-generated impressions develop as they do is because there are two related processes – of agenda-setting and agenda-cutting – in which certain themes are reiterated while others tend to be ignored.

In election campaigns the explicit goal of broadcasters may be presumed to be that there is no important agenda-cutting; indeed, that the role of television journalism in the democratic process is to set a full and balanced agenda before the populace. A successfully informed electorate would then take an interest in voting for its preferred political representation. Testing these assumptions takes the form of looking for increased interest, knowledge and turnout in studies of election campaigns. Some claims have been made of success in these ways. However, the evidence seems based on less sophisticated data collection methods (retrospective claims of both attitude and behaviour together, rather than separated observations of these measures across time); and it is not easily supported by aggregate observations of declining turnout rates across elections since 1960 and of very small turnouts in 'new' elections such as for the European Parliament which do not increase at a second election in spite of increased campaign coverage.

Conclusions must be tentative; but the impression seems to be that explicit dispersal of information by television – the most ubiquitous, heavily-followed mass medium – is educationally inefficient. On the other hand, non-intentional communication of attitudes through the entertainment and non-explicitly political part of the programme spectrum can occur, especially where there is no independent source of information; however, evidence for coherent inculcation of particular ideologies is less widely supported or convincing. One of the principal differences between the American setting, in which the most marked claims have been made that there is a covert political socialisation process going on, and the British case where there are no parallel claims, is that in the former the television culture springs organically from a market-controlled system; the latter however has buffering institutions of control which interfere with a direct link between viewers' demands for entertainment and the freedom of the television companies to provide it. The diet has to have an element of information balance; and not only the information but also the entertainment components are expected to strive to avoid undue political bias. No direct experimental comparisons of institutional arrangements and the functioning and effects of national television systems have been made; however, in the absence of such specific comparisons, the hypotheses outlined seem to be reasonably plausible ones to help account, at least in part, for the differences between television systems and their alleged effect in the United States and in Britain. There are also to be taken into account the perhaps less easily quantifiable factors of differing social backgrounds and values.

Note

1. These correlational findings have been reinforced and clarified by recent experimental research based theoretically in cognitive psychology. This shows that information uptake from a television news bulletin can be influenced to a significant extent by structural production features of these broadcasts. The use of film (Gunter, 1980; Berry, 1983), the way stories are positioned (Gunter, Clifford and Berry, 1980; Gunter, Berry and Clifford, 1981; Berry, 1985), the narrative structure of news stories (Larsen, 1981; Berry, 1985) and the matching of visual illustrations to the narrative (Findahl and Hoijer, 1976; Davies, Berry and Clifford, 1985) have all been found to mediate broadcast news comprehension (see also Berry, Gunter and Clifford, 1982 for further reviews).

4 Television portrayals and the cultivation of sexism

Introduction

The way women are treated socially and professionally by others may depend to a large extent on prevailing stereotypes and images of women in society. The impressions held by the public, and especially by men, of the way women *are, should be* or *would want to be* may influence the range of social and professional opportunities open to women. In recent years, the emergence of women's rights movements and a more loudly-voiced concern over sexism and the restrictions it is held to place on the range of roles deemed appropriate for women, have together resulted in a closer examination of portrayals of women in the mass media and their influence upon images and conceptions of women in the real world.

Early studies by the Annenberg group, which centred primarily on television violence, also noted a pronounced stereotyping of women in prime-time programming. This stereotyping was characterised by two principal features: first, far fewer women than men appeared in action-drama shows; this under-representation has been referred to by one writer as the 'symbolic annihilation of women' (Tuchman, 1978). Secondly, even when women did appear, they were portrayed only in a very narrow range of roles. In television's fictional life, women tend to be most often found at home, rarely at work. Television has also been accused of portraying women as incompetent, especially when they appear in anything other than marital or familial roles. Cultural indicators research showed that whenever women on television were involved in violence, they were more likely than men to be the victim than the aggressor (Gerbner, 1972; Gerbner and Gross, 1976; Gerbner *et al.*, 1977). Tuchman (1978) has argued that television plots symbolically derogate women, so that even when they are portrayed in leading roles and outside the home, they are attacked, surrounded or rescued by males. What impact, if any, does such stereotyping have on the audience's perceptions of women, especially among young children?

Beuf (1974) presented evidence from interviews with small groups of four- and five-year-old children which suggested that the limited variety of female television portrayals may cultivate stereotyped sex-role beliefs among boys and girls. Young girls particularly seemed to believe that only a restricted range of opportunities would be open to them when they grow up. Frueh and McGhee (1975), who studied kindergarten children and second, fourth and sixth graders, found that the amount of time spent watching television was positively related to the strength of traditional sex-role beliefs, resting on the view that woman's place is in the home.

In this chapter we shall examine the possibility of cultivation effects of television on the audience's beliefs about the sexes. We shall begin by looking at the characteristics of female portrayals in television drama. Then we shall examine evidence on the ways in which viewers encode and may be influenced in their impressions of women by television portrayals. Finally, new British data will be reported on sex-role perceptions and their relationships with television viewing among audience samples in the United Kingdom. The authors' own research in Britain has examined not only perceptions of women, but also of men.

Respondents' opinions on women's roles were related not only to *amount* of television watching but also to the *types* of programme they saw most often. Analysis of American television drama content has shown that, although male portrayals tend to outnumber female portrayals on television generally, this pattern of dominance varies markedly from one programme type to another. Males grossly outnumber females in action-drama shows, particularly those featuring a great deal of exciting and often violent activity, whilst the differential representation of the sexes in romantic serials and situation comedies is much less marked. However, according to some writers, even where women are portrayed in more or less equal numbers with men, as in advertisments (Livingstone and Green, 1986), male dominance still abounds in the form of subtle variations in the *nature* of roles played by men and women. Even American soap operas, in which women are numerically prominent, have been interpreted as symbolic representations of a world in which men are powerful and women are subordinate (Turow, 1974; Greenberg, Richards and Henderson, 1980) because the former make many of the decisions and set the limits within which women develop their options for what they will do.

As we have already seen though, it is one thing to classify and describe the content profiles of television programmes, but quite a different thing to establish that the messages supposedly conveyed by television portrayals are reflected in rather than led by public attitudes and opinions. Clark (1972) has proposed that the influence of television content follows a two-step process. The first important factor is the sheer presence of the group – the *recognition* given to it on television. It is hypothesised that the more frequently a social group is depicted on television, the more the viewer comes to believe that that group is an important segment of society; whereas a group seldom seen on television comes to be regarded as relatively insignificant. The second factor involved in television's influence on the viewer's impression of the group is the nature of its portrayal and, in particular, the degree of respect afforded to that group. The social and occupational status assigned to representatives of the group are important here, as is the degree of competence and independence of the personalities these group members project. Even groups that appear frequently on the television screen may be assigned an inferior status by the public if they are usually portrayed as having undesirable characteristics. This, as we shall see, is a common source of criticism of the way women have been treated in television drama over the last quarter of a century.

The presence of women on television

This is a question which has occupied researchers right from the start of television. Head (1954) and Smythe (1954) both reported that only one third of leading characters in American prime-time programming were female. Later, content analysis studies have indicated that not only does television portray women less often than men (in a ratio of about 2:1) but more especially so in central dramatic roles. In an analysis of prime-time network dramatic programming aired during the 1969–72 seasons, Tedesco (1974) found that, on average, only 28 per cent of all major roles were played by women, and several further studies during the first half of the 1970s corroborated this finding (Cantor, 1979; Turow, 1974; Miles, 1975; O'Kelly and Bloomquist, 1976).

The most extensive long-term analysis of television drama content is the one routinely conducted each year on prime-time American network television output by Gerbner and his colleagues. From 1967 to 1972 Gerbner (1972; Gerbner and Gross, 1976) noted that women accounted for only one quarter of all leading characters. From the same research group more recently, Signorielli (1984) reported that from 1969 to 1981 women were generally outnumbered by men by about three to one and year-to-year fluctuations in this ratio were very slight.

Female presence and programme type

While television generally appears to be characterised by a gross under-representation of females, the visibility of women on television does seem to vary across programme types. This point is well illus-

Table 4.1   Male and female characters on American prime-time pro-
gramming in two studies

	1967[a]		1969[a]		1974[b]	
	Males	Females	Males	Females	Males	Females
	%	%	%	%	%	%
Cartoons	90	10	90	10	(—	—)
Crime/detective/westerns	86	14	87	13	84	16
Action-adventures	—	—	—	—	71	29
Other dramas	79	21	77	23	—	—
Comedies	73	27	78	22	—	—
Situation comedies	—	—	—	—	56	44
Family drama	—	—	—	—	55	45
Feature films	53	47	59	41	91	9

Sources: a. Gerbner (1972); b. Miller and Reeves (1976).

trated by some early sets of comparative data as shown in Table
4.1. Certainly, men are more numerous overall, but this imbalance
is far less pronounced in soap-operas and situation comedies than
in action-adventure programmes (e.g. crime-detection series and
westerns).

Women in action-adventure, comedy and soap opera
In American television drama as a whole, Miles (1975) noted that
39 per cent of major characters were women. However, when action-
adventure programmes were analysed in isolation, the disparity
between the sexes was much greater; only 15 per cent of leading
characters were women. Meanwhile, in situation comedies, nearly
equal porportions of male and female characters were recorded.
    Miller and Reeves' (1976) examination of one week's prime-time
television drama output on the American networks indicated that
males outnumbered females in both major and supporting roles,
but that female characters more closely approached males in frequency of appearance in family dramas (soap operas) and situation comedies. Although these figures suggest that the representation of the
sexes has recently been more evenly balanced in situation comedies,
Signorielli (1984) found that even in situation comedies men generally outnumbered women by two to one, when figures from the
end of the 1960s to the early 1980s were examined. A similar ratio
was observed by Barcus (1983).
    Numerically, women in televised fiction seem to get the best deal

in soap operas. Such programmes are populated almost equally by women and men (Katzman, 1972; Downing, 1974; Turner, 1974). Downing (1976) reported that 50 per cent of the characters in soap operas she studied were female, whilst Turner reported 54 per cent males and 46 per cent female characters. Whilst they are more visible, however, many writers have argued that the range of roles female characters are given tends to be very narrow and emphasises certain stereotyped characteristics such as being quarrelsome or wanting to be mothers.

Women in children's programmes
A series of studies conducted during the early and mid-1970s indicated that children's programming on US network television tended to be even more unbalanced in its representation of the sexes than was adult programming. Levinson (1975) reported that male characters outnumbered female characters by three to one in Saturday morning children's cartoons on the three major US networks. Even three out of four of the *animal* characters were identified as males. In another study of US network children's programmes, O'Kelly (1974) found that males heavily outnumbered females by 85 per cent to 15 per cent, and that, not surprisingly, adult male characters appeared more frequently on the screen than did adult females. Males also enjoyed a much broader range of occupations than did females, with the latter most often portrayed in marital or familial roles. Cantor (1979) observed that male characters were more likely to have paid occupations than female characters in these programmes.

The physical portrayal of women observed in children's programmes, as indicated elsewhere in television by US researchers, emphasised youth and attractiveness. Women on television, whether single or married, were invariably slim and attractive. Not only did female characters appear as very attractive, they were also portrayed as very concerned with the way they looked (Long and Simon, 1974).

The other great concerns of women in children's programmes were their home and their families. Female characters were more likely to be married than were male characters, but even though more numerous in the marital context, they were not dominant in it. The status of married women observed in children's and family shows assessed by Long and Simon (1974) was one of deference to and dependency on their husbands. Women were no more likely to be portrayed in authority at home than at work. This was so even though married women were shown as attractive and youthful while their partners tended quite often to have gone to seed physically (Busby, 1975). The conclusion consistently reached by content analysis researchers during the early 1970s was that television represents women and men in a highly stereotyped manner and, if it influences children's sex-role perceptions, it probably reinforces the view that mothers are subordinate to fathers, and that fathers are breadwinners, while mothers do all the domestic work.

Further American studies of children's programmes conducted throughout the latter half of the 1970s and into the early 1980s revealed few changes in the way women were portrayed. Barcus (1983) analysed 899 characters from weekday and weekend children's programmes and found a ratio of three male characters to one female character. At weekends, the margin of difference was four to one in favour of males. This imbalance was found to be characteristic of all types of fictional and entertainment programming. More recently, Barcus (1983) replicated these ratios following an analysis of an even larger sample of over 1100 television characters from children's programmes.

In the context of occupations and careers, men on children's television continued to enjoy more variety and greater success at work. Schechtman (1978) assessed portrayals of male and female occupational prestige on six television shows which had been most frequently viewed by a group of pre-school children – *Batman, Bugs Bunny, The Flintstones, Happy Days, Road Runner* and *Sesame Street.* Schechtman divided occupations into four ranges of occupational prestige – high, medium, low and very low – and explored patterns of distribution of occupational portrayals. From this analysis, he concluded that television, as a source of incidental learning about the world of work, offers the child a male-dominated picture of the occupational world. Women were generally portrayed in inferior occupational roles and in proportions not representing real world numbers. Men outnumbered women in all occupational prestige categories. No women at all were portrayed in the high-level occupational prestige category. Schechtman went on to assess possible relationships between television portrayals and the career awareness of pre-school children. Of the children he questioned, 95 per cent named an occupational choice for adulthood. Furthermore, there was a strong relationship between the occupational choice prestige level of boys and girls and the occupational prestige level of their favourite television character's occupation, with girls choosing occupations of lower prestige and boys choosing occupations of higher prestige.

The portrayal of women in TV advertisements

In 1972 the *New York Times Magazine* published the first major content study of television commercials conducted by the National Organisation for Women (NOW). Over 1200 television commercials were content analysed over a period of $1\frac{1}{2}$ years by 100 NOW supporters in New York city (Hennessee and Nicholson, 1972). Over one third of the advertisements they monitored, showed women as the domestic agents of men and as dependent on men. Nearly one fifth showed women as sex objects and a similar proportion showed them as unintelligent. More than four out of ten commercials portrayed women as household functionaries – in particular, in advertisements for food or cleaning products. NOW monitors also noted that women never seem to tell men what to do in television commercials while men are constantly advising women.

Published for a general readership, exact details of the NOW methodology were not given, but it seems that the study may have been unreliable. There is some uncertainty surrounding the professionalism of the monitoring techniques employed. Some doubt must also be cast on whether the large number of coders were consistent in how they classified women in advertisements along subjective judgemental dimensions such as 'submissive', 'intelligent' and 'dependent'.

The first major academic study of female stereotyping in television commercials was conducted at around the same time as the NOW survey. Dominick and Rauch (1971) sampled almost 1000 television advertisements, again from network stations in New York City, during April 1971. These researchers coded commercials for, among other things, the products being advertised, sex of voice-over, sex of prime purchaser, the role played by the women in the advertisement, and the apparent occupation of the female presented. The appearance of men in a selection of commercials was also monitored for comparisons between the sexes.

Once again, a pronounced pattern of sex-stereotyping was reported, with 75 per cent of all advertisements using females being for products generally found at home in the kitchen or bathroom. According to the authors, the television commercials they studied conveyed the message that a woman's place is in the home; 38 per cent of women in the sampled commercial population were shown inside the home versus only 14 per cent of men. The single largest occupation for females was housewife with over half so portrayed. Men in commercials were generally more often in authority roles. When women were shown outside the home in some sort of occupation, they were usually in a job subservient to men. Voice-overs were predominantly male; 87 per cent of coded commercials used a male voice, 6 per cent a female one and 7 per cent a chorus. In addition, 60 per cent of the on-camera product representatives shown were male.

Courtney and Whipple (1974) provided a longitudinal and comparative analysis of the portrayal of women in television advertisements drawing on four studies conducted over a two-year spell between April 1971 and February 1973. The major conclusions reinforced earlier findings. Women were shown mainly as housewives and mothers, while men were shown in at least twice as many occupations as were women. Almost 40 per cent of women were shown in domestic settings at home compared to about 15 per cent of men. Female product representatives were shown most often performing domestic duties, while males may have demonstrated product features but did not actually use the products. Men were responsible for the vast majority of voice-overs (85 per cent) and dominated as on-camera product representatives on prime-time television advertisements. Over the two years of the study, Courtney and Whipple noted, however, that the number of female product representatives did increase significantly, particularly on daytime television where they appeared as often as male representatives.

McArthur and Resko (1975) examined 199 television commercials from US prime-time television in the spring of 1971 with a particular scrutiny of authority roles. Amongst men 70 per cent were presented as authorities, but only 30 per cent by virtue of product use. Of the 14 per cent of women who were product authorities, 86 per cent were portrayed as product users. Men were also much more likely than women to give an argument for the use of products. In other words, the authority of women was seen to rest on the fact that they *used* the products, that of men in spite of the fact that they didn't.

Throughout the mid-1970s, further American studies continued to find pronounced stereotyping in the way women were portrayed in television commercials. Focusing yet again on the relative portrayed expertise of males and females, Maracek et al. (1978) reported a more even distribution of voice-over experts between the sexes across three years of monitoring (1972, 1973 and 1974). However, female voice-overs were associated with a fairly limited range of product categories – food, household or feminine-care products. Within these traditionally female product categories, there was a marked increase in the extent to which the female had the last word of authority heard. During the second half of the decade, further studies indicated that while males and females appeared in equal numbers as product representatives, women still were predominantly found in commercials for domestic products and invariably appeared in the home. Men, on the other hand, dominated the non-domestic product categories and settings. The male also continued to be the voice of authority (O'Donnell and O'Donnell, 1978).

Schneider (1979) reported trends in sex-role portrayals on a sample of 300 television commercials in Minneapolis–St Paul during October

1976 which they compared to Dominick and Rauch's 1971 sample. Over this time they observed certain changes in the patterns of sex-role portrayals, but found that stereotyping was still prevalent. More older people were shown in the 1976 commercial sample, though there was still more emphasis on youth among women than among men. It was also found in 1976 that fewer members of both sexes were portrayed as employed compared with 1971, but the gap between men and women had narrowed. Although women were no more or less likely to be in out-of-home settings, more men were shown in the home in the latter half of the 1970s.

Pesch and her colleagues (Knill *et al.* 1981) reported a content analysis of over 1600 commercials aired on daytime and prime-time US network television, and examined changes in sex-role portrayals since the mid-1970s. On daytime television, over 90 per cent of voice-overs were supplied by males. Female product representatives far outnumbered males in afternoon television commercials, but there was a distinct variation in the occupational settings of female and male characters. Over 80 per cent of female product representatives were shown in family or home occupations, while nearly 70 per cent of male product representatives were portrayed in business or management occupations.

During prime-time 90 per cent of voice-overs were male, dominating all product types. Males and females were equally likely to be seen as product representatives in prime-time, but the majority of women were still shown in the home and the majority of men in business settings. Television commercials persisted with 'traditional' images predominantly, though the margin of difference between professional women and professional men shown in advertisements was decreasing.

Sex-stereotyping in British TV advertisements
Using a coding frame modelled very closely on that developed by American researchers McArthur and Resko (1975), Manstead and McCulloch (1981) analysed 170 commercials from prime-time television in the North-West ITV region over one week. The analysis revealed that men and women were portrayed in markedly different ways. Women were more likely than men to be shown as product users. Women were displayed in dependent roles more often than men were. Finally, women provided no arguments in favour of the advertised products with which they appeared. Men were typically portrayed as having expertise and authority, as being objective and knowledgeable about reasons for buying particular products, as occupying roles which are autonomous, and as being concerned with the practical consequences of product purchase, although, as in American commercials, their authority was abstract and not based

on practical experience of using the product. Manstead and McCulloch noted many similarities in the way the sexes were portrayed in commercials in Britain and America but they found one major difference: this was in the way arguments were used by central figures. McArthur and Resko in the US reported that 30 per cent of their female central figures used no argument, whereas Manstead and McCulloch in Britain found that 63 per cent of central female figures used no product argument.

Another difference concerned the relation between sex of the central figure and the types of rewards associated with particular products. McArthur and Resko found no reliable correlation between sex of product users and the rewards suggested by these consumers, whereas Manstead and McCulloch found that females were significantly more likely than males to be shown suggesting social approval and self-enhancement rewards, rather than practical rewards. These British researchers concluded that on balance the portrayal of adults is more sex-role-stereotyped in British than in American commercials. More recently, Livingstone and Green (1986) repeated Manstead and McCulloch's procedure, examining 175 separate advertisements broadcast in the London region in November 1983. Stereotypes had, if anything, intensified. More males were shown as central figures, fewer were depicted as product users, and only two per cent appeared in family ('dependent') roles. Additionally, the authors found that women (38 per cent) were more likely than men (5 per cent) to be seen but not heard. No women were associated with depiction of expensive products in authority or user roles, in spite of the fact that many such products – television sets, furniture and heating appliances – occupy the domestic world.

The nature of women on TV

According to some writers, sex-role stereotyping is woven even more deeply into the fabric of television drama programming than the obvious numercial discrepancy between the sexes suggests. Frequency counts of the distribution of women in different types of role in television drama have revealed a number of basic and recurring characteristics of female portrayals. Stereotyped 'propositions' about the appropriate activities and behaviour for women are assumed to be learned by television audiences, thus cultivating a distorted public consciousness about the way women are, should be or want to be in reality (Tuchman, Daniels and Benet, 1978; Butler and Paisley, 1980).

The nature of women on television can be discussed in terms of the roles in which they are portrayed and the personality attributes they display. Two areas of sex-role stereotyping and four aspects of sex-trait stereotyping will be examined according to the following scheme:

(a) *Sex-role stereotyping*
    1. The social roles of TV women.
    2. The occupational roles of TV women.
(b) *Sex-trait stereotyping*
    1. The emotionality of TV women.
    2. The sexuality of TV women.
    3. The power and competence of TV women.
    4. The assertiveness and ambitious nature of TV women.

Sex-role stereotyping

1. The social roles of TV women   Implicit in the sex-role portrayals of much of television drama is the suggestion that marriage and parenthood are of greater significance to a woman's than to a man's life. Tedesco (1974) reported that over a four-year period, marital status could be identified and coded for 51 per cent of female characters, but for only 32 per cent of male characters. Studies of dramatic television content have indicated furthermore that not only are female characters usually depicted in domestic settings but that they also seem to be much more concerned about family and personal matters than are men both *outside* the home as well as in. McNeil (1975), for example, showed that personal relationships associated with romance or family problems accounted for 74 per cent of female interactions but only 18 per cent of male interactions. On the other hand, professional or work-oriented interactions constituted only 15 per cent of women's versus 35 per cent of men's relationships on television drama programmes.

The personal or familial orientation of women's relationships on television is evident in the case of soap operas and situation comedies whose settings are predominantly domestic. In soap operas, women appear in almost equal numbers to men and are usually more central to the plot in these programmes than in action-adventure programmes. In addition to their higher visibility, females in soap opera often hold respected positions in the family and immediate social environment (Downing, 1974); but the further analysis of 300 episodes from fifteen television serials revealed a persistence of sex-segregated role divisions in which women were concerned mostly with their physical appearance and marital relationships; while the world of work was still largely the preserve of males.

The major action in most soap operas and situation comedies consists of conversation, the nature of which centres on romance, familial and other interpersonal relationships, and problems with these relationships – once again reflecting the traditional female stereotypes (Katzman, 1972). Thus, in these programmes even when women are shown outside the home environment (e.g. at work), their conversations tend to revolve around domestic matters.

2. The occupational roles of TV women   Society's attitudes towards women's roles have been undergoing great changes. In particular, there have been changes in beliefs about the value of the family, the manner in which childcare can best be implemented, the role of marriage in people's lives today, and the possibility of self-fulfilment through work. Nevertheless, in American television drama, the overall pattern is still one of under-representation of female characters in employment relative to male characters *and* compared with the participation of women in the labour force in the real world. Downing (1974) reported that in the sample of prime-time television output she examined, 58 per cent of men were shown in professional occupations against just 19 per cent of women. McNeil (1975) found that almost 75 per cent of the male television population were depicted as gainfully employed, while less than 50 per cent of female characters held jobs. Among married characters the disparity was even greater – few married women and fewer mothers were portrayed as employed. Working wives and mothers generally appeared in comedy shows where their work status was rarely elaborated. According to McNeil, in the few instances when television women held prestigious positions, they played less important roles and their work activities were not central to the plot.

Sex-trait stereotyping

1. The emotionality of TV women   A prominent stereotype of women in western cultures is that they are more obviously emotional than men. (The fact that men are shown more frequently as being violent and aggressive does not count as emotionality, according to these stereotypes.) The emotional woman is believed to become flustered in the most minor crises; she is seen as sensitive, often fearful and anxious, and generally dependent on male help and support in all kinds of personal and professional situations. There is a significant sex bias in the way behaviours have been labelled emotional (Sherman, 1971). Emotionality tends to refer most often to those reactions – fearfulness, anxiety, moodiness and neuroticism – which are typically associated with women, but less often to other responses – aggression and dominance – which are regarded as masculine traits.

Is there evidence that females are in fact more emotional in these particular ways? The answer seems to depend on the type of measure of emotional responsiveness that is used. With regard to fearfulness, females have been found to be somewhat more emotional when rating scale measures are used (e.g. Wilson, 1966; 1967; Spiegler and Liebert, 1970), but observational studies of sex differences in response to a frightening stimulus in young children showed that there were no consistent differences between the sexes (Bronson, 1969; Maccoby and Jacklin, 1973; Stern and Bender, 1974). Apparent sex differences in adulthood may arise as a result of males being less willing to report their anxieties and fears than females (Frieze *et al.*, 1978). In some studies supporting this hypothesis (Wilson, 1967; Spiegler and Liebert, 1970), people who reported few fears or anxieties were also likely to score high on a measure of social desirability – the tendency to respond in culturally approved ways. Much less ambiguity is evident in the way women are characterised and portrayed on television, however.

While men are frequently faced with problems related to the outside world and work, television shows women to be much more involved in family and romantic conflicts (McNeil, 1975) in which their 'characteristic' emotionality is highlighted. Greenberg, Richards and Henderson (1980) reported that on peak-time programmes women were portrayed as needing emotional support more often than men. Men, on the other hand, more often needed physical support of various kinds. Together, these findings indicated a generalised sex-stereotyping pattern in which male television characters were oriented more towards physical needs, while female characters were oriented towards emotional needs.

2. *The sexuality of TV women* A traditional expectation of women in our society is that they should be physically (or sexually) attractive. Indeed, although appearance is considered important in initial judgements made of men and women, a much greater emphasis tends to be placed on a woman's attractiveness than on a man's (Schwartz, 1974). Women are aware of the importance of their physical attractiveness and may use it as a means of gaining influence over men (Frieze *et al.*, 1978).

Feminist writers have been critical of the common tendency for women to be judged in terms of their attractiveness in spheres of life where this is not relevant, that is, virtually everywhere outside show business and professional modelling. It has been argued that a woman's success at work depends more often on the way she looks rather than on her ability to perform the duties demanded by the job. Advertisements as well as programmes have often been

Table 4.2   *Patterns of dominance in total appearances for men and women in situation comedies and crime-dramas*

Genre	Sex	Total appearances		Relationship: Dominant	Equal	Dominated
Situation	Male	302	%	19	64	16
comedy	Female	118	%	14	66	20
Crime	Male	311	%	35	41	24
drama	Female	109	%	7	54	39

Source: Lemon (1978).

blamed as important sources of cultivation of these sexist stereotypes in the mass media.

3. The power and competence of TV women   Television is frequently criticised for emphasising the dominance of men and the subordination of women. Focusing chiefly on demographic indicators of dominance, Lemon (1977) described an *intersex measure* which divided two-party interactions between men and women into those dominated by men, those dominated by women and those where men and women were portrayed as equals. She found that in situation comedies, men and women were about equal, but in crime drama, men were far more likely to be dominant and women to be dominated (Table 4.2.) However, even in crime dramas, more interactions between male and female showed them as equal than as unequal. For Lemon, one of the most important defining attributes of power and competence was occupational status. Men tended to be portrayed more often than women in high-prestige occupations – and they also gave more orders. However, even during interactions between the sexes where professional status was irrelevant, men still generally dominated women, though there were variations between different programme genres see (Table 4.2).

Other researchers have been more precise than Lemon was in their definition of measurement of dominance between sexes, analysing several categories of behaviour to show differential patterns of power and competence among males and females in television drama. Thus Turow (1974) studied patterns of advice-giving and receiving, and order-giving and receiving between men and women in a sample of twelve hours of daytime programming and twelve hours of prime-time programming, consisting mainly of soap operas and other drama. In 70 per cent of all episodes of advice or order giving, men were giving the advice. Results of this analysis were interpreted to show that, in the world of television drama, characters are apparently selected, occupations assigned and plots developed in such a way as to minimise the chances of women displaying superior knowledge or abilities to men. Furthermore, even when female characters were given such opportunities, the advice or order-giving tended to be concerned with traditional female topics.

Sternglanz and Serbin (1974) examined male–female interactions in cartoon programmes, finding that the outcomes of male-instigated and female-instigated actions differed significantly: males were more often treated with positive (or rewarding) outcomes for their actions, whilst females tended to experience neutral or negative outcomes. Elaborating on this finding, Sternglanz and Serbin suggested that children would be 'taught' different lessons by these portrayals according to whether they identified with male or female characters. The sequences analysed from these cartoons involved making and carrying out plans. Young girls who identified with female characters, who were generally unsuccessful in their achievements, would be shown that it is inappropriate for a woman to make plans and carry them out because she will probably be punished for doing so.

4. The assertiveness and ambitious nature of women Manes and Melnyk (1974) carried out two studies in which they examined the models of female achievement available to television viewers. The first study compared female characters at four levels of achievement and showed that only those at the lowest level of achievement were depicted as having successful social relations with men. The message thus offered is that women who are ambitious in a professional sense may have to forfeit a happy social and private life.

In their second study, Manes and Melnyk compared the marital status of male and female job-holders on television. Compared with male job-holders, females were depicted as less likely to be married, less likely to be successfully married, and more likely to be unsuccessfully or unhappily married. Content counts revealed that female characters who held jobs were ten times as likely to be unsuccessful in marriage than were housewives. The authors suggest that female occupational achievers portrayed on television are depicted in a way that would not encourage female viewers to imitate their behaviour given that, for female viewers generally, a happy marriage is assumed to be important. This might discourage external achievement-oriented behaviour in female viewers who valued their home life.

Television portrayals and perceptions of the sexes

Content analysis has indicated that portrayals of women and men on television are very stereotyped and limited, and, according to some writers, lag far behind the social changes that are taking place in the world today (Butler and Paisley, 1980). Mass audiences can assimilate information, often incidentally, from television programmes which may thus influence the way they think about the world around them. Continuous exposure to television may cultivate public beliefs about various social entities in line with the way these entities are portrayed on television, rather than with their reality. In particular, stereotyped messages concerning sex roles on television may give rise to stereotyped beliefs about men and women in society among children whose opinions on these matters are in an early stage of development. Sex-role development and the adoption of sex-appropriate attitudes and behaviours can be observed early in children's lives and television may provide raw material for these attitudes.

Effects on children

There are a number of developmental theories about how children learn sex-roles. One such theory is that children learn during the first few years of life that their gender is unchangeable and are therefore motivated to value highly those attributes and behaviours culturally expected of their own sex in order to maintain self-esteem (Kohlberg, 1966). Another is that children are rewarded for imitating members of their own sex and therefore attend more closely to and learn more from same-sex models (Mischel, 1970; Grusec and Brinker, 1972).

It is difficult to isolate the relative contribution of the media to children's sex-role development. Since television viewing is so prevalent, even among pre-school children, it is not easy to find an adequate control group who have not been exposed to the medium. Some investigators have therefore tested a weaker hypothesis which states that the more a person watches stereotyped television content, the more likely it is that he or she will be affected by it in terms of stereotyped opinions or behaviours. However, measures of *amount* of viewing of television may not be sufficient indicators of television effects, because television content and viewers' preferences for that content vary considerably – two heavy viewers who watch totally different kinds of programme may hold two quite different sets of beliefs as a result. As we shall see in the sections to follow, even where direct measures of social attitudes towards women have been employed, researchers have usually not related these reactions to specific viewing habits and preferences of individuals.

We need to know not simply *how much* television individuals watch but also what kinds of content they prefer to watch most often. Which particular portrayals are most salient to viewers and most likely to hold their attention? And finally, to what extent are the messages conveyed by television portrayals assimilated by viewers into their existing knowledge structures? If it is true that boys and girls learn to value most those attributes and activities which are presented by society as appropriate for their own sex, then it follows that they may also be likely to pay close attention to and show strong preference for television portrayals featuring same-sex characters. People also learn to ascribe certain personality attributes as well as behaviours to men or to women. Analysis of television content profiles has indicated that television portrayals tend to emphasise these sex-typed characteristics in men and women (Tuchman *et al.*, 1978; Butler and Paisley 1980). What evidence is there though that these traits are salient to viewers?

Children's perceptions of the sexes on TV
Mayes and Valentine (1979) asked young viewers to attend to male and female characters on television and found that they perceived sex-typed attributes in cartoon characters. In this experiment, however, viewers were primed to focus on certain aspects of programme content, a feature which is not typical of ordinary viewing. It is also important to know to what extent young viewers pay different amounts of attention to the presence and nature of male and female television characters when they are not given specific instructions to do so.

Evidence on this was provided by Sprafkin and Liebert (1978) who showed groups of youngsters film sequences which featured female characters displaying female-appropriate behaviour for example, or male characters displaying male-appropriate behaviour for example, or males and/or females engaged in less rigid sex-role portrayals. While boys selected and attended to male-focused programmes more than to female-focused programmes and attended specifically to male-dominated scenes in those programmes, girls were more likely to prefer programmes or scenes that revolved around female characters and activities. Boys and girls also identified with same-sex characters – same-sex characters were named as favourites by 84 per cent of children.

Adults' perceptions of the sexes on TV
Research on adults' perceptions of the sexes on television has investigated awareness of the relative presence of males and females on the screen and ratings of the personality traits of males and females

in television programmes and advertisements. Some of these studies have revealed that viewers' perceptions of the characteristics of males and females on television do not always correspond with the ways in which the sexes are stereotyped, according to traditional content analytic research.

Schneider (1979) asked fourteen male and female viewers to rate 48 television commercials originally screened in 1976, using adjectival scales describing the personality characteristics of the men and women portrayed. Some confirmation of earlier content analyses did emerge from Schneider's findings. Female characters in the commercials were perceived, for example, as more concerned about the appearance of their home and more dependent on the opposite sex than were male characters. Schneider's findings, however, revealed interesting differences in perceptions of characters appearing in prime-time and daytime commercials. In general, female characters were perceived as less able spouses, less mature, more foolish and less successful than male characters, but in daytime commercials the situation reversed and women were seen in a more positive light than men on similar dimensions. Schneider concluded that, with respect to personality traits, male characters are as often portrayed in a positive or negative manner as are female characters. The real difference comes with the time of day when the commercial is shown.

Sharits and Lammers (1983) extended Schneider's findings about perceptions of male and female personalities in television commercials. Using similar methods, male and female business school students were asked to rate their perceptions of the roles portrayed in over 100 television advertisements. Females in the commercials were rated more favourably than men in terms of many attributes. Females were perceived to be portrayed as better spouses and parents, more mature, more attractive, more interesting and more modern than males. Little difference was found in the perceptions by male and female judges.

It was reported for the first time that men seem to be increasingly filling sex-object roles in television advertisements. In a study of the perceived personality traits of male and female characters in dramatic television programmes, Peevers (1979) recruited six judges to evaluate the principal males and females in selected television dramas by using Bem's Sex Role Inventory. Bem's work on psychological androgyny (1974; 1975; 1976) analyses individuals in terms of the degree to which they possess both masculine and feminine qualities. For Bem, the androgynous person is mentally healthy, able to act competently in situations which require either traditional male or traditional female characteristics.

Peevers reported two studies conducted one year apart. In the first of these, 85 per cent of all male characters were classified towards the highly masculine end of the Bem scale while only 44 per cent of all females ratings fell in the feminine range of characteristics. In addition, 28 per cent of female characters' sex-role scores were in the masculine range, compared with only 4 per cent of male characters who had opposite sex scores. More than twice as many female characters scored in the androgynous range as did male characters (28 per cent versus 11 per cent). The second study replicated the first and indicated that males were perceived as being more stereotypical than females. This evidence suggests that the traditional male role is considered to be so appealing to viewers that it is *over*-dramatised in TV programmes. The sex-role scores of many male characters were so extremely masculine that they could hardly be achieved by real people. The 'super-masculine' portrayal of the male role abounded on the TV screen, presenting a continuing picture of an unattainable but possibly desirable role model.

Analysis of the female role portrayal, on the other hand, revealed that it was more diversified, more flexible, and more human, in the sense that female characters' sex-role scores fell within the limits attainable by real people. According to Peevers, these results dramatically illustrated the acceptance of greater flexibility in the female role in our society. Deviations by female characters in the direction of masculine qualities were acceptable because those qualities are valued. Conversely, male deviations from the male role remained highly unacceptable.

Perceptions of the sexes in TV and in everyday life
Recent British research has attempted to shed more light not only on how the sexes are seen by viewers in television, but also how these television perceptions differ from the way in which the sexes are seen in everyday life (e.g. Wober, 1981; Gunter, 1984; 1985a). In the most recent of these studies, questonnaires were placed with a representative quota sample of 640 people in the Yorkshire Independent Television region, from which 505 usable returns were retrieved, a 79 per cent response rate. The questionnaire listed ten propositions and asked respondents to say how often each proposition was true of men, and of women 'as they appear in television'; they were asked to repeat this exercise for men and women 'as they actually are in real life'.

Striking differences emerged between perceptions of men and women both on television and in real life. There were some variations as well beween male and female respondents in the way that they perceived women and men on television and in real life. These findings suggest that viewers do make subtle distinctions between the

TV images of the sexes and real world appearances and characteristics. These results are set out in Table 4.3.

Qualities under the heading 'womanly attributes' are those which respondents considered as more characterstic of women in real life than of men. The characteristics listed under 'manly attributes' were more usually attributed by respondents to men than to women in real life.

Overall, perceptions of 'womanly' attributes in both real life and television females were not very different for either male or female viewers. Likewise the extent to which these five more 'womanly' attributes were noticed in men, showed little overall variation between real life and television. There were, however, some noteworthy differences. People thought women in particular, and to a lesser extent men, were shown as likely to get on well if they were good-looking on television much more often than they felt applied in real life. Women respondents were less likely to say that women in real life needed to be good-looking to get on than were men. Both sexes thought television underplayed males' needs to be gentle and affectionate compared with what they considered was true in real life. With regard to more 'manly' attributes, again, the overall perceptions were that they applied more to men than to women, but similarly so on television and in real life. Again, there were particular item differences; women were more likely than men to be aware that women in real life might be interested in politics, and this perceived difference also applied to the portrayal of women's interest in politics on television.

Overall, male respondents showed a slightly greater polarisation in attributing characteristics to women, both on television and in real life, than did women. While men again showed slightly more polarisation than women in linking more male and fewer female characteristics to real-life men, this did not occur in men's description of television portrayals of men. Many of the inter-respondent cross-contextual and sex-role-related differences are significant, and tests for these significance levels have been reported in Gunter (1984). The cross-contextual differences, in particular, raise an important question; for if perceivers can and do recognise that television portrayal differs from their own real-life experience, they are unlikely to infer that television portrayal is an accurate picture of real life. In short, if people recognise television is different, this may insulate them from the 'shortcircuits' of perception that are implied in the Gerbner theory.

The social effects of television sex stereotyping
The evidence linking television sex stereotyping with public attitudes

Table 4.3 Percentages of female and male respondents who perceived each characteristic as true of women and men in real life and on TV

	Real Life				Television			
	Women		Men		Women		Men	
Those evaluated:								
Perceived by:	Women	Men	Women	Men	Women	Men	Women	Men
'Womanly' attributes								
Likely to get on if good-looking	68	82	50	46	93	92	85	85
Like to be romantically involved	91	94	94	91	96	97	95	94
Want to settle and have a family	99	97	95	94	87	91	66	70
Need to be gentle and affectionate	89	93	74	69	84	87	56	52
Could not survive without the other sex	77	76	84	77	62	73	80	75
Averages:	84.8	88.4	79.6	75.4	84.4	88.0	76.4	75.2
'Manly' attributes								
Get on well with own sex	85	79	96	95	59	64	86	87
Successfully hold own against own sex	76	80	91	90	85	84	91	91
Interested in politics	56	42	84	82	42	31	83	77
Need a good job to justify life	38	34	85	85	57	49	91	91
Need to feel they dominate other sex	32	40	81	75	51	51	88	81
Averages:	57.4	55.0	87.4	85.4	58.8	55.8	87.8	85.4
Difference between upper and lower averages	27.4	33.4	−7.8	−10.0	25.6	32.2	−11.4	−10.2

and behaviours derives from two research perspectives both of which are faced with problems of methodology and theoretical interpretation of data. Some of the evidence is correlational; such studies examine the relationship between the amount of time spent watching television and the degree to which viewers hold certain sex-typed attitudes or engage in sex-typed behaviours.

While correlational data can offer useful indications of where relationships between variables may lie, they do not establish that one event causes another. Let us take an example to explain what this means more clearly. Gerbner and Signorielli (1979) examined patterns of television viewing among adults and correlated them with answers to a series of questions measuring sexist attitudes. They reported positive relationships between amount of viewing and beliefs that women should stay at home and that a woman should not work if her husband can support her. These findings were explained in terms of a television influence upon sex-role attitudes. This interpretation must be treated with caution, however, since more than one explanation would be consistent with the data. It is possible that television viewing causes sexist attitudes; it is also possible that people with sexist attitudes watch more television than do less sexist people. The correlational findings support either interpretation.

Another source of evidence consists of experimental studies which are designed to overcome the causation problem. In such studies, the quantity and quality of television viewing can be held constant for all groups of viewers, other relevant extraneous factors such as age and social class can be controlled in advance, and cause and effect can be more easily established. Despite the greater precision of experimental studies, however, methodological problems still arise. Sample sizes are usually small and non-representative, television viewing conditions are normally artificial, and usually (though not always) only short-term effects on attitudes or behaviours are measured. Nevertheless there is a growing body of convincing experimental research which suggests that television may influence children and adults. It can affect intellectual development, change attitudes and teach ways of behaving. Its effect may not always be direct and immediate. Rather, television's influence operates in a subtle or incidental fashion through reinforcing or shaping individuals' views about men and women. Research on the impact of television portrayals on attitudes towards the sexes can be conveniently divided into four sections according to two principal criteria – the type of methodology (correlational survey or experimental) and the sample age group (children or adults/adolescents).

Correlational studies with children

Research has established that children know what sex they are by between 18 months and three years of age (Money and Erhardt, 1972), but do they also begin to limit their life options because of a mental association between role and sex? One of the areas in which sex-role stereotyping occurs most on television is with respect to employment (Downing, 1974; Tedesco, 1974; Butler and Paisley, 1980). To what extent does this content influence children's perceptions of the kind of job to which they will be most suited in later life? To test this question Beuf (1974) conducted interviews with children of both sexes between the ages of three and six.

As well as specific questions about television viewing habits, each child was asked, 'What do you want to be when you grow up?' Then they were required to imagine what they would be if they were a member of the opposite sex (i.e. boys were asked, 'If you were a girl, what would you be when you grow up?'). Finally, the children were given a game called 'The OK Picture Game' in which they were shown several pictures, some of which depicted something unusual or out of place, such as a five-legged cat. The interviewer explained to the childen that the object of the game was to see whether a picture was 'OK' or not. Among several 'dummy' pictures were three scenes in which traditional sex roles had been reversed – a father feeding a baby, a man pouring coffee for a woman, and a female telephone-line repair person. In answer to the first part of the test about what they wanted to be when they grew up, boys tended to nominate traditionally 'masculine' professions such as policeman, sports star or cowboy; girls preferred quieter occupations such as nursing. Over 70 per cent of boys and 73 per cent of the girls chose stereotypical careers for themselves. Even when asked what they would be if they were a member of the opposite sex, in nearly all cases, these youngsters selected occupations which are normally regarded as appropriate for that sex. Responses to pictures indicated that sex-typing increased as images moved from child-care to husband–wife roles to occupations. The children's beliefs reflected their experience of fathers helping around the house, but they found pictures of women doing 'men's' jobs less acceptable.

Beuf claims that such sex stereotyping of career aspirations was more likely to occur among heavier viewers of television, but she presents no data to back up this assertion. Furthermore, Beuf's sample was small and unrepresentative, and her findings need to be replicated with other groups of children before they can be confidently accepted.

In a subsequent study, Frueh and McGhee (1975) asked boys and girls in kindergarten, second, fourth and sixth grades about television viewing, and then presented them with a projective measure of sex-role stereotyping. The latter was a paper and pencil test which examined children's choice of sex-typed toys. Strength of traditional sex-role beliefs as reflected by choice of toys showed a clear, positive association with amount of television viewing. Frueh and McGhee also found that boys and older children made the greatest number of traditionally sex-typed choices on the test. The conclusion of the study is that children can learn about traditional sex roles from television. A number of crucial questions remain unanswered, however. Why were boys and older children more traditional in their attitudes? Was it their traditional attitudes that made some children heavier television viewers in the first place? What role did parents play, not only in teaching children about sex roles, but also in helping them to interpret what was seen on television? How accurate was parental monitoring of actual viewing among the youngest children? Was the sample of 40 girls and 40 boys representative of their age groups? Was the projective test a valid measure of children' sex role development?

Perhaps the strongest correlational evidence so far that television viewing influences children's sex role attitudes comes from a longitudinal study of American adolescents (Morgan, 1982). Measures of television exposure (hours viewed in the 'average day'), acceptance of sex-role stereotypes and educational or occupational aspirations, were taken over the course of two years, and the method of cross-lagged panel correlations was applied to the data. The results support the view that television inculcates certain sex-role views, although the effects are limited to girls. Television viewing in the first year of the study significantly mediated girls' third-year attitudes; heavy viewers were more likely than light viewers to agree that men are more ambitious than women, that women are happiest raising children, and so on. There was no evidence that early degree of sex-stereotyping among girls mediated subsequent television viewing patterns. Among boys, on the other hand, existing sexism foreshadowed greater viewing at a later date, although television had no apparent long-term effects on sex-role attitudes.

Among girls the effect of television was greater among the middle-classes. Both lower-class females and males generally were more sexist regardless of viewing levels. These findings suggested that television viewing is most likely to have an influence among those individuals who are least stereotyped in their views.

Morgan also reported – again for girls only – a relationship between amount of television viewing in the first year of measurement and subsequent educational and occupational aspirations. Interestingly, however, the heavier viewers were the ones who two years later set their sights *higher*. This result, although predicted by Morgan on the basis of television's over-representation of professional women, runs contrary to the traditional influences reported by most other studies.

One of the main problems with the above studies is that exposure to sex stereotyping on televison is measured purely in terms of *gross* viewing behaviour. It is assumed that heavy viewers will automatically see a great deal of the sex sterotyping contained by television programmes. As we saw earlier, however, viewers may not perceive portrayals and events in programmes as having the same characteristics as those described by researchers' coding analyses of television content. Furthermore, gross estimates of television viewing do not tell us whether people have actually seen programmes in which sex-role stereotyping is supposedly most commonplace. If overall television viewing does not relate to sex-role attitudes, is it because television has no effect, or is it because it has more than one kind of effect, with one effect counterbalancing the other? In other words, if programmes contain stereotyping and counter-stereotypical portrayals of the sexes, are viewers' attitudes influenced by both types of portrayal in a complementary fashion? There is correlational evidence (and, as we shall see in the next section, experimental evidence) that the precise influence of television on sex-role attitudes may depend on the particular kinds of portrayals viewed.

Miller and Reeves (1976) surveyed adolescent schoolchildren to explore this possibility and began with the fact that objective content analyses of US television programmes had indicated that men and women are depicted differently on a number of social dimensions. For example, women are less likely than men to be employed, more likely to be married, more likely to hold jobs which are less varied and have lower status, and so on. They then located five programmes which countered this social profile, showing women in traditionally male occupations and other social roles, and measured extent of viewing these shows. Their results revealed a strong positive association between frequency of viewing counter-stereotypical programmes and young viewers' sense that it was 'OK' for girls to aspire to the kinds of non-typical roles portrayed in these shows – school principal, police officer, park ranger and TV producer. Boys and girls were equally accepting of non-traditional aspirations as a consequence. In this case, it was not the overall amount of viewing that contributed to this effect, but the frequency of viewing a particular *type* of programme.

Experimental studies with children

While the above correlational studies indicate a degree of association between amount of television viewing and sex-role stereotyping among children, we cannot be certain about the meaning of this relationship. Experimental studies permit more precise definitions of cause and effect and a small number of published experiments have indicated that viewing of televised sex-role portrayals may influence children's sex-role attitudes and behaviours. Experimenters have been concerned not only with the effects of viewing certain kinds of television on sex stereotyping but have also examined the potential of television, through the portrayal of the sexes in non-traditional roles, to cultivate counter-stereotyped beliefs about men and women.

It is only through the precision of viewing control provided by experiments that the specific effects of viewing these different types of sex-role portrayal can be effectively measured. Atkin and Miller (1975), for example, showed 400 children, aged between six and ten years, a fifteen-minute videotape of children's programmes consisting of a news show, a cartoon and several commercials. One of the commercials was for eye glasses and featured a woman modelling glasses who, in different versions, was portrayed either as a judge, a computer programmer or a television technician. In a fourth condition the commercial was not shown to children at all. After the television presentation, the children were given a list of jobs and asked to mark which ones they thought would be suitable employment for women. The children who saw the versions showing the women as a computer programmer or television technician did not differ in their judgements about the suitability of these jobs for women from the children who did not see the commercial. But the group who saw a female judge were more likely to endorse this as an appropriate occupation for women (51 per cent versus 31 per cent for those who did not see this version). Girls and older children were most strongly influenced in this respect. There was also evidence of generalisation of non-traditional beliefs to other occupations. Children who saw the female judge were also more likely to think that women could be doctors. Flerx, Fidler and Rogers (1976) found that five-year-olds who saw a film depicting men and women in non-traditional roles produced significant changes in beliefs about 'working mothers', 'nurturing fathers', and the kinds of games and activities appropriate for girls and boys.

McArthur and Eisen (1976) showed pre-school children short videotaped vignettes which depicted adult male and female models engaging in a number of activities. Under one condition the models behaved in ways normally associated with their sex, while in a second version they reversed their activities to perform non-sex-typical behaviours. It was found that children tended to recall and reproduce,

imitatively, more of the behaviours of the same-sex than of the op-
posite-sex television model. So, even when the same-sex model displayed behaviours normally not thought of as associated with his
or her own sex, the children still recalled and imitated them better.
Thus, boys were more likely to remember and imitate nurturant,
domestic and artistic behaviours than leadership, bravery and prob-
lem-solving activities of a television model when the former behaviours were performed by a male and the latter by a female. On
the other hand, when the sex of the models performing each set
of activities fitted current sex-role stereotypes, so did the boys'
behaviour. Similar results were obtained for girls, although their
tendency to show more imitations of a same-sex model was weaker
than for boys.

Drabman and colleagues (1981) investigated the immediate impact
on pre-school and elementary schoolchildren of a televised presentation in which the traditional sex roles of physician and nurse were
reversed. After watching a videotape of a male nurse and a female
doctor the youngsters were asked to identify photographs or names
of the doctor and nurse. Pre-school children and those aged five
and nine years selected male names or photos for the doctor and
female names or photos for nurse, thereby reversing the genders
they had seen for these occupations in the television portrayal. Their
immediate recall appeared strongly influenced by their stereotypes
rather than by the television portrayal they had just viewed. However,
twelve-year-olds were able to identify correctly the names of the
doctor and nurse on the basis of what they had been shown on
television.

Davidson, Yasina and Towers (1979) showed members of a group
of five-year-old girls one of three cartoon shows. One cartoon showed
a girl in a counter-stereotyped way, successfully behaving in various
traditionally male pursuits including sports and building a clubhouse.
The second cartoon showed a girl in a stereotyped fashion, and
the third paid no particular attention to sex roles. The reverse-
stereotyped version produced significantly less sex-stereotyping of
personality characteristics than the other two programmes, although
as the authors admit, it is impossible to be sure which of many
differences, both related and unrelated to sex-role perceptions,
among the programmes, were responsible for producing the effects.

In another study, television commercial portrayals were used to
influence children's sex-role attitudes. Pingree (1978) presented
seven to nine-year-olds with television commercials showing either
traditional or non-traditional female characteristics with instructions
either that the characters were all real people or that they were
all acting, or that the commercials were just like the ones at home

(neutral). Children's perceptions of reality were successfully affected; those in the reality-set condition believed the commercial portrayals to be more realistic than did those in the acting-set condition, with children not given specific indications about the reality of the portrayals falling in between the latter two groups.

The overall effects of traditional and non-traditional presentations of women on attitudes were contradictory. Children who saw the commercials did not differ significantly in their attitudes towards women from a control group who saw no commercials. However, for children who received instructions about the reality of the commercials, attitudes towards women were less traditional after viewing non-traditional commercials. Non-traditional portrayals had no effect on children's attitudes towards women when no specific instructional set was provided. It seems likely that the duration of these commercials (five minutes) was too brief to effect attitude change unless something else was done to heighten their impact, such as saying that they depicted real people. In attempting to facilitate changes in sex-role beliefs among children, through a specially-produced television series, Johnson and Ettema (1982) reported that such changes depended upon further, external reinforcement of the programmes' lessons in the form of classroom discussions and written assignments about the programmes.

Finally, it is useful to report a real-life 'field' experiment in which the various changes exemplify what comes about when changes involving television are made in a particular way. Reporting what happened in three towns in Canada, Notel (which started without television, but acquired it), Unitel and Multitel (which had one, rising to two channels and four channels, respectively) across a two-year period, Kimball (1977) focused on scores on a sex-role differentiation scale. The scale was filled in by children and showed how accurately the items described children of their own age, and how accurately they describe parents. It was found that before Notel acquired television there were no differences between boys and girls in attitudes towards peer behaviour; after Notel had television, as in the other two towns at both stages of the experiment, boys developed more traditional sex-role perceptions than was found amongst girls. In real life, therefore, the kind of television introduced in a small Canadian town appears to have fortified traditional expectations of how boys should behave.

Experimental studies with adults
Most of the work done on television's influence on sex-role beliefs has dealt with children who are supposed to be most susceptible to such influence. According to several recent experimental studies,

however, the effects of televised sex-role portrayals would seem not to be restricted to younger viewers. Television commercials containing traditional or non-traditional sex-role portrayals have also been shown to influence adolescent high-school girls and female college students.

One study by Tan (1979) found that adolescent girls fed a heavy dose of beauty commercials were more likely than a control group of girls who did not see these commercials to believe that being beautiful is an important female characteristic and is necessary to attract men. Twenty-three high-school girls, aged 16 and 18 years, viewed 15 commercials which emphasised the desirability of sex appeal, beauty or youth (e.g. advertisements for soap, toothpaste, beauty products, etc.) 33 girls viewed commercials which contained no beauty messages (e.g. advertisements for dog food, soy sauce and nappies). Each girl was then asked to rank order the relative importance of ten attributes (e.g. pretty face, intelligence, sex appeal, hard-working, competence, etc.) in each of four areas (career/job, wife, to be liked by men, and desirable personal attribute). The girls who saw the beauty advertisements ranked the importance of the beauty and sex appeal qualities significantly higher than did the non-beauty advertisement group for the item 'to be liked by men' and with marginal significance in the same direction also for the item 'personally desirable'. One difficulty in testing the effects of media sex-role stereotyping on sex-role learning and sex-role behaviour is that of locating a control which has never been exposed to stereotyped media portrayals.

Jennings, Geis and Brown (1980) sought to overcome this problem by testing a contrast hypothesis. Rather than expecting that stereotyped commercials depress women's self-confidence and independence of judgement, they tested the contrast of this, that commercials which *break* sex-role stereotyping raise women's self-confidence and independence of judgement. They found that female college students who saw non-traditional depictions of women subsequently expressed more career aspirations than those who saw traditional sex-stereotyped commercials.

Building on these findings, the researchers investigated whether commercials could have effects, not only on the attitudes of female college students, but also on their behaviour. Eight television commercials were devised; four showed women in traditional, dependent and subservient roles vis-à-vis men; the other four exactly reversed the roles within the same scenarios and showed women as dominant and men as subservient. After viewing one or the other set, viewers were questioned about the female and male roles shown. Then, half were given an Asch-type conformity test. In this, they were asked to rate cartoons and were shown a set of falsified ratings supposedly supplied previously by other people. The degree to which their own opinions differed from the falsified ratings was interpreted as a measure of independence of judgement. Other participants in the experiment were asked to give a short, impromptu speech, and their degree of confidence in so doing was rated. Those women who had seen the role-reversed commercials were more independent in their ratings of cartoons and more self-confident in giving a speech than were those who had seen the stereotyped versions. Given the absence of any similarity between the situations in the commercials and of the subsequent situations in which the women had to perform, it is unlikely that the observed behavioural effects arose from the explicit content of the advertisements. Indeed the women were, it seems, unaware of the influence exercised by the commercials. When the women were asked if they identified with the people in the commercials, all reported a low level of identification regardless of the version seen. Nevertheless, there was an apparent behavioural effect which led the authors to point to an implicit message power in the commercials, assimilated unwittingly by viewers.

Effect or selectivity?

Much of the empirical evidence discussed so far has pointed to a relationship between sex-role stereotyping on television and popular beliefs about the sexes. Correlational surveys have shown a link between amount of television viewing and degree of sex-role stereotyping among viewers. Experimental studies have demonstrated that, when individuals are shown sex-stereotyped TV portrayals, their beliefs may be influenced, in several instances in the short term and in one case across a two-year period, in the direction of increased stereotyping. Counter-stereotyped portrayals, on the other hand, can have the reverse effect, producing an increase in non-traditional perceptions of the sexes.

Correlational studies have attempted to reveal possible long-term effects of television viewing on beliefs about the sexes, but have often failed to demonstrate carefully enough that viewers have actually seen particular, critical programmes or portrayals: neither do such studies show that real-world beliefs about women or men correspond with their perceptions of the sexes on television. The interpretations of correlational relationships is a problematic issue: results can be fraught with ambiguity and directions of effects may be extremely difficult to disentangle. Is a significant correlation between television viewing and a stereotyped belief about some social entity to be interpreted as an influence of television, or is viewing behaviour affected, at least in part, by the antecedent belief? There is some evidence that the latter 'selective viewing' hypothesis may have some validity, especially among adults whose lives provide them with established contexts with which to interpret and even to choose, new experience and evidence as it comes along, fittingly.

Like the earlier mentioned work of McArthur and Eisen (1976) a study by Sprafkin and Liebert (1978) demonstrated that children tend to focus more carefully on television characters of their own sex. These researchers observed the way children selected television programmes and found that youngsters tended to choose programmes that featured characters of their own sex. Furthermore, girls and boys paid more attention to same-sex characters and attention was greatest when the same-sex character behaved in ways normally deemed most appropriate for that sex. This study indicated that children may use television selectively to find confirmation of previously developed stereotypes about their own sex. Such early established stereotypes are likely to be inculcated by a mixture of influences including experience, behaviour of parents and the influence of early peer groups, as well as of what is seen on television. Indeed, evidence is accumulating that influences of televised sex-role portrayals on children's beliefs about the sexes may be mediated by the ways in which characters are perceived and evaluated. Character perceptions may in turn be affected by pre-formed sex-stereotyping among young viewers.

Reeves and Greenberg (1976) used multi-dimensional scaling techniques to explore the cognitive dimensions used by children in judging television characters. They found that children of different age groups used virtually the same dimensions to describe the characters. Boys were more influenced by physical strength and activity; girls were more influenced by physical attractiveness. Reeves and Greenberg concluded that the dimensions identified are strong predictors of the children's desire to copy the social behaviour of television characters behaving stereotypically.

The importance of other social forces for reactions to television portrayals of the sexes was indicated in research by Williams, La Rose and Frost (1981). Preconceptions about sex-appropriate traits and behaviours influenced children's ratings of male and female TV characters. Further, children's belief that their own friends and peers in real life would approve of the way a particular character behaved was found to be an important determinant of their reported intentions to imitate or 'want to be with' that character.

Sex-typed biases in character perceptions seemed to rely as much on the sex of the character as on the sex of the viewer. Strength, for example, figured more prominently in the character preferences of boys than of girls. Likewise 'good looks' were more important for girls than for boys, but also related well to the preferences of boys for female characters. In sum, this research suggests that children's preferences for television characters and the way they behave are mediated by pre-existing beliefs concerning whether others in one's social environment are likely to approve of those characters and their behaviours. If this early evidence is accurate, then the *quantities* of males and females shown on television (something emphasised frequently by content-analysis research) are considerably less important than the *qualities* portrayed, and how these qualities are perceived.

Recent British research has further examined relationships between sex-role and sex-trait perceptions and television viewing among adults. This research has been concerned with elucidating associations between particular beliefs and particular patterns of programme watching.

Different programmes portray women in different ways. Do individuals who watch a great deal of one type of programme hold different beliefs about women than the individuals who watch another type of programme? And if such distinct patterns of relationships do exist between programme preferences and beliefs, are they to be interpreted as evidence of selective viewing or specific television influences? A further question investigated by this work is whether viewers' perceptions of the sexes as seen on television are the same as their perceptions of the sexes in real life, and whether both sets of perceptions relate in similar ways to patterns and preferences of television viewing.

Gunter and Wober (1982) reported a survey in which diary measures of television viewing were related to questionnaire responses concerning perceptions of women on television and in real life. The questionnaire was in three parts. In the first part, respondents were asked to say how true or untrue it was that women on television in daily life serials (e.g. soap operas), in situation comedies, or in advertisements are portrayed as 'not being interested in politics', 'wanting at some time to be mothers', 'quarrelsome with other women', 'very interested in jobs and careers', 'very keen on romantic affairs with men', 'depending on men to help them out of trouble', and 'more likely to get on if attractive'. If the second part, respondents were required to say how true or untrue each of these items was of women in real life. And in the final part, slightly re-worded versions of these items were presented concerning the way women *ought* to lead their lives.

These items were chosen to reflect prevalent characterisations of women on television which had previously been identified by content analysis studies, and which supposedly functioned to cultivate sexist stereotypes among viewers (see Lemon, 1977; Tuchman, 1978; Butler and Paisley, 1980). From their completed viewing diaries, respondents were scored for the total number of programmes viewed during the survey week and for amount of viewing of several programme types: namely, serious action-drama (consisting of crime-detection series and feature films), soap operas, comedy shows, and news and current affairs programmes. Respondents were then divided into light, medium and heavy viewers of television in general and of each of these programme types.[1]

A series of multiple classification analyses were computed to assess relationships between television viewing patterns and beliefs about women, with statistical controls employed simultaneously for sex, age and socio-economic class of respondents. These analyses revealed a number of significant relationships between television viewing behaviour and perceptions of women both on television and in actuality, but only with respect to viewing of serious action-drama programmes. Significant relationships between viewing of other kinds of programme and perceptions of women were not found.

Amount of serious action-drama viewing and endorsements of how women are portrayed on television, how they appear in real life, and how they should be in real life were significantly related for four attributes: 'women as interested in jobs and careers', 'women as keen on romantic affairs with men', 'women as dependent on men to help them out of trouble' and 'women as getting on better if they are attractive'. Further significant relationships emerged between serious action-drama viewing and perceptions that 'women want to be mothers' in real life and that they 'should want to be mothers' as an ideal.

The results, reported by Gunter and Wober (1982), show that heavy viewers of serious action and drama programmes were significantly more likely than light viewers to perceive that women in serious drama serials are interested in job and careers, keen on romantic affairs with men, dependent on men to help them out of trouble, and as likely to get on if they are attractive. The same paper reports the five attributes of real-life women on which perceptions were related to amount of serious action-drama viewing. Heavy viewers of this type of programming show conflicting perceptions: they were more likely to say that women are keen on romantic affairs. But they also perceived women in everyday life as more career-oriented than did light viewers. On the other hand, light action-drama viewers saw women as less dependent on men when in trouble and less dependent on their own attractiveness in getting on, than did heavy viewers. So, in some cases the light action-drama viewers had 'stereotyped' perceptions and in others, the heavy viewers showed more stereotyping.

The study went on to show that viewing behaviour was significantly related to opinions on the same five attributes, on this occasion concerning perceptions of how women should be ideally in real life. These results indicate that heavy viewers of serious action-drama programmes were more likely to agree that women should want to become mothers and that they should be interested in sexual relations as much as men. Heavy action-drama viewers were also more likely than light viewers to feel that women should be interested in jobs and careers, but were less likely to consider that women should be self-reliant when faced with problems, rather than depending on men to help them out of trouble. Heavy action-drama viewers also were more likely than were light action viewers to feel that women should get on well with other women, and that women should be judged on abilities rather than looks.

Content-analysis studies have, over the years, identified a number of prominent images of women on television and inferred that, through regular viewing of these, stereotyped beliefs about women are cultivated amongst the general public. The results from the present study afforded the opportunity to examine actual public perceptions of female portrayals on television *and* to see whether or not these perceptions corresponded with the 'images' of women defined through content analysis of American programming, which forms a substantial part of action-drama material seen on British television.

In serious dramas, content analysis studies have indicated that women are portrayed mainly in domestic, familial roles, and much less often in professional career-oriented roles. Women are often shown as preoccupied with romance and as dependent on men to help them whenever they get into trouble, especially outside the home (see Seggar and Wheeler, 1973; Lemon, 1978; Tuchman, 1978). Perceptions of women on television serials obtained from viewers by Gunter and Wober (1982), however, did not indicate particularly strong tendencies for viewers to see women in television as wanting to be mothers, as more likely to succeed if they were attractive, as depending on men when in trouble or as interested in jobs and careers. Viewers' subjective perceptions on the first three of these attributes did not coincide with the 'images' of television women identified by objective content analysis. Agreement between viewers' perceptions and objectively-coded qualities of women did occur on the item concerning women shown as keen on romantic affairs with men. There are also differences in women and men viewers. From separate surveys and measurement of viewing behaviour there is evidence that not only do women view more programmes than men do, overall, particularly fiction and light entertainment, but they appreciate what they see there, better than do male viewers (Wober, 1984c). As regards advertisements women do not, in spite of the content analyses of British television reported by Manstead and McCulloch (1981) and Livingstone and Green (1986), consider that advertisements portray women in a demeaning way.

There was no consistent evidence from these studies corresponding with the cultivation of stereotyped beliefs inferred from content analysis. Heavy viewers of serious-action drama actually perceived women in television serials as *more* independent of men; content-analysis relating amount of viewing to stereotyped attitudes would predict the opposite. There was no marked relationship between amount of action-drama viewing among this British audience and perceptions of television women as wanting to be mothers and settled with a family, even though American content analyses have often indicated that this is the way women are shown (Tedesco, 1974; Tuchman, 1978). Heavy viewers of serious action-drama were more likely than light viewers of these programmes to perceive women on television as career-oriented, and on this item, audience perceptions run counter to content analytic descriptions of the way women are portrayed (see Butler and Paisley, 1980; Manstead and McCulloch, 1981).

One reason for the evident lack of effects among British viewers with regard to stereotypical portrayals of women and of men may well be because viewers do not perceive the portrayals to be as the content analyses indicate. In the field of advertisements, Livingstone and Green (1986) have shown, as did others before them, that men are much more often portrayed in superior status roles and with greater initiative than are women; yet one national survey (Wober, 1980e) showed that equal porportions of women and men said they had been annoyed with a TV advertisement (only just over one quarter of viewers); sex was related to a composite scale of attitude statements critical of television in general (e.g. the swearing in some plays) but was independent of scores on a similar composite scale of attitudes towards television advertisements (e.g. the amount of advertisements shown between parts of programmes). Had women been dissatisfied about the portrayal of their sex in advertisements there should have been a link between attitudes on this scale, and viewers' own status.

In the realm of programme perception an ongoing study has collected perceptions from large samples of viewers on a set of 17 descriptions of each of 25 programme series. Three factors emerge in the analysis of these data and point to clusters of descriptive characteristics, one being the representation of women (specifically, exploring their portrayal as strong or as weak characters). Examination of possible links between attitudes on these factors showed that the concept of realistic portrayal was associated with levels of appreciation; but attitudes towards the items in the factor describing the representation of women were not any kind of pointer to the degree of appreciation recorded for programmes. Average scores indicating the extent to which each scale applies to each series show that women and men differ very little, if at all; and the British soap operas in particular, but also action-dramas and situations comedies, studied are perceived as depicting women as strong characters.

Another important question is whether viewing behaviour relates to perceptions of women in real life, and also whether real-life perceptions are consistent with perceptions of women on television. Gunter and Wober's study found that beliefs about women being interested in careers, being keen on romance, being dependent on men when in trouble and needing to be attractive to get on were each related to action-drama viewing for television and real-life perceptions. But how consistant in direction were these relationships?

Heavy action-drama viewers perceived women on television serials as not interested in jobs and careers more than did light-action viewers and also believed that this is the way women *are* and *should be* in real life. In addition, heavy action-drama viewers perceived women more as keen on romance both on television and in reality, and believed that they should be interested in romantic relations with men in everyday life. There was a positive relationship between the amount of serious action-drama viewing and the belief that women relied heavily on their attractiveness to make progress in life. Heavy action-drama viewers also tended to believe (more than did light viewers) that women should not be judged on looks alone but on their ability. Finally, heavy action-drama viewers perceived women as dependent on men in television serials or in real life more than did light viewers, and believed less that women should be self-reliant. Clearly, there is consistency in many of the beliefs held about women as they are depicted on the television screen in certain programmes and as they appear in real life, but these beliefs in several cases do not match the images of women on television identified by objective content analysis.

A resolution of the various problems of inconsistency in these viewing and perception relationships was offered by Wober (1983). The method proposed was that if there were a link between a real-life perception or an ideal belief and some measure of television viewing, then the chance that there was causal reinforcement of these beliefs would be supported by an essential piece of added evidence. This was that there might also be a parallel link between the same measure of television viewing and testimony that portrayals resembled what was observed in real life, or what was described as an ideal. These conditions were met in the case of two measures: wanting to be mothers, and being interested in jobs and careers. In both cases those who viewed more soap operas tended more strongly to see such characteristics depicted there; and these heavier viewers also tended to affirm these descriptions as true in real life. In the first instance, heavier viewers were also more likely than lighter viewers to feel that women should concentrate on child-raising.

The use of this subjective perception measure corresponds with what many critics (Hobson, 1983; Newcomb and Hirsch, 1985) call for in terms of understanding how viewers interpret the possible meanings present in programmes. Television, then, is seen as producing 'influences' not as in a 'hypodermic' analogy, but as an interactive process. In this, viewers come to what they see, and interpret what they see, both in the light of their own preconceptions and also as reinforcement of such notions. It is in this sense that television apparently influences certain (adult) beliefs and the information reported here shows how and in some cases where this had occurred.

Note

1. For the four programme categories, relative proportions of total viewing time devoted to each were computed by dividing the number of programmes seen in a category by the total number seen overall. This was done to obtain an accurate measure of how viewers shared out their total viewing time among different types of programmes. Frequency distributions were then computed on proportions data so that respondents could be divided into light, medium and heavy viewers within each programme category.

5   Television and the cycle of life

Introduction

William Shakespeare divided the lifecycle of man into seven ages; and it is remarkable to note how, in that early point in the Gutenberg revolution of print which some say had made widespread literacy and education possible, the picture Shakespeare gives us is in several ways recognisable in today's reality. Shakespeare, the modern layperson and Piaget can all agree on the first stage of growth – infancy, the age of total dependency and rudimentary cognitions. At the far end of the scale, Shakespeare engagingly distinguishes two kinds of agedness; one in which the person enters in slippers and dressing-gown, thus implying a withdrawal into a private from a public world, when faculties remain in reasonable working order even if physique is somewhat impaired; and finally, a condition of severely impaired sensorimotor functioning (though Shakespeare does not imply that this necessarily means mental deterioration).

In an interesting modern theory, Postman (1982) has claimed that childhood as it is known (still) today is a social product and came about as a result of the development of print. Print has facilitated widespread literacy and education and it was only by mastery of these that the individual gained access to the fastness in which adult secrets about sex, violence and death were now secluded. Postman treats the decade from seven to seventeen as until recently that of childhood, and the implication is that whether lengthy or abbreviated, childhood led the person, without a 'teenage' phase, into the adult world. For Postman, the effect of television (at least as he describes its content in America) has been to shortcircuit the pathways to adult knowledge hitherto presented gradually via literacy and formal education. By shamelessly parading sex and violence before all, including child viewers, children (in America) are now made to witness adult 'secrets' that had last been accessible to all young people before the spread of print, 500 years ago. Postman presents the young adult now as 'a grown-up whose intellectual and emotional capacities are unrealised, and in particular not significantly different from those associated with children'. This process is complementary to that in which children have become in superficial ways 'adultified'. The tone of Postman's book is unquestionably pessimistic and he sees the disappearance of childhood as something to be regretted, but which cannot be restored by any measures that he can envisage in America, in the face of an unbridled electronic communications environment; perhaps as a last resort the computer might provide a new competency barrier behind which secrets might recede. This suggestion is not, however, very convincing, as it seems unlikely that the computer will constitute an apparatus which practically the whole population would wish to (and successfully) master, as is the case with print. It could only thus provide a partial barrier across society, while the kinds of matter that the computer might seclude seem unlikely to resemble the life secrets hidden in books or disclosed by television.

It is not easy to be sure with Aries, Eisenstein, Elias and Postman that childhood arose only because of print, and to explore this it would be necessary to examine non-literate cultures and the history of family life in partially literate societies in the centuries before print became widespread. It is important, however, to try to pin down this alleged causality because it has a bearing on the subsequent argument that the advent of television, either because of the way it is organised in itself or in part because it supplants print, may abolish childhood.

In an analysis of anthropological literature on pre-literate cultures, Wober (1971) noted that in many instances there were structures akin to boarding schools, in which youngsters left their families and were grouped into 'societies' where they were given adult lore over an extended period. It would seem valid to interpret the stage up to this educational phase as one of childhood; and clearly it existed in many societies without a precondition of widespread literacy. In the Bible, Leviticus 27 explains the significance of vows made by different people and gives values according to sex and to age; the age bands run from one month to five years, from five to twenty years, and from twenty to sixty years. The milestone for adulthood seems, then, to have been twenty, for the subsequent book (Numbers 1) names those who are 'able to go forth to war' as aged twenty and above. This evidence from pre-literate societies does not disprove Postman's contention that universal print literacy did bring about childhood as it has recently been experienced in western societies; but it undercuts the possibility that it is *only* such a literacy that will 'generate' childhood as a social entity. By the same token, the notion that the medium by which ideas and feelings are communicated may not be the only or even the most powerful determinant of a lifecycle phase loosens the argument that American television may somehow be dissolving childhood.

Television and childhood

There is an extensive literature on children and television. Much of it rests on the assumption – and goes on to fortify it – that children and adults relate to television in different ways. We wish now to examine some of the evidence on this point; we shall seek to verify that adults are well aware of the phase of childhood (since Postman alleges that it is the very concept of childhood that is being dissolved) and that adults treat children as different from adults with regard to their uses of television. We shall seek to establish that children watch television, at least in Britain, in different amounts and patterns from adults, and that they appreciate what they see on television in different ways than do adults.

A large study of children in four British regions (IBA, 1974) showed that not only are there many programmes made for children, but they also figure prominently in children's perceptions of the medium. Asked to recall the programmes they saw the day before the interview, children aged from five to seven mentioned 56 different children's programmes and 46 adult titles; among those aged 8–11 the adult titles outnumbered the children's by 61 to 40; but even among those aged 12–15, there were still 24 different programme titles mentioned of material made for children, as against 75 'adult' programmes. Many of the latter, while not expressly made for children, are examples of 'family viewing' material. The same 12 to 15 year olds, asked to give examples of their favourite programmes, far more often cited comedy and light entertainment material than any other type (children's magazines, and adventure action came next). Few children recalled seeing soap operas (though these are normally broadcast when children are available to view) or said they liked them.

A few years later, the BBC published a major survey (BBC, 1979) which showed the percentage of children in the viewing audience, half hour by half hour, over two seasons. For weekdays in winter, 30 per cent of the audience between 4 and 5 p.m. were children aged 5–9 and 25 per cent were aged 10–15. At weekends, this obvious 'children's hour' was not in evidence, primarily because children's programmes are not provided by the broadcasters at this time. ITV's audience measurement (Wober, 1979a) also showed that between 30 and 40 per cent of 4–9 year olds were watching television during children's hour and so were 20 per cent of 10–15 year olds. Later that year another analysis showed that among children's programmes drama was the best liked type, followed by entertainment: general interest and information was clearly less well liked (Wober, 1979b). There is evidence, however, that young children are sometimes allowed to watch late-night programmes such as horror films (Wober,

1982d) and that they enjoy such films. This has given rise to well-publicised concern about how to protect young children from material that is not suitable or intended for them.

Teenage viewers

If childhood is a period after infancy which is catered for by providing formal schooling and, on television, particular programmes at particular times which achieve fairly widespread viewing among the target audience, the question of what follows is not so clear. The age of consent, when it is considered, in Britain, that a girl may legally set about becoming a mother, is sixteen; one may not vote until eighteen; one must remain in full-time schooling until sixteen. Thus there is a set of different milestones marking a transition from childhood to adulthood; and the age band is distinguished in popular and marketing culture as 'teenage' territory. The situation in the United States is yet more complex, with considerable cultural and legal variations across individual states; it is one of Postman's particular points that many portrayals on television both in programmes and in advertising bring the ambiguities of innocence and knowledge which were early on projected in *Lolita*, and later personified in Brook Shields to blur the lines supposedly recognised more clearly before the advent of television, between childhood and the adult world. To determine whether television recognises and knows how to cater appropriately for this age band of viewers it is part of the solution to survey the public and discover where, if at all, in the lifecycle they locate the teenage category (see below).

A number of audience studies have set out to identify the teenage group as something behaviourally distinct from adults and children. Evidence from one study (Wober, 1980b) came from a sample who filled in a week's viewing diaries. Ten to fifteen year olds had patterns of viewing and appreciation distinctly different from those of children, while from sixteen to nineteen, people behaved in a manner more like adults. The first group (aged 10–15) showed very little appreciative interest in informational programmes; this may coincide with their presence in formal education where such material is offered during the day. From 16 to 19, there was some minor sign of kindled interest in informational programmes, as evidenced by increasing viewing and appreciation of news, current affairs and documentary programmes. An analysis of secondary-school pupils' political awareness (Wober, 1980c) found that these non-voters had very limited levels of political knowledge. There was little evidence that television viewing had anything to do with enhancing such knowledge.

A second viewing diary study (Wober, 1982d) showed that there were teenage audiences markedly different in size, for different programme types and their appreciation averages did not necessarily reflect audience sizes. Thus, while teenagers viewed adventure action in greater proportions than did adults, and liked what they saw more than adult viewers did, teenagers provided much smaller audiences for sport, but almost as great an appreciation as did adults. Both age bands provided smaller audiences for news and general information than they did for other programme types, but teenagers also showed less appreciation in doing so than did adults. Audience size and appreciation among adults did not always match, but there *was* a positive link for these two measures amongst teenagers. This suggests that teenagers are more selective viewers who choose to view what they know they will appreciate.

Television and adulthood
While these kinds of study show that childhood and adolescence are recognised and treated as distinct lifecycle phases by television programme-makers, and their existence is reflected in patterns of viewing behaviour, adulthood is commonly regarded as a kind of existential plateau which lasts for several decades. To be sure, marketing practitioners distinguish parenthood from the experience of adults without children, and they distinguish mid-life turning-points such as marriage, divorce, bereavement and change in employment status; but these fluctuations, while marked, may occur within any of a number of five-year age bands between the ages of 25 and 50; thus television audience studies can afford to – and do – deal with the adult world as a homogeneous unit. However, within this unit, age can act as a variable which relates in various ways with a number of other measures.

To assess demand for different programme types, eleven of these were on one occasion arbitrarily defined (e.g. documentaries, plays, news, sport) and a national sample of UK viewers were asked if they wanted to see more or less of each kind (Wober, 1984c). Those wanting less were subtracted from the percentage wanting more to provide a 'net demand' figure for each programme category. Results were analysed for six age bands and showed larger differences between top and bottom demand for different age groups than between sexes or across socio-economic class categories. The demand differences did not, however, show a linear variation in all programme types. For documentaries there was an inverted U-curve with greatest net demand amongst the 35–44 year olds; for soap operas and news, there were something more like linear relations with older people wanting each type progressively more. A recent large study (Wober, 1982c) showed that with soap opera, news and sport, there were marked and linear increases in the use made (of what was available) with increasing age of viewers; but with adventure, single films and general interest material there were no effective differences in consumption rates across the whole adult age range.

A number of distinctions emerge from all this material. One is that 'television' is not a homogeneous entity, and that different parts of it, or programme types, appeal in different ways to people of different ages. Appeal here means both declared interest or desire to see it, or actual numbers of programmes seen. Next is that age bands labelled as entities in popular parlance, such as children, teenagers, adults and the aged are not homogeneous in their media interests and uses. Each group is split within itself in the ways in which they deal with television, and there are also differences between the age groupings themselves.

Television and the aged

At the senior end of the adult span (in America, at least) there is now a political lobby which interacts with the work of social scientists and mass communicators in wanting to influence how 'the truth' about old people and age is generated and presented. Advertising in the autumn 1974 issue of *Journal of Communication* (p. 112) the National Gray Panthers declared: 'Victims of Ageism, Unite'. They point to the 'very real, frightening and continuous ageism which we find everywhere in our society'.

One of the principal difficulties for any retired person in western societies is adapting to the fundamental life change associated with giving up the highly valued work role. Acceptance of retirement may not be helped by the negative stereotypes which are often associated with getting older and which some gerontologists believe contribute to many of the dysfunctions associated with old age. Derogatory stereotypes of the elderly may deprive older people of the status they enjoyed during their earlier years. Indeed, old people often attempt to deny that they are old because the designation is felt to be degrading (Tibbitts, *et al.*, 1963; Rosow, 1974). It has been suggested that unfavourable characterisation of the elderly on television serves to reinforce and may even engender negative 'ageist' stereotypes (Gerbner *et al.*, 1980).

Television plays a singularly important role in the lives of the elderly for whom it provides a main source of information, entertainment and companionship. Research into the use of leisure time has shown that viewing television is the one activity reported most often by retired, older adults (De Grazia, 1961; Schramm, 1969; Ward, 1979). British figures indicate that people aged 61 and over watch an average of 26 hours a week in summer and 33 hours a week in winter, which is on average about one-third as much again as the amount watched by those aged 60 and under (BBC, 1978).

Elderly viewers now represent a substantial proportion of the potential television audience. In the United States, for example, recent Census figures have confirmed a dramatic rise in the proportion of the population made up of elderly people (Dans, 1980). In 1979 there were over 24 million people in the United States aged 65 years and over and another 20 million aged 55–64 years, giving a combined total of nearly 21 per cent of the US population (US Bureau of the Census, 1981). It has been anticipated that aged groups will increase rapidly in the next two decades both numerically and proportionately. In Britain, recent figures indicate that old age pensioners constitute one in six of the population (Central Statistics Office, 1980). With decreasing birth rates, improved medical treatment and health care, and earlier retirement, this proportion is likely to grow considerably as the end of the century approaches.

While the aged population continues to grow, some researchers have claimed that, on television, the elderly are barely visible, and whenever they do appear it is more often than not in an unfavourable, disrespectful or degrading light. It is argued that this medium upon which so many people, especially elderly and retired individuals, depend for entertainment, information about the world and simply to fill time, may be cultivating negative public images about the aged which may lower their self-respect.

American television's apparent obsession with youth in both programmes and commercials has been accused of impairing the effectiveness of older persons (Francher, 1973), although this is not apparently related to amount of viewing. Francher's claim was not based on any testing of audience perceptions but on a content analysis of age portrayals in 100 television commercials, so a TV influence cannot be proved. Furthermore, even the content-analysis method used by Francher has recently been criticised in that the author did not say how or from where commercials were selected, nor was any information on coding reliability reported (Ostman and Scheibe, 1984). Where audience perceptions were in fact investigated, as in a survey by Louis Harris and Associates (1974), it was found that heavy viewers, light viewers and non-viewers differed little in their attitudes towards old age.

Before any cultivation effects of television on perceptions of the elderly can be demonstrated, a number of questions clearly need to be answered. First, in what ways are different age groups, but particularly older people, shown on television? Secondly, are there any relationships between television viewing habits and perceptions of the elderly, either amongst the elderly themselves or amongst younger age-groups? Thirdly, do perceptions of the elderly as shown on television coincide with or differ markedly from perceptions of the elderly in real life? Fourthly, in what ways, if any, does television act as a mediator of perceptions of the TV elderly and do these portrayals affect real-world perceptions of old age?

The portrayal of the elderly on TV

According to Davis and Kubey (1982) television presents stereotyped characterisations of the elderly which perpetuate myths about old age; for example, that being old involves loss of libido and of mental faculties. Such stereotyped portrayals, which are commonplace on prime-time and daytime television, do not reflect the way the elderly necessarily are and may thus cultivate distorted public impressions of older members of society. For this reason American researchers have compiled detailed inventories of role models on television implying that these provide a profile which will shape viewers' impressions of themselves and their position in society.

Content analyses of television output have indicated that television does not give the elderly as much coverage as it gives to younger people. Mertz (1970) analysed over 500 television programmes on the American networks to assess the role played by older persons. He found that not only were older people under-represented but also that over 80 per cent of elderly role portrayals fell into what he categorised as stereotypical characterisations. In an examination of prime-time American television from 1969 to 1971, Aronoff (1974) reported that the elderly are typically omitted from major character roles on peak-hour television shows. Out of over 2700 characters who were monitored, a mere 5 per cent were classified as 'elderly'. This was about half their share in the US population at the time. Furthermore, Aronoff observed, even when they did appear, elderly characters were usually cast as evil, unhappy and generally dependent on more youthful characters.

Peterson (1973) sampled 30 US commercial network half-hours between 8 and 11 p.m. in 1972. She counted as old those people whose real-life age was at least 65 and those playing roles judged by an observer to be at least 65. In all, out of 277 characters observed, she located 32 old people, three of whom were women. Old people comprised 13 per cent of that TV population, substantially discrepant from the Aronoff study, but based on a smaller sample. Observers rated these elderly characters along 21 bipolar adjectival scales. Eighteen per cent were rated negatively and 59 per cent positively, but no comparative data for other age-groups were provided so we do not know whether old people were perceived as significantly better or worse than any other character type.

Under-representation of the elderly was observed to occur also in weekend children's programmes. Levinson (1975) reported a study of all continuing cartoon series appearing on one local and three network channels in Atlanta over three consecutive Saturday mornings in May 1973. Of 644 human characters observed, just 4 per cent were described as elderly, among whom 77 per cent were male. This study, like several others, however, did not indicate how 'elderly' was defined.

A subsequent study of one week's prime-time drama programming on the major US TV networks in 1974 indicated again that the elderly are both under-represented and negatively portrayed relative to other age bands (Northcott, 1975). In this analysis, 'older adults' were those in their late fifties to mid-sixties and 'aged' were late sixties and over. Just seven (1.5 per cent of the 464 characters recorded) were judged as aged over 64 years, compared to their actual census incidence of 10.1 per cent in 1973. Television was found greatly to over-represent the vigorous and competent adult male and attractive, youthful adult female. The elderly, on the other hand, were more often presented as incompetent, in bad health and involved in crime, usually as helpless victims.

While Northcott's study (1975) could find little evidence of specific stereotypes traditionally associated with old age (such as poor physical health, senility, poverty, institutionalisation) it must be remembered that during the period of the study only seven significant portrayals of elderly characters were recorded at all; hence the study failed to accumulate sufficient data to suggest in what specific ways TV may routinely stereotype the elderly.

Harris and Feinberg (1977) collected data on the frequency and nature of elderly role portrayals on the three US television networks for programmes broadcast throughout the day among seven days of the week over a six-week period. Older characters, it was found, were most often seen on comedy shows and news and talk programmes. Kubey (1980) has observed that when the elderly do make more frequent appearances it is often in a comic context. They may be shown, for example, involved in behaviour normally associated with people a lot younger, such as riding motorbikes or performing modern dance. However, because such portrayals, which are in sharp contrast with traditional stereotypes, are presented in a comical way, they may actually reinforce those stereotypes.

The portrayal of the aged on prime-time television during the mid-1970s was analysed extensively by Greenberg, Korzenny and Atkin (1979). They assessed the frequency of portrayal, personal attributes and social behaviour of the elderly for composite sample weeks of national network TV fictional series at the beginning of the 1975, 1976 and 1977 seasons. One episode of each regular series broadcast between 8 and 11 p.m. and on Saturday morning between 8 a.m. and 1.00 p.m. was videotaped. Specials, sports events, variety shows and network movies were excluded. Altogether about 60 hours of programming were recorded per sample week. Each speaking character in each series was included in the analytic framework, giving 1212, 1120 and 1217 characters respectively for the three years.

The crucial measure of *age* was assessed by coder decisions on age to the nearest full year. Other manifest attributes coded included sex, race and programme type, and also whether the character was a law-breaker. In addition, social behaviours performed by these characters were coded and analysed which included various displays of pro-social, affectionate and aggressive behaviours.

Variations in the distribution and number of the aged occurred as a function of the time and type of programme. Larger percentages of older characters appeared on Saturday morning shows during the second season and larger percentages were also observed in late night shows. Considerably fewer older characters were found from 8 to 9 p.m.

Characters assessed as aged 60 and over were found more often in situation comedies than in any other programme type. All age groups dropped in representation in crime shows during the third season because there were fewer of these items broadcast, but the two oldest age groups declined in occurrence by twice as much as did characters aged 20 to 49 years. In summary the oldest characters on TV were found in equal proportions in situation comedies and crime shows; all other adults were found primarily on crime shows.

There were differences between age groups in some social behaviours but not in others. There was an absence of any strong or systematic differences between older and younger characters in the display or reception of either affection or altruisim. There were differences, however, in the commission of acts of physical aggression. The two oldest age groups were much less likely than others to perform physical aggression; older characters though were more likely to be verbally aggressive.

This content analysis revealed that the aged represented a small and decreasing proportion of all TV characters, with a decline in their presence occurring from 4 per cent to 2 per cent of the TV population over the three seasons monitored. Greenberg *et al.* (1979) compared the age distribution of TV characters with census data from the same age groups. Relative to the real world, the TV world was overpopulated by those in the 20–34 and 35–49 age brackets,

Table 5.1   *Age distribution of television characters across three seasons of US network prime-time series*

Age	1975–76 %	1976–77 %	1977–78 %	1970 Census* %
10–12	4	4	5	29
13–19	8	10	15	9
20–34	31	33	32	20
35–49	37	39	32	17
50–64	17	11	14	15
65+	4	3	2	10
Base	1212	1120	1217	

*The first two Census age categories are 0–14 and 15–19.
Source: Greenberg *et al.* (1979).

while the over 65s were clearly under-represented (see Table. 5.1.). It should perhaps be noted that the 'pre-aged' group was not under-represented, even by the coder rating method used; and further, as the coders were not themselves described as elderly, they must be considered likely, as implied in subsequent studies (Gerbner *et al.* 1980; Wober, 1984a) to have overestimated the age of portrayed characters.

The most extensive content analyses of prime-time television in the United States, spanning the period 1968–79, revealed a distribution of age groups on television differing substantially from that manifest in actuality (Gerbner *et al.*, 1980). The television age curve bulged in the middle years and grossly under-represented both young and old people. More than half of television's dramatic population was between 28 and 55 years while those over 65, representing in actuality about 16 per cent of the US population, made up only 2.3 per cent of the fictional population. Children's programming had even fewer elderly people than prime-time – only 1.4 per cent of all weekend daytime characters were over 65.

Ratings of elderly programme characters by coders along several personality attribute scales indicated that more older characters are treated with disrespect on screen than are any other age groups. About 70 per cent of older men and 80 per cent of older women were judged to be held in low esteem and treated discourteously. Also, older characters were frequently portrayed as foolish, incompetent, eccentric, held in low esteem, and lacking in common sense.

This research went further and claimed that heavy viewing of television was not only related to, but probably also resulted in the development of, a negative image of the elderly. Heavier viewers were ready to call a person 'elderly' at an earlier age on average than were lighter viewers.

Ostman and Scheibe (1984) report that a month's network TV commercials (taped in March 1981) portrayed fewer aged than their proportion in the population. The television elderly population had, nevertheless, risen significantly above the coverage level noted in previous content analyses. They attributed this to a feedback process involving research and pressure-group activity; but another interpretation could well be that it represented a sampling fluctuation. They also report that a previous study by the first author found that perception of TV as real increased with age, despite controls for the other interacting variables. These pieces of American evidence suggest, therefore, that the amount of TV viewing may affect the ways in which people perceive the demographic structure of the television population, and their ideas about characteristics of various segments of the real-world population. In contrast, however, the only available content analysis of the elderly on British television, carried out by an elderly group (the University of the Third Age) themselves (see p. 140, below) reported that age as such was not devalued. They did emphasise, however, that old women were less fairly represented than were men.

TV viewing and conceptions of old age
In support of their contention that television's portrayals of ageing and old age do more than simply reflect and may positively contribute to the formation of public ideas about the elderly, Gerbner *et al.*, (1980) reported survey findings which indicated an association between TV characterisations and audience conceptions of old people, the strength of which varied with amount of viewing. Heavy viewing was related to a negative image of the elderly and the quality of their lives but was never associated with any positive images of older people. Heavy viewers, for example, tended to believe more often than did light viewers that the elderly are unhealthy, sexually inactive, narrow-minded and largely helpless. Conceptions of the young about when people became old were also distorted. When groups of adolescents were asked, 'At what age does a man (or woman) become elderly or old?', light viewers tended on average to say 57, while heavy viewers felt it was 51.

An individual's perceptions of the self and society are based largely on interactions and comparisons of oneself with others. Retirement, for many people, usually results in meeting fewer people and under these circumstances, television may become an important social reference from which an elderly person derives information about his/her current role and status in society. Content-analysis studies of American prime-time TV drama have indicated infrequent and highly stereotyped portrayals of the aged on television which may in turn cultivate a severely distorted public image of the elderly in real life. It is possible, furthermore, for this material to carry its influence to the British viewing public, as it is largely US prime-time drama that makes up the 14 per cent of imported material used on British television, again mostly in prime-time. However, the interpretations and conclusion drawn by Gerbner and his associates depend on the fundamental assumption that overall *amount of viewing* is the crucial variable in the relationship between television portrayals and audience response. Yet the effects of television portrayals on public attitudes are mediated by and may depend more importantly upon the ways in which viewers use and perceive television content than simply on how much of it they actually watch.

Korzenny and Neuendorf (1980) examined the links between television viewing habits and the self-perceptions of groups of elderly people and indicated the necessity to qualify such relationships with, (i) the functions served for the viewer by television; and (ii) the viewers' perceptions of television portrayals of elderly characters. Neither of these factors was considered by Gerbner and the cultural indicators team and this restricts quite seriously the value of their findings. For most of the elderly people sampled by Korzenny and Neuendorf, television performed two main functions – escape ('it helps me to pass time', 'it alleviates boredom', 'it takes my mind off things') and information ('to gain new knowledge', 'it provides useful information'). Elderly characters on television were seen as being portrayed in four different ways by older viewers: as assets to society; burdens on society; respectfully treated; or humorous. The following relationships between these factors were observed.

Elderly people who watched television mainly for escapist reasons from everyday problems tended to view more fantasy content, perceived elderly characters on television as burdens on society, and also tended to have somewhat negative self-images. The aged who watched mainly for information, however, saw more real (i.e. news) content and perceived elderly characters on television and themselves in a less negative light.

To sum up so far, research in the United States has indicated that 'ageism' is a discernible and influential feature of prime-time network programming which falsely shows old people as less effective than they really are, and in so doing distorts (for the worse) both the public image and self-image of the elderly. However, these findings may not be generalisable to non-US audiences, even in countries such as Britain which import substantial quantities of dramatic television programming from America.

Previous research has shown that relationships among American samples between television viewing and public attitudes concerning personal safety and trust are not always found to occur with British samples (Chapter 2). Furthermore, American investigators have not comprehensively examined relationships between viewers' impressions of different kinds of television portrayal of the elderly and their perceptions of old people in reality. Thus, although Korzenny and Neuendorf (1980) showed that information on amount of viewing by itself is not sufficient to predict effects on attitudes towards the elderly, in reality their study suffers from two limitations. First, their sample consisted of old people only, who tend to give biased opinions of their own age group anyway (Schreiber, 1979); and secondly, they did not examine how perceptions of the way old people are depicted on television vary from one type of programme to another – which they might be expected to do if different categories of television content have different functions for viewers.

In British research (to be discussed below) efforts were made to explore these distinctions and also to distinguish viewers' perceptions of the elderly in the real world. Further, perceptions of old age portrayals were distinguished for further types of programme, and in relation to amount of viewing among different age groups, of these different kinds of programmes.

British research

To examine among British viewers the Gerbner *et al.* (1980) contention that the perceived age of onset of elderliness relates inversely to amount of viewing, members of an appreciation diary panel in London were asked: 'What is the first age at which you consider it is fair to describe a person as *old?* (Wober, 1980d). The modal age which emerged was 70. In addition, the position of the perceptual threshold of elderliness was compared across respondents of different ages. Overall amount of viewing was unrelated to the perceived age of onset of old age when respondents' own age levels were partialled out.

Most people had very positive responses to questions on the nature of old age. Further, heavier viewers had a more positive attitude (in one item where the significance of the correlation survived partialling out own age) on the statement that old people are generally very cheerful in spite of their handicaps. With regard to portrayal in different types of television programme, viewers felt that old people are treated with respect in 'actuality' material (news, documentary and game shows); but they did not consider, on balance, that old people were treated with respect in comedies. For that matter they may not have felt that young people or intermediate ones were treated with respect in comedies, either.

Exploring distinctions between parts of the television world further, and partialling out relevant interrelated variables, it was found that more viewing of television linked with a better impression of how old people are portrayed in comedy programmes and with impressions that old people are treated with respect in news, and in adventure-action programmes. Thus overall, the interpretation was developed that at least for this one sample, television viewing related – if at all – in a positive way with perceptions of the chronological definition and character attributes of old age (Wober and Gunter, 1982b).

There may be several reasons for this benign finding. One has to do with the institutional control over the content of television. While there is certainly freedom of expression in both actuality programming and fiction, there is nevertheless an overall climate of decency within which this freedom is exercised. The atmosphere is not a strident one in which the interests of minorities or weaker (though sizeable) segments of society are brushed aside if they get in the way of what may be a war between marketing powers. A recent study by members of the University of the Third Age in Cambridge showed that elderly people did appear less on British-made programmes and advertisements than their proportion in the population, but that the roles they played and the treatment they encountered were largely positive. Secondly, distinctions have been made as between types of television, news and comedy, for example; and it is realised by viewers that old people are treated with respect in news if not altogether so in comedy. Had the American research sought such discriminations it might well have found them.

The need to distinguish between viewing preferences relating to programme types when examining TV influences is reinforced by content-analysis research revealing variations in the way the elderly are depicted in different categories of programming. A recent analysis of daytime soap operas on American network television revealed a favourable image of older people. Cassata, Anderson and Skill (1980) observed in these programmes that older adults tended to be more emotionally stable than younger people, and physically healthy. The overall good health of older characters was reflected in their living arrangements. Three-quarters of these characters lived in their own home, either alone, with their spouses, or with their children – not in hospitals or institutions. The health of these older people was reflected further in their physical appearance which was generally judged in positive terms. The profile of the older person that emerges from the observations of Cassata and her colleagues is one of an attractive individual, usually employed in an important position, who lives independently and makes up an important part of the daytime soap opera world. A further possibility was alluded to in the British research (Wober, 1980d) in some of the explanatory comments which the respondents provided on their own initiative. These suggested that when an old viewer sees an old film in which the characters, then young, were those with whom the present viewers identified in their youth, they do not 'age' the film stars to correspond with their own age now; instead, they take themselves back to the films of their youth. In effect, the number of old films seen may function as a source of images of young people with whose vigour and style the old viewers still feel something in common.

Some of these points were explored in a viewing diary study which was sent to well over 1000 adults nationwide (Wober, 1984a). Scheduling controls within the public service broadcasting institutions may produce types of programming to suit particular parts of the age spectrum, so people were asked whether certain kinds of material were, in their opinion, more rare or more common 'these days'. Highest scores indicating commonness were for 'programmes for adults and not suitable for children', and next, not far behind, for 'programmes for children and of little interest to adults'.

Programmes 'which appeal to and are suitable for all ages' were thought to be not much more rare or common latterly in television. Thus television programming was seen to be developing in terms of increasingly serving the particular interests of the different ends of the age spectrum rather than aiming for a greater homogeneity of appeal.

Estimates of the ubiquity of programmes of particular types depended in part on the judges' own age, and in one case also on the amount of television viewed. Older viewers were more likely to say there were nowadays more programmes available of an adult nature and unsuitable for children; and they were also more likely to say there were more frequent programmes for teenagers. However, while heavier and light viewers tended to have similar estimates of the provision of programmes especially for children, for adults of all ages, heavy viewers were more likely to believe that programmes for teenagers were currently more rarely on display. This result is more likely to be a compound of several elements including the tendency for heavier viewers to watch more soap opera and other items which do not have a manifest teenage appeal.

The same survey also asked people, as before, to estimate the 'first age at which you consider it fair to describe a person as old' but this time they were also asked the 'first age at which you consider it fair to describe a person as adult', and similarly the age at which a person is 'no longer a child' and 'no longer a toddler'. Results were that, on average, the toddler stage was seen as ending at five, and the child at just under 15; adulthood was seen as beginning at just under 19, on average, and old age at 62. These milestones define a perceived span of childhood and of the teenage phase with the first tied fairly closely to the formal years of compulsory schooling and the second rather shorter than the actual teen numbers.

A further finding was that for people who watched more television overall, and most of its separate categories (except news) there were small but significant negative correlations linking amount of viewing with perceived onset of old age. These correlations applied when any mutual relationships with age, sex and class were partialled out. A similar effect, though at a weaker level and located mainly with news and soap opera material, linked heavier viewing with earlier perceived age of the start of adulthood. Two explanations are available for these findings. One supposes that it may be an 'effect' of watching more television to believe that adulthood, and more noticeably old age, have an earlier onset. The other is that people with such beliefs tend for some reason to watch more television. In attempting to judge between these possibilities, or to suggest any other, it should be noted that there is no connection whatsoever between amounts of viewing and the perceived age of the end of childhood and no significant link overall (though tiny positive relationships involving soap opera and sport viewing) with the perceived age of the end of toddlerhood. This tends to dismiss any possibility that there may have been a 'polarisation' or extremist tendency expressed in the judgements of those who prove to be heavy viewers.

Detailed examination of the actual average scores of perceived onset of old age, amongst sub-groups who are themselves of different ages or who watch television in differing amounts, shows that the 'effects' if any are very small; and they are not unidirectional. Thus, among those aged 20–29, heavy viewers give a younger onset of old age than do light viewers. However, if it is argued that this is an 'effect' of registering impressions from the content of television it might be expected that people a decade older, who have been watching television that much more, would show this pattern equally or more clearly. Instead, amongst viewers aged 30–39, heavy and light viewers have an equal point of perceived onset of old age (medium viewers place it higher). In fact, the highest average values of perceived onset of old age occur among light and medium viewers aged 50–59. It seems probable therefore that the overall result – which is a small one in any case – of a link between amount of viewing and the first age at which people are thought to be old is not a result of the amount of television watched. Instead, both this perception and the amount of television watched are an outcome of other, as yet unidentified, personal characteristics.

Discussion

While infancy is clearly one of the stages of the lifecycle, the existence and nature of which most people agree on, infants are not expected to distinguish in a critical way between programmes; nor, obviously, do they understand most of the verbal content of television. Therefore there is no programming (other than the whole of television as a flickering, noisy display) particularly for infants. The infant stage develops into that of the toddler, and here there are programmes on British television designed to appeal to 'pre-school' children (that is, aged from, say, three to five), while in America, Palmer (1984) has made it clear that such material is much less ubiquitous on network television. Instead, specialist children's material is increasingly found on cable channels where it has to be paid for. A number of studies (Dunn, 1977; Morris, 1977; Murphy, 1983) have shown children of this age watch programmes made for them but obviously much else as well, for if they watch an average of two hours a day (see Murphy, 1983) over three-quarters of this is likely to be material not meant specifically for them. They learn incidentally from what they see, including familiarity with simple elements of 'pictorial codes' (such as camera direction) but their grasp can be improved by talking with them about what they have seen.

Viewers consider that the toddler stage ends at age five, and this perception is little affected by viewers' own ages and not at all by the amount of television they see. The most likely determinant of this perception is that this is the start of statutory school attendance. Childhood is thus lent definition as a social category by an institution designed to establish universal literacy (none too quickly, according to the modern fashion) and the leisurely nature of this move towards literacy is not seen as being frustrated by television. People believe that programmes especially for children are increasingly ubiquitous, and this belief is not diminished by one's experience of seeing more or less television oneself. Parents generally favour 9 p.m. as a time after which programmes that are less suitable for children should be shown, and there is a noticeable drop in the number of children viewing after that time. It is also acknowledged that in special cases (which include items that may be thought particularly unsuitable for children) they do stay up to watch, and may record great appreciation for what they have seen. Part of this appreciation may well lie in infringing the norm, which is thereby acknowledged in the breach.

It may be alleged that television is invading the territory of childhood with adult experience, at least in the programming conditions existing in the United States (Postman, 1982); and in so doing, that television is dissolving the precious phase of life that had been brought into being as an outcome of the spread of literacy. However, the minor diminutions of literacy skills that have been reported as a corollary of heavy viewing (Morgan, 1982; Singer and Singer, 1983; Williams, 1986) do not in themselves mean that television, even in North American conditions, has aborted childhood. In some cognitive aspects it could be interpreted as having prolonged it. In Britain, explicit efforts are made to provide material just for children and this is recognised and to a considerable extent used appropriately.

Whereas in the early days of widespread literacy there seems not to have been a social category of teenagers in an ambiguous situation following childhood and before adulthood, such a category now amply exists. It has been said that the teenage phenomenon has been partly created by marketing strategies in the music industry (Coleman, 1961; Larson and Kubey, 1983). Television in Britain has now turned to providing programmes which cultivate the phase. The principal way in which teenage identity and tastes are promoted is by music, but it need not be thought that music is not facilitated by television because the former is only auditory; television has developed imaginative ways of bringing music to the viewing listener. The Channel 4 programme *The Tube* was well patronised by younger teenagers, as is *Top of the Pops*, while certain kinds of anarchic comedy (such as *Monty Python*, *The Goodies*, *Spitting Image*) also appeal to this age group, even if not to them alone. In providing thus for teenagers, television not only reinforces their social entity but provides a contrast to the earlier phase of childhood. It has been observed that, whereas *The Tube* set out to appeal to older teenagers and younger adults (say, 16–24) it did in fact appeal to a younger age band (say, 11–16); and in this respect television may be helping to erode the upper limits of childhood, though not by a direct transposition to adulthood.

At the upper limits of adulthood is another and quite broad age band which is treated as an entity for a number of reasons. People retire and qualify for pensions, they are more likely to be (or to be viewed as) grandparents, and in a world which (through television as well as other media) admires youth and beauty and mobility, they stand in physical contrast to this ideal condition. Shakespeare's sixth and seventh ages correspond in a new term with the 'Third

Age' by which title certain Universities in France and in England have called themselves.

We have found an average figure at which people feel ready to begin to apply the label old; we know from audience studies that old people tend to view more television and that it affords them greater satisfaction than it does younger people. A study has shown that viewers consider old people by and large to be sympathetically portrayed on television in Britain, even if the same cannot be said by American researchers of the United States. Perceptions of television as providing homogeneous programming equally appealing to all ages, are less generally found than perceptions which see television as addressing designated age groups in specifically different programmes. Thus at a level of explicit awareness, people appear to feel that television in Britain has variety in catering appropriately for all ages, and do not see it as imposing damaging stereotypes about different age groups.

6 Television and ethnic minority groups

Introduction

We are concerned in this chapter with three kinds of questions: facts, functions and philosophy, not necessarily in that order of importance. We deal mostly with the United States and Great Britain, but we invite reference as well in readers' minds to parallels that exist in, for example, Sweden, Holland, Australia and New Zealand. The three topics or areas of concern do not, of course, hold apart from each other. The field of 'philosophy' deals in part with goals, or what people ultimately want their society to be like, and these have to take note of initial facts and the ways in which ingredients of a situation combine together and function. If there are differences in what people see as their goals, then factions or individuals will try to alter the ways in which matters function; and short-term functioning can also affect longer-term goals. All these items are connected.

In focusing on ethnic groups we are dealing with problems that are both sensitive and profound. Ethnic groups comprise whole communities each with a past, present and the problems of a future, and, in western society, they are living in a majority community which does not share their particular histories. The past of an ethnic group may either lead or withhold momentum from the development and enjoyment of dignity in the present and the prospect of a harmonious future. This dignity and potential harmony involves the management of economic, political and cultural attributes and relationships. Television can indirectly affect economic processes through advertising and its impact on politics; but culture is very extensively mediated by television.

In the present chapter, we shall consider both factual and philosophical aspects of television's relationship with ethnic minority groups.

The facts are principally demographic ones, involving the numbers of people comprising ethnic minorities both in society and on television. The presence of ethnic groups raises two philosophical issues for broadcasters: the larger problem is whether a society (usually embodied in a nation-state) that contains several ethnic groups, each with its own culture and distinct identity (however much there may be overlaps with others') should move towards homogeneity; or whether it should contrive to remain a collection of parts, known now as a pluralistic society, which is to say a 'multiracial' nation. Secondly, should television come under some kind of central guidance in dealing with such sensitive issues, or should it do without such social control, instead being subject to the constraints and pressures of market forces?

The first control option may imply that a goal of eventual cultural homogeneity is in view, though if the dominant culture decides accordingly, it could attempt to conserve cultural heterogeneity. To leave television to evolve under the influence of market forces seems likely, on the other hand, to conserve for certain groups a congruence of cultural, economic and political minority. Thus smaller or impoverished ethnic minorities would not provide the base for appealing television services directed to them alone and their members would have to put up with an inferior product, or be drawn to use the services of the majority and, in so doing, would tend to become assimilated or alienated. These considerations are so far purely analytic and have not as yet been fully empirically investigated. Nevertheless, some material is available with which to make useful commentaries on these goals and the methods of control by which they can be pursued.

The minority demography of society

The United States contains three major ethnic minorities whose members are relatively conspicuous because of language or of colour: these are the blacks, Hispanics and Asians. A minor minority are 'Native Americans' or 'Indians'. Irish, Poles, Jews and others could also be seen as equivalent ethnic minorities, on whose predicaments similar research should be done. This has not happened, however, and the implication is that, for all the ethnic self-consciousness of such groups, they are not sufficiently visible or different from the majority to excite the kind of attention that has been paid to the first three named minorities.

According to Poindexter and Stroman (1981), the proportion of blacks in the US population during the 1970s 'was estimated at 10–11 per cent'. Seggar *et al.* (1981) gave a figure of 11.5 per cent. Hur (1981) reported that Asian Americans (i.e. of Japanese, Chinese, Filipino and Korean origin) are 'one of the fastest-growing ethnic groups for the last ten years', rising from an estimated one per cent in 1970 to 6 per cent a decade later. Valenzuela (1981) caps this in saying that the Latinos (or those of Hispanic language or heritage) 'are the fastest-growing population in the United States with a rate of national increase ... estimated to be three times that of blacks.' The Latino population was given as between 16 and 20 million, excluding over 3 million in Puerto Rico. The upper limit amounts to about 9 per cent of the US total of 220 million (although Seggar *et al.* give 8 or 9 per cent as the figure comprising both Hispanics and Orientals). Whichever estimate is closer to the truth, the Latinos seem destined to place the blacks in second place as a numerical minority within the next decade. Altogether, these figures mean that well over one quarter of the national population already consists of people who may be termed visibly or audibly distinct from the English-speaking white majority.

These 'major minorities' have two counterparts in the United Kingdom. According to Troyna (1981), 'the black population in Britain currently stands at 1.9 million; that is, 3.6 per cent of the total population'. Although the term 'black' has been used by some to emphasise a common experience of underprivilege, and so includes people of Asian origin, it may not necessarily be what Troyna means by his usage. Troyna uses the term 'Afro-Asian origin' (p. 15) and a focus on the majority white population's antipathy to immigrants 'from the New Commonwealth and Pakistan' (p. 24) to sustain the impression that the size of the 'black' minority includes both black (originating in Africa, nearly all via the West Indies) and Indo-Pakistani sources. During the crisis following the assassination of Mrs Gandhi, however, press estimates were given of half a million each of Hindu and Sikh people in Britain, to which should be added half a million Muslims (mostly of Pakistani or Bangla Deshi origin). The British 'major minorities' are thus thought by some to total some three million altogether, approximately half of African and half of Asian origin, comprising about 6 per cent of the overall population. The Office of Population Censuses and Surveys have stated that, on the basis of a 1983 Labour Force Survey there may be half a million people of Afro-Caribbean origin, 1.2 million from the Indian subcontinent and some from Africa making 1.8 million in all. These comprise, as Troyna wrote earlier, about 3.5 per cent of the overall population. This then, sets some kind of target to which a number of observers imply that television should aim in the proportion of its characters in drama and other fields who are played by minority actors and broadcasters.

While ethnic minorities are thus clearly smaller in Britain than in America one additional demographic and one cultural feature should be considered. The demographic feature is the degree of dispersion of the minorities. If such populations are concentrated in particular centres, then this fact will both be visible and should be reflected in the structure and content of local mass media. A mainly networked mass medium such as television, however, may seek to base its content or appeal on the national pattern and thereby fail to reflect strong local departures from this broader pattern. The cultural feature that requires attention is the extent to which language or political links attach a minority to one or more nation-states else-where. If this is the case, as with the American Hispanic window on Mexico, or its consciousness of the Argentine experience in the conflict with Britain, then a Latino minority may find itself occasionally at odds with the perspectives of the majority of the population. Such predicaments can impede integration. In Britain the war between India and Pakistan, the birth of Bangla Desh and the invasion of the Sikh temple in Amritsar concerned minority Britons in ways that contrasted with the marginality of these events to the majority.

For television, the question is whether reporting events in another country, and especially the relationship between the host country and those to which minorities may particularly relate, will function so as to unite or to divide the consciousness of the minority with or from that of the majority. A different version of the same underlying situation arises when sporting competitions are televised. In such a case Mexican or Chinese athletes at the Los Angeles Olympic Games are potentially looked upon differently by members of the related minority and majority sub-cultures, when television tends to seek and celebrate the success of representatives of the host nation-state. Similarly, cricket teams from the West Indies, India or Pakistan play matches in Britain and are differently supported by members of minority and Euroamerican majority sub-cultures, television being a prime medium of access to such events. In America the Latino and black minorities will probably respond differently from the Euroamerican majority to the ways in which television news deals with civil wars in Central America or the invasion of Grenada.

The minority demography of television

Many researchers have analysed the ethnic composition of the characters appearing on television both in the US and the UK. Greenberg (1982) points out that in the early days of nationwide television, 'classic stereotypes' of blacks, such as the characters of Amos, Andy and Beulah, prevailed; or, in Fife's terms (1981): 'Black Americans simply did not exist outside of their highly stereotyped occupations as shoeshine boys, maids or tap dancers'. However, by 1953 the Amos and Andy show had been cancelled. There followed a decade of non-portrayal, but by the late 1960s Dominick and Greenberg (1970) reported that 10 per cent of all day and evening characters on network television were black. Lemon (1978) counted 21 out of 56 shows that featured at least one black performer.

In contrast to the near numerical parity between the proportion of blacks on television and in real-life society, Greenberg reported that Hispanics comprised only about 2 per cent of characters on television and Orientals a similar number, compared with their real-life proportions of approximately 9 and 5 per cent, respectively. It would seem therefore that blacks were not numerically under-represented overall on US television, though Hispanics and Orientals were. There is some disagreement over the details of the latter group. As Signorielli (1981) states, 'in prime-time and weekend-daytime network dramatic programs, only one racial minority, Orientals, has been over-represented in relation to its numbers in the US population'. Part of the difficulty in assessing these claims is in the presence or absence of different qualifiers (such as programme-type segment studied, or year of sample) and more often than not an omission of quotation of the census basis with which the television figures have been compared.

In the US the overall black population in the mid-1980s is not markedly expanding in proportion to the total, while its television portrayal stands numerically slightly under par. The Hispanic and Oriental populations are expanding, probably faster than their network television visibility. Seggar *et al.* (1981) state that the white percentage of drama and comedy characters had increased from 82 to 86 per cent over the decade 1971–80 mostly at the 'expense' of non-black minorities, which confirms that there was no overall increase in minority representation over this decade. Another estimate, based on a one-month sample, made over a decade ago, found fewer than 5 per cent of over 2300 characters coded black, Oriental or native (O'Kelly and Bloomquist, 1976). But Greenberg (1982) found that this had increased to 15 per cent. Spanish speakers 'are the only ethnic group to have a coast-to-coast television network, Spanish International Network (SIN)' (Valenzuela, 1981); further Barwise and Ehrenberg (1982) have shown that these stations are heavily viewed by Spanish speakers who may therefore be proportionately less concerned with seeing themselves represented on English-language television.

This introduces one of a number of hypotheses that arise from considering simply the numbers of minority characters on television. One hypothesis is that adults in all such ethnic groups would tend to feel disadvantaged, and their children led to reduced self-esteem or to look to majority group peers for friendship and cultural assimilation, if there is a shortage of their own ethnic reference group to be seen on majority network television. Another hypothesis is that Orientals who may have first- or second-generation ancestors in Asia initially feel themselves to be members of groups more numerous than the white Americans, regardless of what they see on television, and thus they may not feel that they are part of an isolated minority, but relocated members of a majority. Their self-concept and self-confidence may have its roots elsewhere and as such an absence of representation on US television might even reinforce such perceptions. For their children however, as they become assimilated, and even before they become conversant with and in English, they increasingly turn from using 'ethnic' radio and television stations to using English-language network television (Lee, 1979). Ryu (1978) reported that attitudes towards programme types were related to English proficiency among Orientals. Less fluent English speakers liked action shows more than did accomplished speakers. The demographic composition of action drama may therefore be of more concern than that of other kinds of programme.

The same kind of external referent, of belonging in part to a respected and numerous society elsewhere, that Oriental Americans have (especially for Japanese or Taiwanese for whom it may be equally remarkable that the sets on which they view are wholly or partly constructed in Asia, as it is for them subconsciously to count the characters of their own ethnic groups) is not as readily available for Latinos. They, on the other hand, speak a language which the Anglophone majority associate to some extent with Cuba, an ideologically threatening and irritant nearby regime. Spanish-speaking viewers may therefore fear that such characters on screen would covertly be felt to have hostile loyalties; and they may prefer it in some ways if there is a low profile of their peers on screen.

It is not merely the numbers of minority characters appearing on screen that may influence viewers; the *kinds* of portrayals that occur may also make a difference. For Jews, the portrayal of Shylock is no longer taken as a token of commonplace stereotyping; it can be perceived metaphorically as within historical quotation marks. Jewish actors and actresses are so ubiquitous that they are not generally perceived by audiences (and occasionally, not by themselves either) as Jews. This provides an example of cultural assimilation alongside which the position of other ethnic minorities may usefully be examined and compared.

Types of ethnic characters
American programmes have tended to portray blacks in low-status jobs (Northcott *et al.*, 1975), though as industrious, competent and law-abiding (Hinton *et al.*, 1973). Reid (1979) reported that black females tended to appear as low-achievers but high on dominance and nurturance. Lemon (1977) examined crime dramas and situation comedies, finding that blacks were more likely to have equality of status with whites in the latter. Greenberg (1982) states that 'an

early trend for over-representation [of blacks] as law-breakers has passed'. However, some other negative aspects of portrayal have been found. Rainville and McCormick (1977) examined the commentaries provided in nationally televised football games, finding that white players received more play-related praise while blacks received negative references to their past behaviour. Roberts (1975) focused on news and found that, although blacks appeared in one quarter of the segments studied, they tended to be seen but not heard.

In US network television, advertisements occupy a conspicuous role and their *dramatis personae* represent one view of people and activities considered desirable in society. Dominick and Greenberg (1970) noted that the occurrence of blacks in commercials rose between 1967 and 1969, but still left a smaller percentage of black characters in commercials than in the US population (10 per cent). This increase was confirmed by Culley and Bennet (1976) and again by Bush *et al.* (1977). Mere numbers were not, however, the concern of Pierce and his colleagues (1977) who defined as 'microaggressions' interactions which are 'subtle, stunning ... exchanges which are "put downs" of blacks by offenders'. According to Pierce, commercials showed blacks less frequently than animals; they never showed them teaching whites; blacks were shown as more concerned with bodily and sexual matters; and as having less command of technology and of space. Out of 191 commercials in 1972 blacks represented 8 per cent of all characters. No blacks were said to have done voice-overs, dispensed goods or favours, or groomed the self; on the other hand, blacks were much more often than whites shown as working for wages. A different way of examining the data was to take the proportion of each activity performed by blacks and whites out of the array of all actions. This showed that blacks performed a much smaller range of activities than did whites; three types of action accounted for nearly 70 per cent of all black males' behaviour (as distinct from whites), namely working for wages, being at leisure and eating. Pierce clearly considers these differences to be racist in content and in effect.

One feature of blacks' appearance is their 'ghettoisation'. Baptista-Fernandez and Greenberg (1980) examined one week's entertainment shows in 1977, finding 101 black characters and a randomly chosen 101 whites from the 484 available. They made several observations similar to those of other observers (lower economic status among blacks, fewer blacks judged as 'bad', blacks discussing business and crime less than do whites). They also pointed out that 41 per cent of blacks but none of the whites appeared in shows with four or more black characters. A similar clustering is reported by Greenberg and Atkin (1978) for blacks, and by Greenberg (1982) for the portrayal of Hispanics, while criticisms of negative and stereotyped portrayals of Latinos ('bandit, faithful servant, mustachioed overweight slob, and the woman with dark eyes, a low-cut blouse and loose morals') have been summarised by Valenzuela (1981). The prominence of war movies means, too, that the Japanese are still occasionally shown as the enemy, while Chinese could for a decade be associated with the North Vietnamese adversary (even though the Chinese themselves were sometimes in conflict with North Vietnam). Weigel *et al.* (1980) agree that while blacks do appear in realistically proportionate numbers, co-appearance of black and white characters is very rare, with actual interactions shown in only about 2 per cent of total human appearance time. Gerbner and Signorielli (1979) found only 8 per cent of black characters in their samples of drama from 1970 to 1976, with a tendency to occupy minor rather than major roles, particularly amongst women.

In all, in spite of some remaining inequalities of esteem, and of disproportions in numbers, American television has shown a capacity for change and an element of sensitivity in its presentation of minorities (for example, in avoiding 'bad' roles for blacks). This has been due to at least four things. First, research has documented a clearly inequitable prior situation and this has been acted upon; second, statutory bodies exist to oversee performance in fields such as this (for example, the US Commission on Civil Rights); thirdly, there are community pressure groups such as the National Mexican–American Anti-Defamation Committee; and finally, there is the purchase power of minority viewers. To what extent continued research monitoring of less dramatic inequalities may have any further impact on events, if viewing and purchasing continue in sufficient quantity to offset any attempt at economic pressure on the networks, without the mechanism of effective bodies of statutory control over broadcasting, remains an open question.

Unlike the US there is a limited performance in Britain of content analysis (probably stemming from the weaker tradition in British social science of reliance on objectivisation and behaviourism). Anwar and Shang (1982) monitored British programmes selected during six weeks across the end of 1978 and the beginning of 1979. Bearing in mind that approximately 15 per cent of programming in peak-time may be imported (principally from the US) 5 per cent of appearances were by West Indians, with another 4 per cent by other blacks, either American or African; only one per cent of appearances were made by Asians. In light entertainment (the programme type which reaches the greatest proportion of the public each week) they considered that television tended to 'legitimise racial prejudice often by portraying ethnic minorities as silly and stupid'.

With only three channels until 1982, British television has tended to give single programmes and series greater prominence than may occur in the US, and certain formats have received particular attention. Thus *Till Death Do Us Part* appeared to give what Anwar and Shang term respectability to terms like 'nigger' and 'coon' uttered by a manifest bigot. Similarly, a character in *Love Thy Neighbour* used names such as 'chocolate drop' and 'the gorilla from Manila' to refer to his black neighbour (who tended to answer in kind, though not quite as pointedly). Other comedies included *Curry and Chips* and *Mind Your Language* in which a collection of immigrants and foreigners slightly reminiscent of Leo Rosten's kinder creation of Hyman Kaplan in New York some decades ago, make stupid attempts to learn the language and ways of the English. Again, *Only When I Laugh* cast an Asian male nurse who, Anwar and Shang say, 'appears to have the IQ of a chimp'.

Nevertheless, these authors give due credit to 'certain positive initiatives in Light Entertainment since the earlier monitoring exercise'. One comedy, *Mixed Blessings*, about intermarriage put blacks and whites on an equal footing; *Empire Road* was an all-black situation comedy, as was *The Fosters*. In 1982 Channel 4 was created, with a specific responsibility to provide programmes for minority audiences. Apart from this progress, however, Anwar and Shang suggest that there is another way in which harm may be done to ethnic minority groups: this is in the frequency of jokes and sketches in ordinary 'white' programmes at the expense of ethnic minorities. Anwar and Shang conclude their section on content by claiming that 'there is a preponderance of jokes and sketches which almost exclusively reinforce negative stereotypes'. However, unlike the American style systematic content analysis, Anwar and Shang do not provide hard numerical evidence that this is the case, so TV producers and performers can deny the existence of such material. To settle these questions counting has to occur, and this has not been done in Britain to the same extent as it has in the USA.

In Britain there has been some systematic observation of content (though more of impressionistic comment), combined with the existence of pressure groups, which have affected the way minorities are portrayed on television. There is also action by statutory bodies such as the Commission for Racial Equality, and the Independent Broadcasting Authority which monitors programme output as well as the BBC which performs the same function on its own programming.

Viewing preferences and patterns amongst minorities
Greenberg (1982), writing about American television, states that minority community children and adults are more likely to watch

programmes featuring minority characters and situations, as part of their overall heavier viewing. Gandy (1981) asserts that 'minority audiences differ [from majority groups] significantly in their media consumption patterns' and puts forward some explanations why this is so. One element is that 'recreational alternatives . . . have been limited historically by racist practices in the US and . . . many blacks have turned instead to vicarious participation in the wider society through television'. Carey (1965) had shown that though there was an overall similarity in order of programme preferences between black and white viewers there were nevertheless some striking differences between the groups. For example, Carey suggested that blacks preferred programmes in which individual conflict was a theme, while items that had a dramatic focus on a family were less viewed by blacks. Fletcher (1969) with a focus on children found one particular characteristic that marked out programmes preferred by blacks – they involved single parents as leading characters. These diagnoses of sensitive but possibly telling differences went further than the analysis published by Frank and Greenberg (1979) which grouped respondents' claimed needs and patterns of media use. Among 14 viewer types which they identified, one category stood out – low-income blacks who sought escape from urban boredom, and appeared to like all programme types equally.

A series of obvious special relevance to the black community was *Roots*. Surlin (1978) reviewed five studies on this series of which one adult and two teenage samples indicated heavier viewing among blacks than whites. One study used a national random sample but neglected to offer an estimate of viewing rates amongst minority and majority segments. Another study is said by Surlin to reveal 'no racial differences' in the number of episodes viewed, but this conclusion may well be misleading. The actual paper (Balon, 1978) gives no evidence for this assertion; indeed, calculations suggest that the blacks in this survey actually revealed a lower incidence of viewing any episode of the programme than did whites. In view of these apparent discrepancies some explanation has to be sought. It may be that, as a telephone survey, it could have made blacks more reluctant than whites to discuss what they experienced as an intensely personal matter, with an interviewer whom they may have assumed to be white.

Poindexter and Stroman (1981) suggest that blacks were more likely than whites to consider and to use television as their source of news and election campaign information. McCombs (1968) showed that the black community had changed from low to high users of television for political news over a span of twelve years. These claims are at odds, however, with other evidence. Tan and

Tan (1979) found that for local, national news, specials and documentaries, blacks were *less* likely than whites to be regular viewers. They reported that black adults were more likely than whites to report regular viewing of crime and adventure programmes and situation comedies. These conflicting results are likely to reflect real differences from sample to sample, differences attributable to lack of control of the social situational variations in which people are asked to disclose their preferences and behaviour, and lack of controls in the analyses for such features as age and social class which also relate, apart from ethnic minority status, to viewing patterns.

A more consistent finding was that blacks were more likely to claim to be regular viewers of series which featured blacks in long-running parts (Greenberg and Hanneman, 1970). When Tan and Tan (1979) applied controls statistically for levels of education, age and reported public affairs viewing among black adults, a link between low self-esteem and television viewing emerged. It is possible that blacks with less self-esteem spend more time watching television entertainment; alternatively watching this material may produce lower self-esteem. More probably, however, the behaviour and the attitude sustain each other. The paradoxical relationship of black viewers to a television service whose contents do not, on the whole, show them a rewarding view of themselves finds a possible explanation in the views of Bower (1973). He suggested that heavier viewing amongst blacks was not merely an outcome of lower income and education in that minority. One possibility is that blacks were more dissatisfied with the portrayal they found of society and of their part in it, in newspapers and magazines, turning therefore to a less dissatisfying even though imperfect television version.

Allen and Bielby (1979) found that among blacks those with lower education and socio-economic status reported less viewing than did those of higher status (a result opposite to what is usually found among whites). The more educated blacks tended to view both more majority and also more black public affairs programming. This study also found, as the Tans' had, that degree of personal commitment to black identity, together with knowledge of educational level and economic status, could significantly predict total amount of viewing. People who were more secure in their social roots were more likely to watch black public affairs programmes.

These studies point to the importance of the notion of control and a sense of mastery over one's destiny in ordering the relationship with television. People with greater self-confidence and social competence use television in a more purposive way, for surveillance and information as well as for entertainment. At the other end of the scale, those without a sense of mastery are the mastered, spending long hours with principally non-informational television, thereby avoiding the kind of material that might help them to alter their predicament. With economically determined programming rather than public service broadcasting on the increase there may be even less chance of such people altering their status.

The major thesis sustained by the Gerbner group – that the message system of television has a pervasive influence in society – depends on several links of argument. One is that the 'world' portrayed by television is taken for a reasonably accurate representation of the real world by its viewers. In other words, that television is like a plane glass window or a plane mirror. One step towards confirming the argument is to explore whether viewers do treat the television world as real. Greenberg and Hanneman (1970) investigated this question and reported that adult blacks were more likely than whites to say that television content was realistic. Donohue and Donohue (1977) similarly found that, among young teenagers, blacks were more likely than other groups to rate television characters as realistic. Working with a similar age group, Dates (1980) reported that black high school students in Baltimore were more likely to watch series which featured black performers. The probable reason for this was that black viewers identified their own interests as being similar to those of black characters in the programmes, and they did this more than did white viewers for their own reference group. Leckenby and Surlin (1976) had noted that both black and white viewers had similar views of *All In The Family* (the US show based on the British format of *Till Death Do Us Part*) and of *Sanford And Son* (equivalent to *Steptoe and Son*). Viewers who saw more of these series not only found them more entertaining, but also considered them more true to life.

In these studies of the ascription of reality to television portrayals it should be noted that black viewers have been asked to make judgements about television programmes containing mostly white characters. Most black viewers are unlikely to have direct personal experience of white family life, so they are judging something of which television provides the chief source of evidence, which they lack the opportunity to validate. The extent to which black or other ethnic minority viewers feel that television portrayals of their *own* culture are realistic has not been studied in detail. Similarly, when whites assess television portrayals of largely white society they do so from a basis of personal knowledge of what is being shown. If they have to make an assessment of the realism of television portrayals (when they occur) of black family life and culture, white viewers lacking direct knowledge might consider television more realistic than do black viewers. In the absence of many programmes showing black family life, this may explain why television appears more 'realistic' to blacks than to whites.

In Britain, Anwar (1983) has provided the most extensive report yet available about viewing amongst people of Asian and Afro-Caribbean origin. The study was spread over four conurbations and involved over 2000 interviews. Respondents were asked their opinions about special community programmes provided on radio as well as on television, and also about mainstream material. While Asians cited two vernacular programmes amongst their favourite television items, Afro-Caribbeans mentioned *Roots* (which had been broadcast not long before the fieldwork) and *Empire Road*, a BBC all-black serial. However, 'non-ethnic' programmes were widely liked as well including films and the TV series *Dallas*. Asian viewers volunteered that they liked *Mind Your Language* (the comedy which Anwar and Shang had previously decried) while Afro-Caribbeans reported they particularly liked two prime-time soap operas, *Coronation Street* and *Crossroads*, neither of which at the time had featured any noteworthy ethnic minority presence. Reflecting these Asians' opinions, the show *Mind Your Language*, which had been allowed to lapse because of doubts about its propriety, was revived by the actor who had played one of the Asian parts, and reappeared on British television in late 1985.

Although these British ethnic minority viewers appeared to like the basically white network television material, nine out of ten of them also wished to see more programmes reflecting their own people both in Britain and in their countries of origin. They also wanted to see more presenters from their own minority groups on mainstream programmes. This finding was supported in a survey reported by Manuel (1987). She carried out a content analysis of twelve series appearing in prime-time during 1984 and reported that 'black actors accounted for only 2.25% of the total number of actors used. Most frequently, black actors were cast as low-paid workers, students and lawbreakers'. The survey that followed soon after the content analysis showed that three-quarters of a sample of 500 Asians and Afro-Caribbean respondents said they could not identify with any of the characters on British television drama. Two-thirds wished to see blacks more frequently featured in such series. It was also clear that, while people of Asian origin were not dissatisfied with the content of drama on British screens, as regards representation of their ethnic minority group, a majority of Afro-Caribbean people were dissatisfied in this respect.

At the time of writing little if anything is available on American Hispanics' and Oriental viewers' beliefs about the reality of what they see on television; nor is there similar knowledge about what minority viewers in Britain believe about the realism or otherwise of the scenes and behaviours they see on television. Not having direct and historical knowledge about British ways and norms of behaviour, it would not be surprising if recent immigrant viewers tended to take drama portrayals as reasonably closely reflecting British culture, and the behaviour displayed in comedy and light entertainment as representing reality. On the other hand, if immigrants encounter real-life prejudice, and there is little doubt that they do, but see less sign of it on television (because the public services exercise some control to minimise such mischief) then ethnic minority viewers may come to see television as unreal in important ways, and failing to reflect some of the harder realities of life.

Two directions of possible effect exist for minority ethnic group viewers, as also for the majority; and these effects depend in part on the extent to which viewers sense that television offers a real view of life, or whether they tend consciously to discount what they see as artifice. Minority viewers could be led, if their segment of society is under-represented in numbers or derogated in character, to feel that television discourages the view that their presence has a valuable place in British life. It could also be said that, with a relative dearth on television of the kind of prejudice some encounter in real life, some minority viewers could be influenced to feel that ideals of toleration are being protected and that television is, in this sense, benevolent. Another possibility is that some minority viewers, seeing a white society on television that lacks the hostility and prejudice that are felt by some to affect them in real life, will feel that television projects an incorrectly benevolent image which fails to expose and thus erode such wrong-doing.

The perceptions of majority ethnic group viewers are also of importance. Some of them may, with whatever cause or justice, feel that television over-represents minority groups; in this case they are less likely to look on with approval at an external influence on mainstream mores and culture and more likely to feel negative about demographic and cultural change. These negative possibilities are complemented by the positive chance that, if equitable portrayals of ethnic minority citizens are seen, this could reinforce acceptance and help dissolve prejudice. These possibilities are all anticipated by those responsible for devising and regulating television output, and efforts are made to strive towards the latter ideals. What little is known about the possible outcome of the different ecologies of television in the US and the UK can now be explored.

Effects of television's portrayal of ethnic minorities
Greenberg (1982) examines the development of self-concepts among

minority children, in terms of 'role socialisation'. Williams *et al.* (1973) and Van Wart (1974; cited by Greenberg) found no consistent benefit for Latino children from watching *Carascolendas*. Filep *et al.* (1971), on the other hand, showed that child viewers of *Sesame Street* had more positive self images than had non-viewers. Dimas (1970) showed that a single film portraying successful black athletes, entertainers, soldiers and families improved black children's self-esteem.

Greenberg and Atkin (1978) studied fourth, sixth and eighth grade children in two American cities and reported that blacks looked to television to learn how people comport themselves, more than did whites. Blacks chose white characters as well as black ones as role-models, but white children were less likely to name black characters as role-models. Atkin *et al.* (1978) reported simultaneously that black youngsters had more positive perceptions of black role-models in terms of activity, strength and beauty (though intelligence seems not to have been mentioned) than they did of white characters. Johnson (1984) came closer to the matter of target-setting in cognitive abilities in her study of black adults in Pittsburgh and their assessments of photographs of twelve well-known local newscasters, two of whom were black. Here, while significant majorities saw black newscasters as more attractive and credible than white newscasters, slightly less than half the sample ranked the black reporters as better performers.

Hinton *et al.* (1973) had already suggested that black youngsters who saw more white-dominated television did not thereby develop negative self-concepts. A study by Donahue (1975) cast doubt on whether children are more likely to imitate TV characters than other people. He gave New Orleans schoolchildren examples of situations in which some response was required; they were then asked what they would do in each of these situations, and what their parents, best friends or favourite television characters would do. There was no suggestion that white children themselves were more likely to imitate behaviour they attributed to television characters, rather than to parents or best friends. It was inferred that television probably did not have any greater influence than parents or friends might have.

This particular project merely involved black children without implying that it was an ethnic attribute which had a particular bearing on their responsiveness to influence. The theme underlying most of these studies, however, is whether there is a 'white-wardness' in which, by contact through television with the dominant white culture, black youngsters wish to become like whites in attributes and behaviour, and whether any differences that remain are a source of a sense of default, or of dignity. *Sesame Street* had suggested that positive consequences of using characters from ethnic minorities were possible, as did *Fat Albert and the Cosby Kids* (Berry, 1980), but these effects arose through purposely designed programming for children. Children and teenagers also encounter the television of the predominantly white marketplace, and it should be an aim of research to explore in what ways, if at all, the mainstream network has a bearing on the lives of ethnic minority citizens.

There are two possible ways of doing this. One proceeds through the attitudes of the minority viewers, be they black, Hispanic/Latino or Oriental as in America, or black or Asian for the most part as in Britain. The other is through looking at the attitudes of the majority.

As regards the attitudes of ethnic minority groups and their use of media characters as role-models (see p. 160), it should be borne in mind that blacks may say they use television for role-models (e.g. Gerson, 1966) because this is a copious source of such examples, providing apparent entry to domestic 'white' locations; but the validity of any such claims has not really been demonstrated. In Greenberg and Atkin's (1978) report, black children were more likely than whites to say they learned most of what they know about jobs, how to solve problems (does television explicitly illustrate this, other than in the fields of medicine and crime?) and how to behave, from television. What we are now questioning is whether black youngsters really do then copy the 90 per cent or more 'white' forms of behaviour that content analysts tell us television consists of, or do blacks follow their own autonomous cultural, patterns with their roots in its own particular history, religion, artistic mode of expression and approach to family and social life? More fundamentally, should black minority culture be conserved or helped to conserve itself? Or should it be absorbed into the common melting-pot? What do blacks and whites think about these questions? On these underlying goals there is a dearth of material in the research literature, either of an analytic nature exploring what the questions are, or of an empirical kind setting out public opinions of what goals they think should or should not be pursued.

The second available route to producing effects for the minority communities is indirectly via the minds and behaviour of the majority. Part of the mechanism for implementing this process has been envisaged by the Annenberg school researchers under George Gerbner. They say (Gerbner *et al.* 1982) that heavy viewing of television changes viewers' attitudes – whites become more illiberal and more likely to support a range of measures that would restrict or demean blacks. According to the Gerbner group, television creates an oppressive and potentially illiberal environment, in the first place because of its structure and the way it is financed: it is 'shielded from public governance by current interpretations of the First Amendment; and yet publicly licensed and protected in terms that render the medium dependent on private corporate governance' (p. 104). Because 'many millions of dollars of revenue ride on a single ratings point . . . competition for the largest possible audience at the least cost means striving for the broadest and most conventional appeals . . . ' (p. 105). Television thus sets an ideal of white, affluent, middle-class, male-dominated society, and expresses this ideal in different ways in all its genres, news, drama, entertainment and sport.

The Gerbner group argue that 'television's mean and dangerous world' is 'expected to contribute to receptivity to repressive measures and to apparently simple, tough, hard-line posturings and "solutions".' The fact that conflicts have 'their requirements of happy endings' does not alter these researchers' views that American television presents a mean and dangerous world. Instead, they suggest that happy endings produce 'a sense of entitlement to goods and services, setting up a conflict of perspectives'. It is by no means convincingly argued – let alone demonstrated – that such a conflict of perspectives does exist or is felt in viewers' minds; or whether it exists mainly in these researchers' interpretations. Before discussing their case, however, it is necessary to examine the facts they have reported.

Using several national surveys, the Annenberg team have analysed links between measures of television viewing and of social and personal beliefs. One of the focal questions was a seven-point scale on which people assessed where they stood, from extremely conservative to extremely liberal. Eight questions were also asked about attitudes towards blacks, assessing respondents' desire to keep blacks and whites separate, implying that the blacks would remain socially and economically worse off than whites.

It was found that 83 per cent of respondents who described themselves as politically moderate were against bussing children from disadvantaged neighbourhoods to schools elsewhere; 18 per cent of moderates would not vote for a black for president; and 22 per cent said they would object if a black were brought to dinner. The researcher's purpose, however, was not merely to report norms on matters of inter-ethnic attitudes, but to relate these to amounts of television viewing. Overall, heavy viewers (with the usual definition of 'heavy' being over four hours' viewing a day) included a larger proportion with anti-integrationist opinions than did light viewers (who claim less than two hours' viewing a day). This differential is more marked among those with a claimed liberal position than

Table 6.1 *Political identification, weight of viewing and attitudes to integration*

		Average percentages on eight items of those who oppose integration	
		Weight of viewing:	
		Light	Heavy
Self-professed:	Liberal	24	36
	Moderate	36	40
	Conservative	42	43

Source: Gerbner *et al.* (1982).

among moderates; but among conservatives, light and heavy viewers showed similar proportions 'with' anti-integrationist positions. The figures are reassembled from their paper as shown in Table 6.1.

The Gerbner group are unhesitating in concluding that it is television viewing which has actually caused changes in opinion, and more so among particular categories of people. Self-professed liberals are said to have shifted in their opinion towards less liberal positions by their television viewing. This claim is made at first without the benefit of longitudinal panel trend data, although Gross (1984), analysing the same surveys in somewhat greater detail, reports that opinions had intensified across time. The evidence of such temporal changes is not, however, substantially set out. The fact that different panels of respondents were used in these successive surveys means that it is difficult to interpret this increase in intensity as a longitudinal effect.

Alternative explanations for these results can be found. People who claim the title liberal, but who at the same time disclose illiberal opinions, may have other underlying psychological characteristics, such as external locus of control, that are associated with heavy viewing. It is, however, possible that the Gerbner group are correct in their interpretation. They suggest, further, that 'commercial populism', or the desire to enjoy the benefits of copious consumption, may be replacing the earlier ideal of American society as a melting-pot in which cultures combine. Whether or not this is the result of heavy television viewing, the norms reported by the Gerbner group do little to support the notion that America consists of diverse cultural groups moving towards integration; they much more readily provide a picture of a mainstream society resisting integrationist movement.

To some extent a crossroads between the way which pursues an assimilationist integration and that which seeks a society of distinct but possibly equal and overlapping cultures was reached and symbolised by the television programme *Roots*, first shown in January 1977 and seen by over 130 million Americans. Several studies explored the significance of this series for viewers, both for whites and for blacks. Howard *et al.* (1978) interviewed nearly 1000 adults nationwide and found that many people thought that the programme would produce sympathy and empathy, and an increased awareness of black history, and at the same time relatively fewer felt personal guilt, shame or anger at what had happened. While this might argue well for an increased readiness for integration among whites, the researchers also found that over 40 per cent of respondents thought the series would increase black hostility, thus reducing the possibilities for cultural integration. Nevertheless, they state than 'an overwhelming percentage of viewers of both races indicated an inclination to disuss the program with members of the other race'; and over 80 per cent of men respondents actually did so.

Focusing on teenagers, Hur (1978) in Cleveland found that under 20 per cent of whites claimed to have watched all episodes of *Roots*, whereas over two-thirds of blacks watched them all. Blacks who watched more of the series had more positive perceptions of black intelligence, though for whites this link did not occur. Among both black and white teenagers those with more 'liberal racial attitudes' (the questions used to assess this were not reported) rated the series as more enjoyable and informative than did those with less liberal attitudes. This result suggests that any effect the programme may have had on these particular teenagers was to reinforce existing attitudes. Thus, those with liberal inclinations would probably find from their viewing some support for integration based on inter-ethnic respect and esteem; illiberal viewers who did not enjoy and find this series informative are likely to have rejected any pro-integration message it might have had.

Clearly, one circumstance that would affect how people react to a single series of high impact, or to programming in general, is the climate of opinion in which they live. Balon (1978) tackled this in his study of a racially heterogeneous community in Texas. Whites were more likely to say the series would have a positive effect on race relations; but the small number of blacks in the sample were more inclined to say the series would reinforce what they felt to be existing attitudes. While there may be other more effective studies of *Roots*, the ones examined here provide only a limited account of what might have been the significance of the programme for white and black communities of American society. None of the studies, for example, tackled the question of whether seeing the series, or even just knowing about it, may have affected viewers' attitudes towards cultural integration or otherwise. Did the series foster an understanding of the alternatives, and a preference for moving towards cultural homogeneity, or towards cultural heterogeneity? A loose effects inference emerged from a study by Ryback and Connell (1978) which reported that among high school students in Georgia a greater proportion of blacks than of whites served detentions – a sign of anxiety and behaviour disturbance – while the series *Roots* was being shown. But there were no controls introduced for amount of viewing of the series, or even for teachers' involvement in viewing the series. Not surprisingly, Poindexter and Stroman (1981) have to conclude that 'more than 30 years of the published empirical literature provides a dismally incomplete picture of blacks and television'.

Television's portrayal of ethnic minorities in Britain
Ethnic minorities in Britain are primarily blacks and those originating from the Indian subcontinent. There are also Chinese, Mediterranean and many other minorities in Britain, but not in the same numbers or so visibly different from the previous local populations. The Jews, for example, at one time numbered over half a million but are now reduced by over a fifth of that number largely through assimilation: and, apart from a small minority of them who are conspicuous because of what they wear, the rest do not stand out from the majority. Many Asians and blacks are not culturally different from the majority – having regional speech accents, supporting local sports teams, and being active in their local neighbourhoods – but skin colour, and to a lesser extent clothing, make them *look* different and this is more likely to foster a belief that they *are* different.

Conspicuousness need not necessarily give rise to difficulties, but in practice it does. Airey (1984) states that in Britain, 'race and class prejudice and discrimination ... exist in large measures ... younger people, who are less likely than older people to express prejudice themselves, are particularly pessimistic about the growth of race prejudice in Britain.' In detail, while nine out of ten respondents in Airey's large national survey believed there was at least a little prejudice in Britain against Asians and blacks, over one third acknowledged they themselves were at least a little prejudiced. Asking people to label themselves as prejudiced is rather a curious thing to do, and it is possible that the 30 per cent who accepted the designation of 'a little prejudiced' might be more honest and considerate towards minority citizens than are many of the two-thirds who claimed to be 'not prejudiced at all'. The self assessment of prejudice related well to other questions about whether one would mind having an Asian or black boss, or finding that a close relative had married an Asian or black. One quarter of the respondents agreed that not only would 'most people' but also they themselves would mind a lot if a close relative married an Asian or a black.

Unfortunately, this research included no questions on television viewing (or even of personal experience of or contact with minority citizens) with which to relate the results on prejudice. Nor did it take the opportunity to point out a positive role for the mass media; since if younger people are themselves less prejudiced than older ones, they might be more and not less optimistic about the future if only the information about their own attitudes is adequately publicised. Early British studies have not suggested that television had any effect on inter-ethnic attitudes (Hartmann and Husband, 1974; Critcher. *et al*, 1977). Troyna (1981) dealt primarily with newspapers, although he did imply that television functions similarly, for example: 'racial attitudes . . . derive from the complex interaction between "personal" experiences . . . and media experience'. However, the national press is not subject to the 'governance' of society as a whole (as expressed through parliamentary decisions embodied in appointed organisations), while television and radio are subject to such social control.

It is appropriate therefore to look to the broadcasting authorities for evidence that their services have not encouraged prejudice or, better still, that they may have helped to dissipate it. Reflecting this concern that their comedy-drama, *Till Death Do Us Part*, might be strengthening prejudice, 772 people were assembled by the BBC in halls nationwide to watch and answer questions about the show. The problematic character Alf Garnett (later seen as Archie Bunker in the USA) was considered by one quarter of these 'duty viewing' respondents to be unreasonable, but a similar number found his opinions quite often reasonable. The conclusion (BBC, 1973) was that viewers did not change their attitudes much as a result of seeing the programme but that there was 'probably some reinforcement of existing views, both liberal and illiberal'. Not long after this a programme with a similar 'creative' strategy (of depicting prejudiced views in a character with whom it is intended that people will not identify) was shown on ITV: *Love Thy Neighbour*. A survey (Ndumbu, 1975) by a black interviewer with 25 black respondents found that they said they accepted what they saw 'in good' self-negating humour; a minority of better educated viewers among this small sample found the format distasteful.

In separate vein, an experiment by survey (Wober, 1981d) set out to explore whether the level and kind of situational conflict in comedy might in itself predispose viewers to find a programme enjoyable or not; in particular, if the main characters were a mixed-race pair this might affect responses in a way that was not evident with a racially homogeneous pair of leading characters. A series and single-episode synopsis was written and posted to respondents, along with a week-long viewing diary in which they recorded their appreciation of programmes watched. They were also asked to answer some brief questions about the synopsis. The material had been prepared in four versions. In two the name of one principal character was conspicuously English (Terry) and in two it was Asian (Raj). The other main character was English (Helen) in all four versions. The other variation was to have the two working either for the same or for rival organisations. The differences in judged attractiveness of the plot were significant across a comparison of the racial options explored. In the versions with an inter-ethnic principal pair, 44 per cent of those respondents who had a definite opinion rated the plot quality as poor or feeble, while only 28 per cent of those assessing the versions without the mixed-race feature rated the plot similarly poorly. This suggests that, in anticipation at least some viewers might be reluctant to be 'socially engineered'. However, when a comedy series of this kind was shown not long afterwards (*Mixed Blessings*) it received modest-to-good appreciation scores from those who did view it.

Following the lead of the survey experiment just described, another one was designed to establish information about perceptions and attitudes amongst the majority white population concerning three categories of immigrant citizens, those of Irish, Afro-Caribbean and of Asian origin. Two of the television regions were selected (the North-West and Eastern England) in which the numbers of people of immigrant origin differed. The Office of Population Censuses and Surveys provided estimates that in the North West there were 211 000 32 000 and 117 000 people of Irish, West Indian and Asian origin, respectively; while in Eastern England there were 58 000, 28 000 and 59 000 such citizens. It was hypothesised that respondents in the North-West would estimate that there were greater numbers of minority origin citizens in their local region than would be estimated by respondents in the Eastern region, because there are greater numbers of such people in the former than in the latter. In the East of England, in the area surveyed, however, relatively less frequent direct contact with ethnic minorities in real life, might leave people living in this part of the country more prone to a television influence on their perceptions concerning minority groups. Next, since people in these two regions received three television channels (BBC1, BBC2, Channel 4) offering common output to both and one which was basically a national network with just some regional variations (ITV), it was hypothesised that viewers in the two regions would make similar estimates of the proportions of minority group role occupants on television plays, serials and dramas. A third hypothesis drawn from Anwar and Shang's study (1982) documenting under-representation of ethnic minorities on television, compared to their proportion in the nation as a whole, predicted that heavier viewing of television should produce underestimates of the real life numbers of immigrants nationwide.

Fieldwork consisted of two surveys, each split in two. In the North-West, half the sample kept television appreciation diaries across a week, and were given questions about estimates of minority groups perceived on television, and attitude items on integration goals. The other half of the sample were asked for diary and attitude data and estimates about numbers of immigrants in their own region, and in the nation at large. The same procedure was followed in the Eastern England sample (Wober and Fazal, 1984). Not only, therefore, were estimates of perceptions of the ethnic minority demography secured; the data were available to relate the perceptions to relevant attitudes, and to patterns and amounts of television viewing.

The first hypothesis, that estimates of the number of ethnic minorities on television would be similar to real-life estimates, was emphatically confirmed, with significantly larger estimates from the North-West of all three groups (Irish, West Indians and Asians) to be found in the regional population, than was estimated for their own case by Eastern region respondents. The second hypothesis was supported only in part; both samples provided estimates that were not statistically different with regard to the incidence of Irish and West Indian characters in television fiction. People in the North-West, however, provided significantly lower estimates of Asians to be seen on television drama, than did respondents in the East. Enquiries about the programmes screened during the fieldwork fail to suggest any clear reason why the North-West sample provided a low estimate of Asian numbers on the screen. People in the North-West also considered Asians to be more numerous in the nation as a whole. The differences in estimates are represented in Table 6.2. This suggests that in the North-West, where there are objectively more immigrants living locally, the estimates made of their national population levels are closer to the regional estimates than to what is perceived to be the case on television. In the East, the opposite is true; estimates of minority numbers in two out of three cases are closer to the television picture than they are to the local evidence. Since there

Table 6.2 *Region and estimates of ethnic minority numbers on TV and in the UK*

Concerning:	Eastern England			North-West		
	Irish	Asians	W. Indians	Irish	Asians	W. Indians
Differences						
UK – own region	2.7	3.0	2.7	0.9	0.4	0.7
UK – TV fiction	1.1	3.1	1.5	1.6	5.2	2.4

are objectively fewer immigrants in the Eastern region, there is not much social evidence from which to make a national estimate, which is possibly derived in part from information available on television and in newspapers.

We can now proceed to a more complex analysis which relates estimates of immigrant numbers to amounts of viewing of television of different programme types, partialling out attitude and personality scores. The first outcome is that people who watch more fiction and light entertainment are likely to think there are more immigrants living both in their own region, and in the nation as a whole. This is true of both regions. In contrast, there is no significant link whatever between amounts of viewing of non-fiction, documentary-type programming and estimates of immigrant numbers either on television or in the region or the nation. Of greater importance for interpreting the results, however, is that correlations between amount of viewing of non-actuality programming and estimates of the numbers of immigrants to be seen in fictional material are non-significant. These results are represented in Table 6.3.

It can be seen that heavier viewers did not develop higher estimates of immigrant participants in entertainment television as a result of watching more of it. Heavy viewing, therefore, cannot account for higher estimates of immigrant numbers in the nation, and in viewers' own regions. Although attitude measures had been partialled out, there must be other underlying personal attributes that are linked both with heavier viewing and with giving higher estimates of immigrant numbers in real life contexts. The linkages are clearly complex and the conclusion must be that great caution should be exercised in making inferences from single studies, when variations in different regions are readily observed. Secondly, measures of viewing of television as a whole undoubtedly obscure important differences between phenomena related to viewing of different programme types.

The research involved a measurement of 'cultural philosophy' with one item each on assimilation ('Immigrants should try to learn the

*Table 6.3   Television viewing, by religion and estimates of ethnic minor-
ity presence*

With estimates of immigrant numbers in	Sample	Average correlations between numbers of programmes seen in types that are:	
		Non-Actuality	Actuality
UK	East	.30**	− .03
	N. West	.15*	.01
Own region	East	.19**	.02
	N. West	.18**	.01
TV	East	.05	.04
	N. West	.03	− .06

* $p < 0.05$
** $p < 0.01$

ways of their new country and live like the local people as soon
as reasonably possible') and cultural pluralism ('Immigrants bring
strength to a country with their variety and should be encouraged
to keep their own ways as far as reasonably possible'). These items
were combined into a single index, a high value on which indicated
support for cultural pluralism. Authoritarianism was measured with
three items (Wober and Fazal, 1984) and it emerged that in three
of the sub-samples there was no significant relation between the
two measures of authoritarianism and cultural pluralism. In one
of the North-West sub-samples a significant correlation of − .5 suggested that more authoritarian people were opting for cultural pluralism. There were three significant correlations (out of twelve,
combining three minorities, two sub-samples and two-real life contexts) linking authoritarianism and higher estimates of immigrant
numbers. Cultural philosophy did not significantly relate to number
estimates in real-life contexts; cultural philosophy did have two (out
of six) significant correlations with estimates of minorities on television programming suggesting that those who want to see assimilation
tend to think that numbers on the screen are high.

The results just discussed involve, of course, only the white population. They do, however bring together a number of characteristics
displaying possible links between some of them and lack of relationships between others. It cannot be asserted from simple correlations
that television viewing causes altered personal estimates of ethnic
minority numbers, or attitude or personality characteristics among
viewers.

Two final possibilities concern the idea that television viewing experience may influence attitudes towards ethnic minorities. It was suspected, from American studies showing that television seldom shows blacks and whites cooperating or even interacting much, that heavy viewing might relate to and even produce 'racist' attitudes. It seems unlikely from the results just discussed, as well as from basic considerations in psychological theory, that viewing overall has 'caused' any effect on authoritarianism. If anything, the present data give more support to a link between non-authoritarianism and heavier viewing.

Both the considerations at the outset of the British study and its findings suggest that the structural possibilities of how ethnic minorities can relate to a mainstream society are not merely a matter of two opposing alternatives. One simple model was of a linear opposition of structural options, with one extreme being a condition of cultural separation linked with an attitude of rejection from one group to the other, and the other pole being a condition of assimilative integration with attitudes of positive evaluation between groups. The suggestion now is that this model be replaced by a 'triangular' one. In this, assimilation is an option at one apex; it is not to be taken for granted that assimilation as a social outcome is always aligned with an attitude of welcome and acceptance. Assimilation may be the goal of individuals who are intolerant of diversity. Thus some may wish the phenomenon of cultural diversity to disappear. This could be accomplished, on the one hand, by newcomers living 'like the local people as soon as reasonably possible' and also by not having reminders of diversity that can occur when seeing what is called 'integrated casting' on television.

Apart from the diversities of assimilation there are two possibilities of cultural pluralism; one is ideally in full parity and harmony (which is what the British Commission for Racial Equality mean when they use the term 'integration'); and the second is a pluralism without social parity of esteem and opportunity. This unequal condition can be called 'diasporate pluralism'. In America this predicament may affect Orientals or Hispanics who to some extent have relatives living in other countries and who locate some of their cultural roots and contacts externally. In Britain this affects some Asians likewise. In both Britain and America the notion of a diasporate condition can less readily apply to blacks, whose roots in known African societies have long since been torn away.

There is a more complex difficulty which faces the ideal of a cultural pluralism of parity. Writing in a volume on *Social Psychology and Developing Countries*, Segall (1983) discussed an aspect of personality called 'Need for Achievement' which considerable research has suggested is established in individuals by the child-raising practices they experience, and by the folktales they are told. Not only do people within a culture differ in regard to their levels of need achievement; so too do cultures, each with their different child-raising practices and folk literatures. Cultures also differ in the definitions of what each considers is desirable to achieve. Since need achievement levels contribute to patterns of economic behaviour and advancement it seems that some cultures place their members in a better position to prosper materially than do others. Part of a maintenance of cultural pluralism then may also entail support of a mechanism for obstructing economic parity. Since television has probably replaced the mechanisms of oral folklore that help to sustain cultural identity, it may be that young people amongst ethnic minorities are moving towards psychological and cultural assimilation. At the same time some community leaders may be trying to drive away from this towards a goal of a cultural pluralism in which different communities are distinct but equal.

In Britain, cable and satellite television may eventually bring to an end the relative cultural homogeneity of the public service broadcasting channels. As in America, cable services for black and other community viewers may be created in which 'narrowcasting' provides cultural foci of a density sufficient to sustain plural cultures, particularly if such channels operate in minority languages. Separate language channels in restricted locations are available in America for Hispanics and in Britain for Asians. The Welsh channel S4C, sets out to satisfy the 20 per cent of households in Wales which are said to practise some Welsh speaking, even though most of them also speak English and watch the three other majority channels. Viewing figures are inconclusive but suggest that the minority channel receives a small share of viewing time, so it is questionable whether the operation serves effectively to reinforce the existence of Welsh language and culture; though it must certainly be true that, without it, there would be even less chance of safeguarding that nation's linguistic identity. The dilemma is that proficiency *only* in the language of the minority will deny access to the culture and economy of the majority; thus in such circumstances cultural pluralism would be fostered, but parity in economic status could be harder to achieve.

It would be well to recognise analytically that if the majority do learn to accept a cultural pluralism of esteem, that this will not of itself establish parity of economic status. Such parity will arise not only when the climate is equally accepting of individuals from whatever cultural source, but also if each sub-culture generates the same levels and direction of achievement orientation. These attributes cannot be supplied by members of the majority culture, and the complexity of reasons for inequalities in performance should be correctly apportioned in public analyses. Television is an important medium for promoting the spread of ideas, whether they be valid or invalid, and it therefore has a role to play in contributing towards accurate conceptions of a multicultural society. Very many questions arise from this discussion, some of which are now listed as an agenda for further research and thought.

1. Should TV develop 'ethnic' channels or sectors providing their own mythologies for children of ethnic minorities, especially if separate languages are involved?

2. Should TV provide homogeneous channels emphasising forward-looking mythologies (like *Star Wars* or *Star Trek*, but attempting to avoid overtones of Eurocentric Arthurian legend)?

3. Should television devise less 'realistic' forms of fiction, like masque, dance or opera, where the ethnic origin of performers has less significance than the identity of characters they portray?

4. If TV provides parochial news from immigrants' countries of origin should this be scheduled so as to find or avoid large audiences of ethnic majority viewers?

5. With what degree of identification should TV handle news of conflicts between immigrants' countries of origin (e.g. in Central America and the Caribbean, Korea, the Indian subcontinent, parts of Cyprus)?

6. If mainstream TV provides comedy, soap opera or drama located in ethnic minority subcultures, might these have a positive impact on majority perceptions?

7. Is there a positive integrative function in sports where British teams with members of immigrant origin meet country-of-origin teams (as in the US, Hispanic or Asian competitors would signify in sport against Mexico, Japan or China)? If there are such competitions what is the significance for public perception and attitudes of TV portrayal of stadium crowds with many members of immigrant origin supporting the non British/American teams?

7 Television viewing and perceptions of health and medical practice

Introduction
There is evidence that television may be an important source of information about health and medical matters (Kline, Miller and Morrison, 1974; Miller, Morrison and Kline, 1974). In the United Kingdom, documentary and magazine programmes concerned with health and medicine have proliferated on television in recent years. These programmes are often scheduled during prime-time and many achieve large audiences each week. Their aim is to convey information about health and health-related matters clearly and appealingly.

As well as these informational broadcasts about health and medical developments, illness and health are among the most common themes in television fiction. They feature prominently in British and American-made television dramas. In American soap operas, for example, up to half of all characters may be involved in health-related events of some kind (Cassata, Skill and Boadu, 1979). Problems depicted most often include psychiatric disorders, heart disease, pregnancies, automobile accidents and infectious diseases.

There has been concern in particular about television's portrayal of certain kinds of behaviour, which although often socially acceptable, nevertheless are known to cause physical harm when indulged in to excess – as is often shown on television. The depiction of smoking, drinking alcohol and the use of other drugs has given rise to concern because of the potential social learning which might occur among young viewers.

Another aspect of health and medicine shown commonly on television is the health profession and the treatment of ill-health or physical injury. US research has indicated that in general there tend to be many more health or medical professionals in American television serials than in real life (Katzman, 1972). Furthermore, television doctors are usually highly competent and nearly always make correct diagnoses even though their patients often withhold vital diagnostic information from them (Liebmann-Smith and Rosen, 1978). In view of the popularity over the years of many fictional medical series (e.g. *Dr Kildare, Ben Casey, Marcus Welby MD, St*

Elsewhere) and the seriousness with which some of their portrayals are taken by viewers (see Gross and Jeffries-Fox, 1978), the extent to which public knowledge and beliefs about illness and health, and the efficiency of the medical profession in treating various ailments, are affected by such programmes is an important question.

In America, it has been claimed that watching television is an unselective pastime and leads to distinct effects (Gerbner *et al.*, 1980). As we saw in earlier chapters, Gerbner and his colleagues have reported that heavier viewers of television (which typically portrays an extremely violent world) tend to give exaggerated estimates of the occurrence of real-world crime and to exhibit greater fears of personal victimisation compared with lighter viewers (Gerbner *et al.*, 1977; 1978).

This chapter examines what evidence there is to indicate that beliefs about health and medical matters may be influenced by television viewing in a similar fashion. We shall begin by looking at the way health, health-related behaviour and medical treatment and practice are portrayed on television. Then we shall move on to examine evidence for the influence of television portrayals on public attitudes, beliefs and behaviours relating to this domain of social reality. Finally, as in earlier chapters, we consider evidence for a selective view of television watching and interpretation of programme content in the context of health and medical matters.

Health portrayals

Research during the 1970s in the United States showed that there were few informational programmes on health issues, and what information did occur was often considered to be useless and inaccurate (see Pearl *et al.* 1982). More helpful were brief public service messages on topics such as heart disease, smoking and crisis centres. Even here, though, information about most major health issues such as cancer, stroke, accidents, hepatitis, venereal disease, child-care, lead poisoning and family planning was virtually non-existent.

Other studies showed that health-related behaviour changes could be effected successfully through the mass media, particularly when the advice given in television health campaigns is combined with organised self-help and other social support (McAlister, 1976; Farquhar *et al.*, 1977). In the absence of additional social support, however, the ability of health programming *per se* to effect changes in health-related behaviour may be limited. Two British surveys assessed the impact of two broadcasting ventures specifically aimed at helping unwilling smokers to give up smoking (a *Good Health Show* programme on Granada television and BBC TV's *Nationwide* Stop Smoking Campaign in 1976: Eiser, Sutton and Wober, 1978).

The first study was concerned with the possible short-term effects of the *Good Health Show*. Similar percentages of viewers and non-viewers of the programme (13 per cent) said they were trying to stop smoking completely, whilst slightly more viewers (40 per cent) than non-viewers (35 per cent) said they were trying to cut down. The second study investigated the possibility of longer-term effects of the *Good Health Show* and of the Stop Smoking Campaign on *Nationwide*. The claimed success rate of those who had been trying to give up or cut down on smoking during the past year was higher among viewers of these programmes than among non-viewers, but not significantly so.

Eiser *et al.* concluded that though the observed effects of these programmes were generally mild, the results suggest that television may have a useful role to play in helping or persuading people to give up smoking. Those who were most likely to be helped by the advice given in the programmes, however, were those individuals who already wanted to give up smoking. The extent to which a television message produces a change of attitude or habit then may depend upon existing predispositions of viewers.

In addition to campaigns and advice programmes on television, however, health-related matters have been given ample coverage on fictional television. In one study, Smith *et al.*(1972) monitored all programmes on a commercial network station in Detroit during one week, focusing on the portrayal of health. Programmes were coded for their depiction of physical or mental illness, medical treatment, doctors, smoking or health in general. This analysis revealed that health-related topics appeared in 72 per cent of programmes monitored, most of them in entertainment programmes and commercials.

In the late 1970s a study by Greenberg (1980) analysed illness and health matters in ten prime-time shows and two soap operas over four days. Of the 40 prime-time shows there were 28 with at least one health portrayal. Several generalisations were derived from this research. First, patients portrayed on television were usually those suffering from complaints requiring intensive medical care and treatment from health professionals; second, health professionals cared about the emotional well-being of their patients as much as about their physical condition; and third, specific health information was given in small doses and was often obscured by comedy in the evening shows and by romantic interludes in the afternoon soap operas.

Diet and nutrition

Television entertainment programmes frequently feature eating and drinking. In many popular soap operas and drama serials, dialogue often takes place around the dinner table or over breakfast – *Dallas* being perhaps the best example of this on prime-time television. Several writers have documented the quantity and quality of food commercials on children's television in the United States during the 1970s. Choate (1976) observed that during any year, the average child viewer was likely to see about 22 000 commercials, 5000 of them for food products, over half of which were high calorie, high sugar, low nutrition items. Barcus (1971) found that 67 per cent of Saturday morning commercials and over half of general children's programme commercials (Barcus and McLaughlin, 1978) were for sugared cereals and sweets, usually presented as snacks to be eaten between meals. Indeed, the sugar-laden products promoted by most food commercials on children's television were of precisely those kinds that the US Senate Select Committee on Nutrition and Human Needs (1977) urged should be reduced in children's diets. Other observers reported that less than one in ten television commercials on US network television generally presented healthy foods such as fruits and bread; most were devoted to mass-produced, packaged and marketed foodstuffs of fairly low nutritional value (Mauro and Feins, 1977).

One American content analysis study has indicated that 75 per cent of all dramatic characters are depicted eating and drinking, or talking about doing so (Gerbner, Morgan and Signorielli, 1982b). Gerbner *et al.* (1982) found that food consumption is emphasised not only in commercials but also in programmes. Eating, drinking or talking about food was observed to occur on average nine times every hour in prime-time network television drama programmes in the US, involving around three-quarters of all dramatic characters. Eating habits in such programmes were anything but balanced and nutritious. Often, eating was not done in a relaxed manner at the table; more often people ate snacks. The diet was seldom nutritionally balanced and frequently consisted of fast food. Prime-time characters grab junk-food snacks (39 per cent of all eating–drinking episodes) as often as they sat down to a well-balanced, relaxed meal (42 per cent). In weekend children's programmes, three US researchers have observed that snacks (45 per cent) far exceed regular meals (24 per cent).

The favourite drink on prime-time American television is alcohol, with coffee and tea next. About one third of the drinking depicted on prime-time television is of alcohol or coffee (White and Sandberg, 1980; Breed and DeFoe, 1981). The kinds of drink consumed on television do not reflect their respective popularity in real life. Alcohol is drunk twice as often as coffee or tea on television, 14 times as often as soft drinks, and 15 times as often as water. Comparison of drinking shown in entertainment programmes and commercials has revealed that most references to drinking occur in programmes (Kaufman, 1980) rather than in commercials.

The nutritional value of the foods referred to and consumed in programmes is no better than that of the foods found in commercials. Kaufman (1980) compared ten top-rated prime-time programmes with the commercials embedded in them. She found that the greatest number of references by far to alcoholic beverages and sugary foods occurred in programmes. On the other hand, three out of four references to highly nutritional fruits and vegetables were found in advertisements.

Over-eating and obesity is a health problem for many people in modern industrialised societies. But on television being overweight seldom seems to be a problem. Kaufman (1980) coded 537 prime-time television actors as obese, overweight, average or thin. Of these 12 per cent were overweight or obese, despite the fact that these characters rarely ate a balanced meal. Obesity was found to be related to age, ethnicity and poverty on television as in real life. Television, however, portrayed a different demographic distribution of obesity from that found in actuality. Children and young people were rarely grossly overweight, while disproportionate numbers of blacks and Orientals were obese. Indeed 90 per cent of all obese people on American television were black – clearly an over-representation compared to the occurrence in real life of obese people who are black (10 per cent).

Drinking and smoking

There has been concern about television depiction of the often liberal use of alcohol, primarily because it may serve as an example to young viewers. Children, it is argued by some writers, could learn that heavy consumption of alcohol is socially desirable behaviour. But what is the picture of alcohol drinking presented on television?

The evidence of the real world is that drinking may result in strained relationships and harm to self or others. On television, however, the consequences of drinking are usually slight. Although as many as a third of all characters are drinkers, very few have drink problems (Gerbner et al., 1982). Alcohol is most often used by leading male characters and the drinking is often done in the home.

Hanneman and McEwen analysed television content for 80 hours in March and 21 hours in November and recorded references to the use of alcohol, tobacco, medically prescribed or licit drugs and illicit drugs in prime-time entertainment programmes. Alcohol consumption was the most common of these, with instances of drinking occurring on average about 1½ times an hour. Such incidents were fairly equally divided among situation comedy and serious drama programmes (McEwen and Hanneman, 1974; Hanneman and McEwen, 1976). Garlington (1977) coded use of alcohol in five episodes of 14 different soap operas. He found that alcohol was used on average three times per episode. Drinking most often took place in the home and hard liquor was the most popular beverage.

Television drinking is not always a casual, social behaviour. Breed and DeFoe (1981) assessed 233 drama scenes about alcohol in prime-time on American television and found that 40 per cent were 'heavy drinkers' scenes (five drinks or more). An additional 18 per cent involved chronic drinkers. The same researchers further observed that alcohol is consumed more often than any other beverage on television and that this is virtually the opposite of drinking patterns in real life. As already mentioned, drinking of alcohol was more than twice as frequent as the second-ranking coffee and tea, 14 times as frequent as soft drinks, and more than 15 times as frequent as water. Of all identifiable alcoholic beverages, 52 per cent were hard liquors, 22 per cent were wine and 16 per cent beer.

Greenberg *et al.* (1979) conducted a content analysis of composite weeks of prime-time programming during the 1976–77 and 1977–78 seasons in the United States. Behaviours coded included consumption of alcohol, tobacco, licit and illicit drugs. Information was also recorded concerning the demographic nature of the television characters who indulged in these behaviours. More than two acts of alcohol drinking per hour were found in both seasons. Tobacco use averaged under one incident per hour and illicit drug use was also recorded at that level. According to Greenberg *et al.*, a viewer had to watch television for two hours to observe someone smoke a cigar, cigarette or pipe, and more than one hour to see someone use illegal drugs; the same viewer could see alcohol being offered and consumed every 21 minutes. Alcohol usage was also found to vary across different types of programmes. During the first season examined, the highest rate of occurrence was in crime shows (3.78 per hour) followed by action-adventure (2.74), family drama (2.50) and situation comedy (1.40). During the next season, however, situation comedy had climbed to the top of the ranks (4.72 alcohol acts per hour) and consumption during crime shows had increased also (4.60). Meanwhile, alcohol usage in family drama and action adventure fell. Similar analyses were conducted for use of illicit drugs and smoking and revealed generally low frequencies of usage. The overall use of the three substances increased from just over three incidents an hour in the first season to nearly four per hour in the second season.

Content analysis studies have shown that drinking is frequently seen on television. What impact if any does this televised behaviour have on alcohol consumption among viewers? A recent study by Atkin, Hocking and Block (1984) examined relationships between attention to advertisements for alcohol on television and in magazines, among teenagers in Michigan, California, New York and Georgia and found that drinkers aged 12–16 or those who intended to drink when older were more likely to have seen beer, wine and liquor commercials. Atkin *et al.* asked their respondents to say whether or not they drank alcohol and, if so, how often. The youngest who were well below the legal drinking age were asked if they intended to begin drinking when they were older. Other questions focused on parental and peer attitudes towards drinking as perceived by respondents themselves. Results showed that peer influence was the best indicator of beer and wine drinking and the second-best indicator of liquor drinking. High-exposure advertising on television, as measured by claimed viewing of television for prime-time and sports programmes when most alcohol advertising occurs, was associated with greater consumption of beer and wine than was low exposure to such advertising on television. A similar finding emerged for liquor drinking in relation to liquor advertising in magazines. For the subset of adolescents who had not yet begun drinking, those heavily exposed to advertising were more likely to indicate that they planned to drink in the future.

In summary, Atkin *et al.* found that the relationship between exposure to advertisements and liquor drinking amongst these American teenagers was strongly positive, while there was a moderate association for beer and a fairly weak association for wine. Peer influence appeared to play a bigger role in beer and wine drinking, while the contribution of advertising was more powerfully related to both beer and liquor drinking than was parental influence.

There were certain limitations to the design of this study – many admitted by the authors – which make the interpretation of the findings problematic. It is possible, for example, that the association between exposure to advertising and drinking might be explained by common antecedent variables. Certain unmeasured personality characteristics or attitude variables could be important, and underlie both frequency of drinking and amount of viewing of television. Second, the direction of causality is not established by this study. While alcohol advertisements may stimulate drinking, it could also be true that heavy drinkers are motivated to attend to advertising for drinks more carefully. The authors point out that adolescents are more likely to see advertisements for alcohol before they start drinking, than the other way round. This assertion does not take into account the possible early examples of and introduction to drinking by parents or other relatives in the home environment though, which may presage attention to alcohol commercials. A stronger point is that adolescents who had not yet started drinking were more likely to say they would if they had been heavily exposed to advertisements.

In a study covering some of the same ground as that of Atkin *et al.*, Wober (1986) used viewers' own perceptions of portrayal of alcohol on television as one measure of their experience of the topic in programming; a diary measure across the week indexed the amount of viewing per person to the two channels carrying advertising (including that for alcohol, which in the relevant period was listed as 14th in the top 20 product categories, by expenditure, advertised on ITV) and viewers indicated how much they drank alcohol at home, and out of the home, each on a six-point scale. Results showed negative relationships between amounts of viewing and reported alcohol use, but these links were located in particular programme sectors. Having partialled out any interrelationships with age, sex and class, people reporting heavier drinking outside the home were lower viewers of news and of sport. Those drinking less in the home revealed less viewing of adventure-action series programmes. It is impossible from these results to infer any interpretation that greater exposure to television (with its advertising) is responsible for heavier alcohol consumption.

The same study examined the possibility of a connection between the amount of television carrying advertising that is viewed, and attitudes towards the merits of alcohol and whether it should be restricted in some way or not (with items, for example, exploring whether the government should seek to reduce consumption by increasing tax on alcohol, or by reducing the advertising allowed for it). It was found that the amounts of viewing of commercial television, or of non-commercial television were unrelated to attitudes towards the control of alcohol. Nor was the amount of viewing of either kind of television linked to the amount of reported drinking at home. A significant relationship beween viewing and drinking behaviour was, however, noted, with a tendency for heavier viewers of non-commercial television to report less drinking out of the home (this relationship being independent of other factors such as age, sex, or class).

The same survey included a question on whether people smoked or not, and if so, how much. Among the sample who replied 26 per cent reported being smokers – not a very different figure from the 32 per cent disclosed in a contemporary survey by MORI. The question now was whether smoking behaviour was related to the amount or patterns of viewing behaviour; if it was so related, it might be possible to sustain explanations of viewing experience affecting behaviour (although there would be no proof of such a process); but if smoking was not related to viewing, it would not be possible to encourage any such hypothesis. There were also at least three separate available hypotheses being advanced by social critics as to how television might be promoting smoking. One idea was that exposure to spot advertising (which on ITV and Channel 4 is allowed only for non-cigarette tobacco products) might associate with heavier personal smoking. Another possibility mooted was that viewing sports programmes would encourage smoking; many sports competitions are sponsored by tobacco companies, while other stadia often show display dvertising for tobacco products. The third contention, put forward by Piepe *et al.* (1986), is that viewing of soap operas would pave the way to belonging to a culture in which smoking was more commonly accepted, since they had shown that smoking occurs in several British soap operas to a more frequent extent than it does in US programmes.

To investigate these hypotheses at a first level chi squared analyses were performed to relate amount of viewing for each of four channels, with smoking behaviour; and similarly calculations were made to explore possible links between smoking and the amount of viewing of programmes in each of seven programme types. The first outcome of these simple calculations is that a significant link implicates heavier viewing of ITV, but also of BBC1 with smoking; taken in terms of programme types heavier viewing of soap operas and also of action adventure serials was associated with smoking, though this was not observed for heavier viewing of sport. At first sight, then, these data may be taken as encouraging the view that watching sport advertising and soap opera may encourage a smokers' culture. However, this initial conclusion is dissipated by more careful treatment of the data. Regression analyses performed separately amongst younger, medium aged and older adults show that only amongst the youngest group (aged 16–34 years) can smoking behaviour be significantly linked to a group of potential predictor measures; and none of the analyses implicate amounts of viewing to ITV, BBC, or to any particular one of seven types of programme as independently linked with smoking behaviour. All those links observed in first-level analyses thus disappear in the more rigorously controlled procedure of multiple regression. Two measures persist, however, as indicators of smoking behaviour; one is sex (younger adult women evidently being more likely smokers, when measures of other personal attributes are held in control) and the other is attitudes towards the restriction of alcohol – a permissive attitude being associated with smoking.

In sum, this research provides no resilient evidence that smoking is attributable to patterns of viewing experience. This does not preclude such possibilities amongst younger teenagers, but these await further investigation.

Although the use of illicit drugs is depicted relatively infrequently on television drama programming, advertising of proprietary drugs is fairly commonplace during peak television viewing hours. Concern has arisen also that use of illicit drugs may be linked to the use of standard proprietary drugs (United States Senate, 1971). Is there any evidence that television advertising for proprietary drugs is linked to their use, and in turn to the use of illicit drugs?

To investigate this question, Milavsky, Pekowsky and Stipp (1975) conducted a five-wave panel study with teenage boys in which they examined the relationship between exposure to drug advertising on television and the use of proprietary drugs, the use of illicit drugs and an attitude of readiness to take proprietary drugs. By combining programme-viewing information with data about the number of seconds of proprietary drug advertising appearing on each programme, Milavsky *et al.* were able to construct a measure of response to proprietary drug advertising on television. They found that viewing of drug advertising showed a weak *positive* relationship with teenage boys' use of proprietary drugs. Additionally, it showed a *negative* relationship to their use of illicit drugs – both marijuana and narcotics. Finally, the authors examined possible indirect links between television drug advertising viewing and use of illicit drugs through the formation of an attitude of readiness to take drugs. Although this attitude was weakly related to use of both proprietary and illicit drugs, there was no evidence that such a predisposition to use drugs stemmed from exposure to drug advertising on television. In conclusion, there was no evidence to support the interpretation that drug advertising–either directly or indirectly–leads teenage boys to take illicit drugs. On the contrary, the data indicated that it was the lighter viewer of drug advertising on television who was more likely to be a user of illicit drugs. Whilst there was some evidence for the development of what the authors called a 'pill-pushing' culture, television did not appear to play a significant role in the formation of this attitude.

Sickness and health on television

American studies have indicated that only about 7 per cent of major television characters have injuries or illness requiring medical treatment. Gerbner *et al.* (1982) carried out a study of health-related portrayals on prime-time American network television drama programming. They analysed cumulative data collected over 11 years of their cultural indicators project and in addition carried out a special study of one weeks' network programming to focus on health matters on television. The analysis looked at 'special aspects of medicine, illness, nutrition, drinking, smoking, body weight and safety' (p. 292).

Though years of extensive content analysis had indicated that the world of fictional television in the US is a violent place, pain, suffering and medical help are not as prominent as one might expect. According to Gerbner and his colleagues 'symbolic violence serves to resolve conflict and to demonstrate who can get away with what against whom' (p. 292). During eleven years of monitoring trends in television content, Gerbner *et al.* (1982) reported that on average only about 6–7 per cent of major characters sustain injuries or illnesses requiring treatment. About 3 per cent of major characters were portrayed as mentally ill, and about 2 per cent as physically handicapped. This meant, according to Gerbner's estimates, that the average prime-time viewer would see about 9 ill or impaired major characters each week. Physical illness, when it does occur, seems to affect the good guys and the bad guys in a like manner. The physically handicapped, however, tend to have a peculiar demographic distribution, usually being confined to older and less favourably presented character-types who are also subject to more probable victimisation.

Early studies of mental illness established that mass-media depictions of pyschologically disturbed people were much closer to public impressions and beliefs about these individuals than to characteristics established by mental health professionals. Instead of cultivating a greater public understanding of mental illness, these early findings suggested that the media served only to reinforce inaccurate stereotypes and traditional prejudices – for example, that the mentally ill are also dangerous (Nunally, 1961; Gerbner and Tannenbaum, 1962). More recent research has indicated that mentally disturbed individuals as shown on TV were the most likely of any group both to commit or to be victims of violence. Compared to 40 per cent of non-disturbed prime-time characters who were violent, Gerbner *et al.* identified 73 per cent of mentally-ill characters as violent at some time. In the victimisation stakes, 44 per cent of mentally balanced versus 81 per cent of mentally disturbed characters became victims of violence. Mentally-ill characters were twice as likely as mentally 'normal' characters to be killers and more than four times as likely to be killed.

The medical profession and treatment on TV

Doctors and nurses and other members of the medical profession have appeared on television since the earliest broadcasts. As well as making fleeting appearances in films and other televised dramas, television series have been built around the lives of particular doctors or hospitals, both in the United States and in the United Kingdom.

The cultural indicators group has observed that professional people dominate the world of fictional prime-time television. And among the professional ranks, health professionals are dominant, numbering, on US television, almost five times their proportions in real life (Gerbner *et al.*, 1982). Doctors, nurses and other members of the health profession are outnumbered on US fictional television by only two occupational groups – law-enforcers and criminals. Gerbner *et al.*, estimated that the average member of the American television audience will see about 12 doctors and 6 nurses (with 3 doctors and 1 nurse in major roles) on prime-time fictional programming each week. Doctors are nearly always male, white and either young or in middle age; while nurses are nearly always female, white and young or in middle age.

To what extent do doctors and patients get information about each other from the mass media, and what kinds of information do the media make available? De Fleur (1964) and De Fleur and De Fleur (1967) found that the media may create an impression among young viewers that nurses are cold, impersonal and detached. Following this, McLaughlin (1975) reported a content analysis of 15 major prime-time programmes on American television dealing with the medical profession. He found that although television's doctors may not always cure their patients, they often manage to solve their problems. Power and authority were identified as primary characteristics of television doctors. Such characteristics often extended beyond the treatment or therapeutic situation into the private lives of their patients, over whom they often exhibited a great deal of control and personal influence. In the case of medical treatment, television doctors often performed unusual, high-risk treatments or attempted experimental treatments with unproven reliability. Given the choice between a safe treatment with a limited outcome or a risky one that, if successful, would effect a complete cure, the television doctor often chose the latter course. In nearly half of the cases monitored by McLaughlin the doctor pursued matters into the private lives of patients.

Many of the above findings were confirmed further in another study of prime-time doctor shows. Warner (1979) noted that 61 per cent of the doctors' duties were performed during house calls or in the field. The television doctor tended to have frequent private relationships with patients, but was rarely shown at home with his own family. Furthermore, the nature of doctors' relationships varied with the sex of the patient, as evidenced in the nature of their instructions to male and female patients. Television doctors gave orders and advice to female patients twice as often as to male patients.

The success of doctors' treatment could be measured in personal terms as well as professional ones. In four out of ten cases there was successful medical treatment and personal crises were solved; in another four out of ten cases, the success of the medical treatment was uncertain but personal conflicts more central to the plot were resolved with the doctor's help. According to McLaughlin,

> Looking at the entire structure of portrayals, it can be said that in 95 per cent of the relationships between doctor and patient at least one of the following took place due to the action of the doctor: (a) people have been brought closer to each other, (b) people have worked out a conflict created by the medical treatment, or (c) people have accepted forces they have realised they cannot control... The role of the medical doctor on television is therefore that of a powerful almost omnipotent healer who performs his duties above and beyond normally expected capacities. (p. 184).

Liebmann-Smith and Rosen (1978) studied the presentation of illness and the medical profession on television since the medium's earliest days. They listed 30 medical entertainment shows beginning with *Medic* in 1954 to the short-lived *Rafferty* series in 1977. Medical shows which ran for more than five years included *Ben Casey*, (1961–66), *Dr Kildare* (1961–65), *The Bold Ones* (1963–67), *Marcus Welby MD* (1969–76), *Medical Centre* (1969–76), *Emergency* (1972–76) and *M.A.S.H.* (1972–82). These authors observed that fictional medical shows tended to fall into two main catgories: dramatic-serious shows and comedy shows. Generally, all dramatic medical programmes over the years have followed a basic formula in which the doctor is viewed as a skilled professional striving to alleviate the problems of his patients. In the earlier shows such as *Medic* and *Doctor Christian*, the focus was on the doctor, his skill and his role in society. In the more popular series which characterised medical drama during the 1960s, such as *Ben Casey* and *Dr Kildare*, the focus was on the newly practising doctor's initiation into the uncertainties of medicine and his professional development through subjective relationships with patients. In other words, these series took on the format of soap operas, in which much of the underlying themes and storylines were preoccupied with emotional and interpersonal relationships between characters. The most popular medical series were those of the early 1970s – *Marcus Welby MD* and *Medical Centre* attracted consistently large audiences. More recent series have lacked the same level of audience appeal, say Liebmann-Smith and Rosen, because of a trend towards greater realism. Series such as *Medical*

Story and *Doctor's Hospital* were less successful because viewers were shown some of the flaws of doctors and the health care system.

Liebmann-Smith and Rosen identified seven medical television comedies. The first was *Doctor in the House* (1970–73), a British television series about a group of medical students who in the later series qualified and were portrayed as young doctors entering their first jobs in a hospital. In 1972 there was a US show called *Temperature's Rising*, but the most successful medical comedy series, indeed one of the most successful TV series ever of any kind, was *M.A.S.H.*, a black comedy set in Korea during the Korean War. Its content dealt mostly with the uncertainties of war and medicine and the demanding role of surgeons. These uncertainties, as Zynda (1984) explains, were played for laughs, however, and the wit of the pro-gramme undoubtedly contributed significantly to the show's popu-larity over many years. However, the realism of the programme was probably reduced to some extent in the United States where as with all comedies, it was accompanied by 'canned' laughter. The real strength of the show was manifest in its success in Britain, where the comedy was not reinforced by any artificial audience response, but where it achieved very high appreciation scores.

Liebmann-Smith and Rosen made a special study of *Marcus Welby MD* in order to examine more closely the portrayal of doctors and patients on television. Unlike most medical shows in which the action takes place in a hospital setting, Welby and his young colleague Dr Steve Kiley practised medicine wherever their patients were. This meant in patients' homes or in remote locations as well as in surgery and in hospital. A content analysis of 50 episodes revealed that twice as many patients were male as female, over one-third were children and over 40 per cent were young adults under 40 years of age. Two-thirds of patients were single, 30 per cent were married and 10 per cent were divorced. Over 90 per cent were middle-class and white.

Examination of doctors' diagnoses, treatment and relationships with their patients also revealed certain patterns other than those which might be expected in real life. Diagnoses, for example, were usually fairly quick and easy. The doctor was nearly always correct first time; incorrect diganoses were made in just 12 per cent of cases. If the doctor did fail to save the patient this was likely to be because the patient withheld vital information: this happened in 18 per cent of episodes analysed.

Nolen (1976) observed that the drama of doctor shows is often fuelled by diagnoses of rare illnesses. Liebmann-Smith and Rosen observed that over half of the *Welby* episodes dealt with rare diseases, and in 20 per cent of cases the treatment provided was experimental.

Episodes were usually further spiced with family conflicts, emotional difficulties and the uncertainty of being able to save the patient. Often patients would resist treatment and only the threat of a sudden attack would force them to realise the seriousness of their condition and agree to the prescribed treatment. In real life, for most people, their relationship with their doctor is strictly professional. However, in 64 per cent of the *Marcus Welby* episodes assessed by Liebmann-Smith and Rosen, the doctor was a personal friend of the patient and his family, and in half the shows, the doctor was shown socialising with the patient or family. The same authors also observed that whilst in the United States these days house calls are relatively uncommon, with many doctors unwilling to make them and many patients unable to afford them, in 82 per cent of the *Marcus Welby* shows, at least one house call was made. On some occasions, both doctors would call at the same time. Furthermore, the doctor would not infrequently go out of his way to make a house call even on a patient who had not asked for one.

In the United States also, though not so much in the United Kingdom, the financing of medical care is one of the major problems and concerns of people. Hospitalisation, in particular, is too expensive for most people without adequate medical insurance. Yet the doctor's fee or medical costs were mentioned in only 10 per cent of the *Welby* shows monitored. Thus the cost of medical care is played down on US television.

In summary, the portrayal of the medical profession in television drama has been observed, at least by American researchers, to differ from what is commonly known about the behaviour of doctors in the United States. Two important questions need to be asked in the light of this observation. First, to what extent are viewers of these programmes aware of the differences between television doctors and real-life doctors, and in being aware of such, do they realise that fictional portrayals of the medical profession do not provide accurate reflections of the real thing? And secondly, when viewers have little direct contact with, experience or actual knowledge of doctors and hospitals, to what extent are their beliefs about the medical profession fostered by the way the latter is dramatically represented on television? These are questions requiring empirical investigation among audiences.

Further studies of sickness and health as portrayed in American soap operas were reported by Casatta, Skill and Boadu (1979). The authors compiled an inventory of all the health-related conditions occurring in 13 daytime serials broadcast during 1977. These conditions were then divided into three categories; accidents and violence, diseases and other health matters. Accidents and violence included such incidents as motor vehicle accidents, attempted suicides, attempted homicides and accidents other than motor accidents. Diseases included neurological, cardiovascular, renal, pulmonary, gastrointestinal, congenital, infectious, neoplastic and reproductive disorders. Other medical matters included psychiatric disorders and pregnancies.

Almost 80 per cent of all ill-health-related conditions fell into the accidents and violence category. About one quarter of these incidents involved motor vehicles. The greatest number of motor vehicle accidents occurred in two medically-oriented soap operas: *General Hospital* and *The Doctors*. There were 13 attempted suicides, comprising 15 per cent of this category of conditions, while another 20 per cent of accidents and violence category occurrences were homicides. Casatta *et al.* found that both suicides and homicides were more likely to occur in these serials than in real life. In daytime serials 0.88 per cent of characters committed suicide compared to 0.013 per cent in real life. There were 2.9 homicides per 100 characters in these programmes compared to FBI statistics of only 0.009 homicides per 100 in the US population.

Slightly over a quarter of ill-health conditions in these serials were classifiable as diseases and such diseases were responsible for around one fifth of all deaths. Cardiovascular disease was the major killer and was four times as likely to be fatal for women as for men. The next most frequently occurring diseases were reproductive and pulmonary afflictions accounting for 40 per cent of all instances of diseases in daytime serials. Psychiatric disorders were much less common – just 25 cases were recorded.

Casatta *et al.* concluded that illness, accidents, violence and death are major elements in the storyline of most daytime serials on television. Problems of physical and emotional health are commonplace among soap opera characters and may often have diverse and extreme effects on their lives. Female characters appear to be more vulnerable to physical and emotional problems than are male characters. A factor related to high incidence of disease and other health conditions in these programmes, observed by Casatta and her colleagues, is that health professionals are frequently represented among the characters. Many of the characters work in hospital settings, 'which are natural dramatic crossroads where new characters and new storylines can be easily introduced (as well as other characters being eliminated)' (p. 79). Despite the preoccupation with such morbid subjects as physical and mental illness, Casatta *et al.*, conclude that soap operas offer a note of optimism in their story-lines. Good characters tend to recover fully, while bad characters often do not. Those who are portrayed as deserving cases therefore usually survive and regain their health, whilst those who have done wrong lose either their well-being or their lives. Thus do we see soap operas inheriting the mantle of medieval morality plays.

Mainstreaming and conceptions of health

What can be done to study whether this fictional television world, so different from real life, may have any effect on it? Gerbner and his colleagues (1982) began to use the term 'mainstreaming' to describe the fact that some differences in social perceptions, attitudes or beliefs between various population groups (such as young and old people) may be reduced if both are heavier viewers of television.

> Groups who share a relative commonality of outlooks cultivated by television (the 'mainstream' view) will often show weak or no associations between amount of viewing and a given perspective. But strong relationships may be found for those groups whose lighter viewers do *not* share that outlook. Thus, cultivation may often imply a convergence into a more homogeneous 'mainstream', rather than absolute, across-the-board increments. (Gerbner *et al.* 1982, p. 299).

Gerbner *et al.* computed secondary analyses on data-sets from several surveys to examine relationships between levels of claimed television viewing and health attitudes and beliefs. In one such exercise, they re-examined data from a survey conducted by Virginia Slims and The Roper Organisation (1979) to compare nutritional complacency among light, medium and heavy television viewers, while controlling for a series of demographic factors (sex, age, income, education and race). In the initial unadjusted comparison, heavy viewers were somewhat more likely to endorse complacent attitudes ('I'm not concerned about weight. I eat whatever I want, whenever I want') and were marginally less likely to endorse non-complacent attitudes ('I diet occasionally to keep myself trim'; 'I pretty much stay on a diet all the time'). The evidence for mainstreaming was found, for example, in the extent to which amount of television viewing was related to complacency about diet across different age groups. In their words,

> ... older people are more likely to be unconcerned regardless of viewing; they are already 'in' the mainstream. Younger and middle-aged respondents on the other hand, show evidence of the cultivation of nutritional complacency. Again, the further away from the mainstream, the stronger the cultivation. (Gerbner *et al.*, 1982, p. 301)

On close inspection of their data, however, it is difficult to understand the logic of the above argument. In earlier pronouncements about the concept of mainstreaming, we have been led to believe that this influence becomes manifest when heavy viewers within different demographic groups exhibit greater homogeneity of beliefs than light viewers in those groups. This pattern is not indicated by the Virginia

Slim/Roper Organisation data we are now discussing. The age-group data from Gerbner *et al.* (1982) shows that there was as much diversity across the three age categories among heavy viewers as among light viewers. As well as this problem there is the additional fact that we are not told what the mainstream belief is (apart from the implication from the content analyses discussed above, that careless gluttony is the example on screen) that heavy television viewers should be converging towards. But since there is no real evidence of any such convergence of opinion among either heavy viewers or light viewers, only among medium viewers, the standard mainstreaming argument is not supported.

Gerbner *et al.* (1982) reported further secondary analyses of data taken from the 1977 and 1978 National Opinion Research Centre (NORC) General Social Surveys concerning television viewing and its relationship with smoking and consumption of alcoholic drinks. In relation to smoking, it was found (as it had also been shown in Britain by Eiser, Sutton and Wober (1978), that cigarette smokers reported significantly more television watching than did non-smokers. Non-smokers averaged 2.65 hours of viewing a day, while smokers averaged 3.01 hours a day. This pattern held across a number of demographic sub-groups, though two exceptions were found. The positive association between smoking and amount of television viewing did not hold for non-white respondents and for those whose self-reported current health status was only 'fair' or 'poor'. Among light viewers, those who said their health was 'good' or 'excellent' differed in extent of smoking from those who said their health was 'fair' or 'poor' by 12 percentage points, whilst among heavy viewers the difference was only one point. This evidence is consistent with the notion of mainstreaming, but does it indicate an influence of television viewing? Before discussing this question let us first examine the findings with regard to drinking.

Secondary analyses of NORC data revealed that light and medium television viewers were somewhat more likely than heavy viewers to say they drank alcohol. Once again there were certain variations in the nature of this relationship across different demographic sub-groups which were identified as consistent with mainstreaming. Individuals with some college education were more likely to drink than those who had not attended college, but the difference between these groups was 24 percentage points among light viewers versus 14 points among heavy viewers. Likewise, whites were more likely to say they drank alcohol than were non-whites, but the difference between these groups was greater among light viewers (28 per cent) than among heavy viewers (10 per cent). A third piece of evidence for mainstreaming was that although those in better health were generally more likely to say they drank than were those who admitted to relatively poor health, the difference between them was greater if they were light viewers (25 per cent) than if they were heavy viewers (11 per cent).

Using partial correlations to control for six demographic variables simultaneously, Gerbner *et al.* found that television viewing was still significantly related to smoking, while its relation with alcohol consumption was reduced to zero. Despite the latter finding, there was nevertheless evidence of mainstreaming in relation to drinking, as well as in relation to smoking as indicated by the above noted convergences of behavioural tendencies among heavy viewers within certain demographic groups. The zero correlation between claimed drinking of alcohol beverages and television viewing could have resulted because correlations between drinking and television viewing were negative within one demographic group and positive within another, thus cancelling each other out. The fact that heavy viewers within certain demographic divisions shared a similar pattern of behaviour, according to Gerbner *et al.*, indicates that the medium 'may be absorbing viewers of otherwise divergent behaviours and outlooks into its mainstream' (p. 303).

Are there any consequences of certain patterns of television view-ing for viewers' actual states of health or for their health-related behaviour and attitudes? Even if poor health and television viewing are positively associated, it could simply mean that people in poorer health choose to watch more television because they are unable to get out and about or because they have a lazy disposition anyway and cannot be bothered to pursue a more active time-filler. According to Gerbner and his colleagues, there is evidence that television watch-ing and health are not causally correlated, but that their relationship can be interpreted to suggest that television perpetuates unhealthy beliefs, values and lifestyles. One question in the NORC General Social Surveys for 1975, 1977 and 1978 asked respondents if they derived a 'very great deal' or 'a great deal' of satisfaction from their health. Gerbner *et al.* computed secondary analyses on answers to this question and found that heavy television viewers were signifi-cantly less likely to say they derived satisfaction from their health. This relationship held across various demographic sub groups.

More recently, Tan and Tan (1985) set out to explore television's potential as a resource in maintaining mental health. Since they considered that the screen stimulus was probably equivalent to doses of an anti-depressant drug, they suggested broadly that 'television viewing is positively and linearly related to positive mental states', which appears to mean that heavier viewing makes people happier, not just while viewing, but possibly thereafter as well. However, they expect viewing of soap operas to be 'negatively and linearly related to a positive mental state' but that viewing of situation comedies and game shows would be 'positively and linearly related to a positive mental state'. Using 446 telephone interviews to provide their data, Tan and Tan report that heavier soap opera viewing was 'negatively related' to positive mental state (and vice versa); heavy soap opera viewers were less happy and adjusted to their lives; conversely game show and situation comedy viewing were positively related to positive mental health as reported over the telephone.

In a study following the Tans' (Wober, 1985), 537 diarists' evidence of the patterns of their week's viewing were analysed alongside replies on a number of questions about the perception of mental health in television portrayals, as well as on measures of attitudes towards the origin and maintenance of mental health and personal acquaintance with the problems of mental ill-health. The actual amount of television seen in a week within each of seven programme types was not independently related to how accurately viewers think that mentally disturbed people are shown in each of such programme types. This lack of 'effect' of heavier viewing upon these particular perceptions gives no encouragement to the further possibility that amount of viewing, in any programme type, might have links (let alone any causal effect) with viewers' own condition of mental health.

To what extent, then, do findings such as Gerbner's and the Tan's indicate an effect of television viewing? As with smoking or drinking behaviours, there are a number of third variables other than demographic factors which might underlie both amount of television viewing and health-related behaviour. Light viewers may be generally more active outside the home and have hobbies and interests that involve them in various sports and forms of fitness-enhancing exercise. Heavy viewers, on the other hand, may be less outgoing types who prefer not to be very active socially or physically. Often, how healthy one feels, as distinct from how healthy one actually is, may be determined by a whole range of attitudes, beliefs and behavioural predispositions whose formation may have been quite independent of the influence of television. Psychologists have found, for example, that people differ in the extent to which they feel they have control over their state of health and recovery from illness. This attribute has been investigated carefully and found to relate to a whole range of health-related attitudes and beliefs quite independently of demographic factors.

Viewers' reactions to televised medicine

Content-analysis studies of prime-time medical shows on television indicate that there are stereotyped portrayals of the medical profession and of the relationships between doctors and their patients on television which are not entirely consistent with the real world. There is also evidence that health-related attitudes differ between light and heavy television viewers. To what extent though do the portrayals which heavy viewers consistently encounter actively distort their perceptions and alter their attitudes?

Robertson, Rossiter and Gleason (1979) investigated the effects of proprietary medicine advertising on children's beliefs about illness. Level of exposure to medical commercials was measured among eight, ten and thirteen year olds using a randomly selected list of 35 programmes combined with actual incidence of commercials by programme. The authors also asked the children four questions estimating the incidence of symptoms in the population (e.g. how many times a month do people get headaches?). Results showed no relationships between children's perception of population illness and level of exposure to medical commercials, despite what the writers note as being 'the considerable depiction of illness on television, both on doctor shows and in medicine commercials'. As other writers have since pointed out, however, there were only two doctor shows on prime-time US television in 1977 when these data were collected (*M.A.S.H.* and *Quincy MD*) and these programmes said little about headaches (Pingree and Hawkins, 1982). Similarly, on the evidence supplied, the children's likely viewing of medicine commercials on television was light, amounting to fewer than 15 commercials a week. At most this would seem to be very light viewing of the relevant content, and a higher level of exposure than this is probably necessary for any TV influence to occur. Another problem with this study, as with so many other cultivation effects studies, is that it was not tied to careful content analysis nor to real-world statistics, without which it is difficult to define 'TV answers' and 'real-world answers'.

Studies of TV viewing and confidence in medical treatment
Buerkel-Rothfuss and Mayes (1981) looked at relationships between level of viewing soap operas and perceptions about people and events in the real world, including beliefs about the medical profession and ill-health. A student sample was asked to check off from a list of 13 soap operas shown on American network television those they viewed in a 'typical week'. They were also asked to estimate the number of females and males out of ten in the population who are doctors, have suffered nervous breakdowns and have had serious operations. We have already seen in the sections on content analysis above that doctors and health problems are frequently occurring features of soap operas on American television. The researchers

found that heavier viewing of soap operas was positively associated with higher estimates of the numbers of doctors in the real world and of people who have had serious operations. It was concluded that this indicated a possible cultivation effect of soap opera viewing. Since British findings had indicated that relationships between television viewing and certain social perceptions could be mediated by deep-seated personal dispositions, information was therefore sought from respondents in a new study (Wober and Gunter, 1985) concerning a relevant personality factor – the degree of personal control they felt they had over their own health (health locus of control).

At the time this research was carried out, there had recently been several health-related series on British television. These series included a soap opera set in a hospital (*Angels*), a magazine programme dealing with different medical topics each week (*Where There's Life*) and a drama-documentary series (*The Nation's Health*) which had been particularly realistic and critical in it portrayal of the standards of national health care and treatment in Britain. Together, these television series provided a context in which to examine the impact of television portrayals or discussions of health and medical matters on public beliefs about treatment of and recovery from ill-health.

A parallel theme of this research, however, was to find out whether beliefs about medical treatment were related more significantly to personal dispositions of viewers than to particular viewing experiences. Research elsewhere has indicated that people differ in the extent to which they consider they are in control of their health and that the nature of this belief can influence their own recovery from illness and whether they think that medical efforts are important or ineffective in the treatment of illness or injury (King, 1982). These 'health locus of control' beliefs seem to be related also to the extent to which individuals keep careful checks on their health (Strickland, 1978). Research has also indicated that internal health controllers (that is, people who believe that they have control over their own health) express stronger intentions to seek out health-related information than do external health controllers (that is, people who believe their health is influenced by outside factors). But such beliefs do not relate to actual information-seeking behaviour (Wallston *et al.*, 1976; de Vito, Bogdowicz and Reznikoff, 1982). To what extent do health locus of control beliefs relate to television viewing patterns? Further, does television viewing in general, or more especially viewing of certain kinds of programmes correlate with perceptions of medical treatment independently of deep-seated beliefs about health as measured by health locus of control positions?

A questionnaire and viewing diary were sent to a panel of 1270 people resident in and representative of the population of London.

The diary listed all programmes broadcast by the four TV channels during one week. Against each listed programme was a six-point rating scale along which respondents gave an evaluation of each programme they had seen. This exercise provided information about liking for programmes that had been watched and also indirectly indicated precisely how much television had been seen during the week.

The questionnaire was in four parts. One part asked respondents about their degree of confidence in hospital treatment for 13 different illnesses, should they require hospital treatment for any of them. A question was also included on whether they or anyone they knew well had actually been in hospital during the previous six months. Twelve other test items followed, assessing beliefs about the causes of health, illness and recovery from ill-health, which were derived from the Health Locus of Control Scale (Lau, 1982). In a third part were six items derived from the Just World Beliefs scale (Rubin and Peplau, 1975). Finally, respondents were asked how often they had seen each of three recent TV series primarily concerned with medical and health matters.

Diaries and completed questionnaires were returned by 551 respondents, and replies were weighted to ensure good estimates of the incidence of the various beliefs expressed for the London population (see Wober and Gunter, 1985). Each respondent was given a score for the number of programmes endorsed in the viewing diary. Viewing behaviour was broken down into seven programme types (action-adventure series, soap opera, sport, comedy and light entertainment, news, documentary and general interest, and films and plays) and a score was given for numbers of programmes seen in each type. From the questionnaire data, scores were given for claimed viewing of the three particular series related to medical and health matters. Single Health Locus of Control and Just World Belief scores were computed by summing over their component items. Factor analyses were computed on 'confidence in aspects of health care' responses and on responses to the Health Locus of Control items. The 13 confidence in health care items were reduced to three factors, labelled *psychosomatic disorders* (Factor 1), *general surgery and medicine* (Factor 2), and *serious functional collapse* (Factor 3) (see Table. 7.1.).

Personal beliefs and confidence in medical care
The results were statistically analysed further using a technique called multiple classification analysis which examined relationships between degree of confidence in medical treatment for different categories of illness and disorder, and Health Locus of Control and

Table 7.1   Factor analysis of confidence in medical treatment items

	Factor 1	Factor 2	Factor 3
Psychosomatic disorders			
Food allergy	.46	.45	12
Stroke	.43	.19	.33
Mental disturbance	.79	.14	.21
Depression	.82	.14	.17
Senility	.62	.11	.36
General surgery and medicine			
Appendicitis	.05	.68	.15
Broken limbs	.06	.70	.14
Gastric ulcer	.23	.62	.24
Plastic surgery	.18	.40	.28
Jaundice	.22	.56	.24
Serious functional collapse			
Heart bypass	.19	.29	.66
Leukaemia	.29	.29	.51
Kidney failure	.23	.17	.56
Eigen value	4.59	1.17	0.50
Per cent of variance	73.30	18.60	8.00

Just World Beliefs, while controlling for any effects due to sex, age and social economic class. There were significant relationships of both health locus of control and belief in a just world with confidence in medical care. With respect to locus of control, in the case of each medical treatment factor, external controllers had more confidence in medical care for all above disorders than did internal controllers. Just World Beliefs did not relate to all medical treatment factors in the same way. Low scores on the just world items were associated with more confidence in medical treatment for *physical problems*, but less confidence with respect to treatment of *psychological problems* and *major surgical problems*.

Respondents were asked to estimate how many episodes they had seen of three medical series recently shown on television. Relationships were examined between total amount of viewing of all these programmes together and opinions about the quality of medical treatment available in hospitals.

The results of further multiple classification analyses indicated significant relationships between claimed amount of viewing of medical series and opinions about treatment of psychological and major surgical problems. In each case, heavier viewers of these programmes had lower levels of confidence in the quality of treatment likely to be received for these problems. These relationships existed principally for the magazine (*Where There's Life*) and realistic drama-documentary items (*The Nation's Health*), but not for viewing of a fictional soap opera, and they survived statistical controls for demographic and other personal differences. However, closer examination of the findings indicated that the relationships between confidence in medical treatment and viewing claims were not linear, but U-shaped; those who viewed just one or two episodes had less confidence in treatment they might receive than was found amongst people who said they had seen none of the episodes, or most or all of them. One interpretation of these results is that those who saw a little of *The Nation's Health* did indeed have their confidence reduced, but those who remained to watch three or even four episodes were people with enough confidence in the treatment provided by the Health Service to sustain protracted attention to a critical portrayal of that service.

Further statistical analyses as above were computed to examine relationships between viewing claims for individual medical series and opinions about the quality of medical treatment. Viewing claims for two out of the three series were significantly related to medical opinions. These two programmes were the magazine show *Where There's Life* and the drama-documentary *The Nation's Health*. No significant relationships emerged between opinions and viewing claims for the fictional drama serials *Angels*. Most of the relationships were curvilinear. Those individuals who said they had seen just one episode of each programme or three or four episodes during the past four weeks had greater confidence in medical treatment than did those who had seen two episodes.

Claimed viewing of *The Nation's Health* was significantly related in this curvilinear fashion to all three confidence in medical treatment factors, while viewing claims for *Where There's Life* were related in this way to confidence in the treatment of *psychological problems* and *major surgical problems* only (See Wober and Gunter (1985) for further details).

At the next stage of analysis, further statistical controls were introduced for respondents' beliefs in the degree of personal control they felt they had over their own health. Using their scores on the health locus of control scale, respondents were divided into those who tended to believe that health and recovery from illness were largely matters under personal control, versus those who thought that these conditions were determined largely by external forces such as luck and the efficiency of treatment. Within each of these two sub-samples, further multiple classification analyses were run in which claimed viewing of the three listed medical series was related to respondents' degree of confidence in medical treatment for *psychological problems*, *physical problems* and *major surgical problems*, whilst controlling simultaneously for the effects of sex, age and social class. Although the numbers of respondents claiming to have seen at least three editions of each programme in the previous month were quite small, nevertheless, the patterns of relationships were fairly consistent across the sub-samples and across medical treatment factors.

Overall claimed viewing of the three television series was not significantly related to opinions about medical treatment, nor was claimed viewing of the hospital soap opera, *Angels* either among internal controllers or external controllers. There were significant relationships, however, between viewing claims for *The Nation's Health* and *Where There's Life*, and degree of confidence in medical treatment for all three kinds of medical problems. The nature of these relationships, once again, was largely curvilinear, with those individuals falling within the 'medium' viewing category for each programme tending to exhibit the most substantial deviations from the average confidence score. The other substantial result was that, among internal controllers, only claimed viewing of *The Nation's Health* was related to confidence in medical treatment, whilst among external controllers it was principally *Where There's Life* for which viewing claims were related to beliefs about medical treatment.

The validity of the subjective estimates of extent of viewing each of the three television series over the previous month was reinforced by significant correlations of viewing claims with diary measures of viewing programmes of the same category for that week. Thus, viewing claims for *Angels* correlated significantly with diary measures for viewing soap operas ($r = .20$, $p < 0.01$); viewing claims for *Where There's Life* correlated with diary measures for general information programmes ($r = .11$, $p < 0.01$); and viewing claims for *The Nation's Health* correlated with diary measures for drama viewing ($r = .09$, $p < 0.05$). No significant relationships emerged between diary measures of overall amount of television viewing or viewing of particular types of programmes (e.g. action-adventure, soap operas, sport, comedy/light entertainment or news) and confidence in medical treatment for various disorders.

Among internal health controllers (i.e. those respondents who felt they had considerable personal control over their state of health or recovery from illness), those who had seen more than one episode of *The Nation's Health* tended to have less confidence in the expected proficiency of medical treatment for a range of problems, though negative opinions weakened somewhat amongst those who said they had seen at least three episodes compared with those who claimed to have seen two. Among external controllers, claimed viewing of *Where There's Life* was related to perceptions of expected treatment for all kinds of health problems, while claimed viewing of *The Nation's Health* was related just to opinions about treatment for *psychological problems*. All these relationships except one were curvilinear. Once again, respondents whose viewing claims for each series fell in what we term the 'medium' range (i.e. two episodes seen in the last month) were the ones who generally tended to hold the most negative opinions about medical treatment. The one exception to this pattern was the relationship between claimed viewing of *Where There's Life* and opinion about the treatment in hospital of physical problems, which was linear. The more editions of this programme respondents said they had seen, the more negative their opinions became.

Finally, comparisons of relationships between claimed viewing of television medical series and confidence in medical treatment were made among sub-samples differentiated in terms of the Belief in a Just World scores. A median split procedure was followed as before, thus dividing respondents into low Just World believers and high Just World believers. Within each of these sub samples, statistical relationships between viewing claims for the three medical series and opinions about medical treatment in hospitals were examined, controlling for sex, age and social class differences. Significant relationships were found only among low Just World believers.

In summary, what emerged here was that claimed viewing of just one series, *The Nation's Health*, was significantly related to opinions about the efficiency of hospital treatment. All relationships were curvilinear, with respondents with medium-level viewing claims (two episodes in the last month) having the most negative opinions about the efficiency of medical treatment for *psychological problems, physical problems* and *major surgical problems*.

The above study examined public beliefs about the expected quality of medical treatment for different kinds of ill-health, including physical and mental disorder amongst a metropolitan sample in Britain. Whilst these data are not representative for the nation as a whole, they do serve to indicate relationships between public confidence in hospital treatment and a range of other factors including beliefs about health care and control, TV viewing, and, more relevantly to the concerns of this book, viewing or claimed viewing of TV programmes concerned with health and medical matters. A theoretical assumption is made in this study that confidence in hospital treatment is a negotiable, flexible and situationally influenced characteristic of individuals. Therefore it may be subject to change in the presence of relevant information from personal experience or from television, or other sources of knowledge about what actually happens in hospitals. On the other hand, it is assumed that beliefs about the role of fate or patients' or doctors' efficacy in the area of health represent a more fundamental aspect of an individual's psychological make-up that is less readily subject to change under various environmental influences. This latter assumption derives from Rotter's social learning theory which proposes that a person who values his or her health and believes that he or she can exercise control over health, will be more likely to engage in health-enhancing or maintaining behaviour. Such beliefs and accompanying health-promoting endeavours reflect an enduring, deep-seated psychological characteristic in terms of which individuals can be reliably categorised. This theorising has been empirically reinforced by subsequent psychological research during the 1960s and 1970s which, according to one reviewer, 'lends credence to the expected theoretical assumptions that individuals who hold internal as opposed to external expectancies are more likely to assume responsibility for their health' (Strickland, 1978, p.1194).

The study by Wober and Gunter (1985) found that those individuals who felt more in control personally of their state of health were certainly not as pessimistic about the efficacy of treatment for various medical problems as were people less self-confident about health matters. Moreover, these two types of person differed in the way their viewing of medical programmes was related to their perceptions of medical treatment, suggesting a mediating function for certain personal health orientation dispositions in this context. These findings do not provide a conclusive demonstration either that exposure to certain television programmes affected real-world perceptions or that individuals who hold certain beliefs chose selectively to watch particular television series. But even if the television-influence interpretation is valid, it is clear from these findings, that the impact of television content may be modified by and even in part dependent upon deep-seated personal dispositions of viewers.

In America it has been claimed (Gerbner *et al.*, 1980) that watching television is an unselective experience and leads to distinct effects. Television presents a warped picture of reality, and heavy viewers' perceptions of and fears about the world (especially the latter) are said by these researchers to correspond more to the television portrayal than to the real world. After this had been questioned (Wober, 1978) from Britain, an American (Hirsch, 1980) re-analysed the data used by Gerbner and severely challenged his conclusions. One of the features of Hirsch's critique was that the Gerbner group had used relatively blunt categories of viewing experience – comparing 'light' with 'heavy' viewers, whereas when attention was paid separately to those who viewed nothing at all, or to those who were extremely heavy viewers, their results were not 'in line' with the simple undirectional relationships Gerbner had been talking about and on which, indeed, some far-reaching claims had been made about television's role in society.

The present results, on a small stage, have some resemblance to those that have been described for instance by Gerbner and his colleagues in America, although there is one important difference as well. The difference is that the American measures deal with overall amounts of viewing and relate to a claim that television drama, drama-documentary and fact are inextricably mixed, so that the content of the medium resembles a hologram plate – any part of it carries the same essential imprint as any other part, or the whole. American television influence is therefore said by the Gerbner school to operate in proportion to the amount of the total that is seen. On the other hand the present study focuses on viewing of particular programmes; by comparing different programmes and by statistically controlling for the effects of age, sex and class (measures relating to overall amounts of viewing) it produces a more explicit account of relationships (which may or may not be validly interpreted as evidence of television influences) between social beliefs and exposure to particular areas of television content thematically relevant to those beliefs. This is especially significant in the context of British broadcasting, whose peak-time television schedules include a varied menu of drama, documentary and general interest magazine programming, not all of which is likely to be relevant in terms of (explicit or implicit) messages carried which relate meaningfully to health or medical beliefs. Additional controls for pertinent psychological factors increase still further the confidence one can have in emergent relationships between TV viewing and public beliefs about aspects of the social environment. The resemblance between these British and previous wider American results lies in the fact that analysis into broad-band groupings can create one kind of conclusion, while more detailed analysis, using narrower groupings of viewing experience, can blot out or even reverse such conclusions. Where the present study departs again from its American predecessors is that it makes room for the possibility of two overlapping processes that may both be at work and which might operate in different directions. Here we have personality attributes that can influence viewing selectively; and the experience of viewing may influence attitudes or perceptions.

Finally, it must be noted that any influence of programmes on attitudes has only been measured in the short term. Research has not yet sought to confirm (or deny) influence in the longer term. It is plausible to argue that small influences, such as we have noted, set in train a process of conversation and observation which builds upon and confirms an attitude that has initially been implanted. On the other hand, it is plausible also to argue that small influences will be assimilated by more durable underlying personality structures so that, in a long-term assessment, any minor programme influence would be dissipated.

8 Television viewing and perceptions of family life

Introduction

The family is the fundamental unit within which people in nearly all societies are brought up and in which the future generation is forged. The family is also the unit within which nearly all viewers form their acquaintance with and their patterns of use of television. Family life has changed rapidly in western societies over the last century, with a reduction in the numbers of children and an increase in divorce and single-parent families. One mordant critic recently suggested that in the next century a common social indicator would be the average number of parents per child. In Chapter 5 we examined some allegations that television was inevitably tarnishing the social category of childhood (though such fears were seen to be probably unnecessarily exaggerated). If childhood survives in the television age, is it, nevertheless, together with family life altered by this ubiquitous asset?

In this chapter we shall examine evidence on the nature of television families, how they are perceived by viewers, and on whether the examples they provide have any influence on attitudes towards marriage and family life. Some writers have argued that television portrays families, as it does most other social entities and behaviours, in a narrow, stereotyped fashion, which is likely to do harm. In her book, *Growing up on Television*, Kate Moody (1978) observes that 'TV's contemporary family portrait includes little love and shows scarcely an intact family. Rather, family life on TV is notably absent.' In other words, television gives a low priority to family life. Moody cites research done by Rose Goldsen, a sociology professor at Cornell University, whose analysis of six months of prime-time family shows on US television in 1974–75 revealed few programmes in which characters had any family relations at all. Few contemporary TV dramas portrayed characters who enjoyed happy family lives.

There are, however, some well-known television families. *The Waltons* are an example of a very happy and contented family group. *The Brady Bunch* is a comedy series about a widow and widower who marry and merge their families. Also well known to British viewers are *The Dukes of Hazzard*, another happy-go-lucky family group. Less contented families can also be found, of course, usually in series such as *Dallas* and *Dynasty*; these families are incredibly wealthy and want for nothing except more power and personal happiness. According to Goldsen (1975) these particular serials are 'anti-family' dramas. Her six-month count yielded 15 marriages, 19 couples living together outside wedlock, and 19 separations or divorces. Bearing children was seldom smooth. Goldsen found 11 pregnancies in her study which resulted in two miscarriages, two abortions under consideration, and three births which almost killed the mother. Only one pregnancy in the six months of television monitoring involved a woman and man who were married to each other and living together in reasonable harmony. According to Moody 'It is likely that soaps injure the image of family commitment by a visual code that implicitly denies that children are important in family living' (p. 122).

In both the US and Britain soap operas in their simpler forms have tended to occupy non-prime-time, that is, daytime or early evening when the audience contains a high proportion of female and older viewers. Serials such as *Dallas, Dynasty, Knots Landing* and *Hotel* have been called soap operas, but they are aired in prime-time, and are expected to appeal to audiences containing an increased proportion of male viewers. They differ in their objective characteristics and ethos from the mainstream of soap opera in noticeable ways.

Amplifying Rose Goldsen's theory, the anthropologists Mary Douglas and Karen Wollaeger (1978) have distinguished between 'dramas of disruption' and 'dramas of social harmony'. They see traditional soap operas as examples of drama of social harmony (abbreviated by Wober (1983) to 'dramony') while the prime-time serials qualify as dramas of disruption. The theory is that if disruptions of 'traditionally' approved norms occur in dramony, they are overcome or even defeated; while the disruptions (fraud, divorce, suicide, incest, and so on) in other serials such as *Dynasty* defy and corrupt traditional norms. It is a moot point as to whether the location of disruptive behaviour in strata so wealthy as to be beyond the everyday reality of the mass audience 'protects' the audience from taking what they see as applying in their own world.

Finally, it will be borne in mind that analysis of situation comedy must be dealt with very differently from that of 'straight' drama. For in comedy the practice is to ridicule that which is entrenched and powerful, and the effect of the ridicule may be to undermine, or simply to reinforce by reminding viewers of the authority models portrayed. Which way each programme functions is something that cannot be determined by 'objective' analysis of content, but has to be done by skilful detection of audience perceptions, and if possible by measurement of behavioural change.

The family on television

A number of content analysis studies were carried out mostly in the United States during the late 1970s and early 1980s which examined the portrayal of families and close interpersonal relations on television. The general pattern to emerge from this work, much of which focused on pre-prime-time material, was that traditional values seem to be the norm where family life is concerned. Families and relationships were observed as being more important to women than to men on television (McNeill, 1975).

While divorce is a more common occurrence on television drama programming these days than it was ten years ago, most women on television are married; if single, individual or divorced, they are frequently preoccupied with getting married. Few television characters have children; over 90 per cent have no children (Phelps, 1976). If a woman is a mother, she is unlikely to have a life outside her family. This analysis also claims that a married woman usually defers to her spouse. This deference is particularly characteristic in the predominant, middle-class television household (Glennon and Butsch, 1982; Roberts, 1982). The female relies on her spouse for support and authority. In contrast, the male partner is more concerned with matters outside the home, and relies on the female to manage domestic and personal matters. This can vary according to the social class of the family. In working-class television families the father figure may be portrayed as relatively less competent and in control than he is in middle-class families.

The successful working woman character must usually pay a price for non-conformity (at least within the world of television) by having problems in her personal relationships with men (Roberts, 1982). On those occasions where a woman's wealth was achieved by work, it was usually gained at the expense of personal happiness (Himmelweit and Bell, 1980).

The lifestyles depicted for men represent a marked contrast to those for women on television, according to Roberts (1982). Male characters seem rarely to have much of a family life, and when it is present, the family usually takes second place to the more fulfilling and rewarding demands of a career. In fictional television programming, the story-line often fails to reveal the marital status of male characters. One study found, for example, that in the case of 46 per cent of men the viewer could not tell if they were married, compared to 11 per cent of women; nor could they identify in 53 per cent of cases whether men were parents, compared to 19 per cent of the women. Among those television characters whose marital status is revealed, however, men appear to be more successful at marriage than women. Fewer men than women on television are likely to be divorced (Silverman *et al.* 1978).

According to Roberts, child viewers could gain the impression that for women, marriage is an all-consuming lifestyle. Women who deviate from this lifestyle put their personal happiness at risk and jeopardise the affection and support of their loved ones. For men, on the other hand, marriage and family may be seen as largely unimportant or as a lifestyle to which the less able and the ineffectual are relegated (Roberts, 1982).

Glennon and Butsch (1977; 1979; 1980) reported an historical study of the portrayal of families on television spanning over thirty years from 1947 to 1977. They collected information about 218 family series, all prime-time shows in which the main characters were members of a family and among whom most of the interactions in the programme occurred. These programmes included mainly situation comedies (86 per cent), but there were also serious family drama, adventure series and cartoons. The content analysis showed that families on prime-time television were much more likely to be middle-class than working-class. Most heads of households were professional or managerial people and fewer than one-fifth of the families observed were headed by blue-collar workers. Many of prime-time television's families were in fact extremely wealthy and successful and rarely had to be concerned with making ends meet. The pattern of family types remained fairly constant for many years, though the authors observed a slight increase in the number of working-class families on prime-time television during the early 1970s.

Within working-class families Glennon and Butsch distinguished between those headed by a rather dumb, unintelligent father and those who were upwardly mobile. They argued that these two themes serve to weaken the dignity of working-class family lifestyle. The inept father may lead working-class families to be regarded in a purely comical fashion. At the same time, while the upwardly mobile family is usually strong-willed and more dignified, the fact that it is striving to attain middle-class status conveys the message, say the authors, that working-class lifestyle is something to escape from.

Middle-class families are shown in a different light. The husband is usually intelligent and mature, although the wife may be depicted as inept in a variety of ways. In many middle-class families, however, both parents are people who seem to be able to deal effectively with any problems. Glennon and Butsch speculated on the possible impact of television's family portrayals. For instance, the comic nature of many working-class families' fathers may suggest to working-class children that their fathers are laughed at by the rest of the world. Another message identified was that the effort of moving from a working-class to a middle-class lifestyle is often underplayed by television, perhaps leaving working-class members of the audience with the impression that the attainment of a higher social status is relatively easy to achieve, which in reality it often is not. The portrayal which paints a picture of the middle-class 'super-family' able to cope apparently with ease with any kind of problem, might lead viewers to question the adequacy of their own family, by setting unrealistic goals for happiness and contentment.

Fisher (1974) explored marital and familial roles on television programmes broadcast by the three major networks in the United States portraying contemporary American families. He was specifically interested in the actions of the televised characters of husband–father and wife–mother and the kinds of behaviour spouses displayed towards each other and towards their children. Fisher found that familial role behaviour was usually conflict-free, emphasising affectionate and altruistic concerns for one's spouse and children. Violent or disruptive behaviour was not evident. There was little apparent concern within the marital setting for financial problems. Television spouses helped each other, did little housework and had few problems with the children. Fisher suggested that marital and familial role behaviours on television can serve as models which viewers might imitate. Television may thus be an important vehicle for teaching unmarried viewers about marital obligations and role expectations, as well as in offering possible solutions to those viewers who may be having marital difficulties. Overall, Fisher felt that television's portrayal of family life seemed to emphasise socially approved cultural expectations.

Hines, Greenberg and Buerkel (1979) reported that there were about 40–50 families on the air every week on prime-time and Saturday morning television in the United States. Of these, about one-third consisted of two parents with children or a single parent with children, and about one-fifth were married couples with no children. The remainder were various family groupings – cousins, aunts and uncles, in-laws, and so on. Half the marriages were first marriages and divorce was increasing. In family series, women seemed to fare better numerically than in television programming more generally.

As well as looking at family structures, Hines *et al.* examined the nature of interpersonal relationships on television. They observed that television's fictional relationships usually concentrated on immediate family members – wife, mother, daughter, sister and their counterpart males roles (see also, Buerkel–Rothfuss and Greenberg, 1978). Within the family setting, husbands were usually a companion to their wives and a friend, guide and teacher to their children; they also managed the family finances. The main topics of conversation consisted of health matters, domestic concerns, jobs, deviant behaviour and personality. Male and female family members initiated conversations about equally according to one wide ranging study (Greenberg *et al.*, 1980).

These authors concentrated on family-centred television series where the story-line revolves around a particular family each week. They sampled 115 such shows across three seasons of US prime-time television between 1975 and 1978. A content analysis frame developed by Borke (1967) was adopted for the systematic description of normal family interaction in ordinary settings. She observed families or parents and children performing a variety of family tasks in their homes. Verbal interactions were categorised according to the functions they performed from the speaker's point of view, and these categories were reduced to a smaller number of primary and secondary modes of interaction, e.g. contributing information, giving support, resisting, retreating and directing. These were then assumed under Horney's (1945) three classifications of interpersonal direction: going *towards* someone, going *against* someone, and going *away* from someone.

Greenberg *et al.* coded acts into each of these three directions. Within each directional category, a series of modes was used to describe more precisely the manner in which characters were approaching, avoiding or attacking. Going away did not occur very frequently during any of the three seasons monitored; going against someone accounted for about 12 per cent of interactions on average over the three years. The mode of going against someone most commonly observed was verbal opposition. Direct physical attacks were infrequent.

The most common category of interpersonal interaction recorded by Greenberg *et al.* was that of going towards someone which accounted for between eight and nine out of ten family role interactions during the period they monitored. Offering information, seeking information and giving directions to others were the most popular modes of positive interaction. Another common mode of interaction was giving support to other members of the family. Asking for and accepting support, on the other hand, were less frequent.

Greenberg *et al.* also decided to take a look at conflictual behaviour in family groups on television. By pairing each nuclear family role they found that conflicts occurred most often between husband and wife and between two siblings (brother against brother or brother against sister). There were of course conflicts between parent and child and between sisters, but these were relatively less frequent occurrences.

Greenberg *et al.* summarised their findings as itemised below:

1. The vast majority of fictional television characters do not have relatives appearing in the stories with them.
2. No particular configuration of family structure dominates; most common are families headed by a single parent or two parents, plus children; childless couples are nearly as frequent.
3. Divorce has increased each season; it has become equivalent to widowhood, as a factor to account for single-parent families; first marriages account for half the adults, and a quarter have never married.
4. Relatives outside the nuclear family are rare; nuclear family members account for 80 per cent of all roleholders.
5. Males and females are equal in number in TV families.
6. Females and males are equal in initiating and receiving family role interactions.
7. Husband and wife is the most active interacting TV family role pair.
8. Parents are more likely to interact with same-sex children, e.g. more father–son than father–daughter interactions.
9. Affiliative acts occur in TV families about eight times more often than conflictual acts.
10. Conflict is more heavily concentrated in husband–wife pairs and dyads that include a brother.
11. Offering information to others is the dominant mode of family interactions.
12. Parents are most likely to give directions; children least so.
13. Parents and spouses are more likely to give support or encouragement, children are most likely to see it. (Greenberg *et al.*, 1980, pp. 171–2).

Some researchers have focused specifically on the portrayal of families in programmes that children are most likely to see regularly. Barcus (1983) assessed the distribution of various family and kinship units in over 90 drama and educationally-oriented programmes. Examples were also found in cartoon and animated adventure programmes. Barcus found that traditional family roles are emphasised. The father is the bread-winner and the authority figure in the household. There are certain respects in which he may be portrayed as less nurturant and competent than the mother. The mother is usually very good in her role as home-maker and source of affection and understanding. Fathers tend to get on well with their sons, but less often enjoy informal relationships with their daughters. Father and son are especially likely to get on famously in adventure settings.

Family life on television, observed Barcus, is not entirely conflict-free, but where problems do arise internally they are usually concerned with disobedience and discipline and solutions generally reinforce traditional values and relationships between parents and children. Marital problems occur also, but these seldom involve the children. This, notes Barcus, does not reflect real life. Whilst children may see televised portrayals of extramarital affairs, problems of parents with in-laws and so forth, there is also a great deal of supportive behaviour to be seen within television families. Family relations are most often close and cooperative. Financial difficulties, divorce, trouble for children at school, ageing members of the family, and other real-life problems, are rarely prominent on television.

The questions that arise from these analyses of televised families are whether viewers actually perceive families – either their own or other people's – in the same way as they are shown on television; next, if television's portrayal differs from how families behave in real life; then, finally, if television's portrayal has any effect on viewers' perceptions of behaviour within their families.

The impact of TV portrayals on beliefs about marriage and the family

Effects among children
Some critics have accused television of undermining the status quo through its frequent portrayals of lifestyles of apparently limitless wealth in popular series such as *Dallas* and *Dynasty*, which are said to cultivate envy, greed and dissatisfaction amongst viewers, particularly those from the lower social classes, who would dearly love to emulate these models of affluence but can never realistically hope to. However, studies of television's portrayals of different family lifestyles have indicated that their message may be that money cannot in fact buy true happiness and that only poor families lead contented lives.

Thomas and Callahan (1982) looked at family-focused series during three months of peak-time network programming in the United States each year from 1978 to 1980. Categorising families as upperclass, upper middle-class, middle-class or working class, they assessed each family for the extent to which its members exhibited high or low levels of sympathy towards each other and pulled together in times of trouble. They also looked at the extent to which family members' intentions towards each other were good or bad. Finally, they assessed each television series on the extent to which individual episodes finished happily or not for the family concerned.

All working-class families portrayed exhibited high degrees of sympathy, whereas only one in five upper-class families did so. Middle-class families came about mid-way between the first two. Similarly, the proportion of helpful family members was much greater in series which revolved around poor than around wealthy families. Thomas and Callahan reported that seven out of ten characters in 'poor family' series were well intentioned and none was ill intentioned towards other members of their family. However, just over three out of ten upper-class family members were well intentioned, and a similar number were ill intentioned towards their relatives.

Shows featuring poor families were by far the happiest too. Nearly all working-class family shows ended happily, whilst no upper-class families ended happier at the conclusion of an episode. In sum, Thomas and Callahan interpreted their findings to show that good will, friendliness, happiness and contentment were characteristics much more likely to be associated with poverty than with wealth among television families. What impact may such portrayals have on viewers?

A research group led by Nancy Buerkel–Rothfuss and Bradley Greenberg of Michigan State University explored this question. This work began with a detailed analysis of programme content which has already been discussed above. The next stage of the investigation involved finding out amongst samples totalling over 1000 children, aged nine, eleven and thirteen years, from Michigan and California, which family shows they customarily watched, and whether they watched shows which depicted families in harmony or in conflict. This was ascertained through the children's endorsement of items on a list of 40 family shows for frequency of viewing each programme. Buerkel–Rothfuss, Greenberg and their colleagues then asked the children how realistic they perceived the behaviours of television families to be. Second, they asked the children whether they believed that they could learn from television about family life. On a separate questionnaire the children were finally asked about their beliefs about real-life families. These items dealt with children's perceptions that, in real life, family members generally support one another or generally ignore or even oppose each other. One example of such an item was: 'Of every ten parents, how many help their kids a lot?' endorsed along a scale from 0 to 10.

Certain relationships emerged beween the types of family shows viewed and perceptions of real-life family roles for these children. In the presence of simultaneous statistical controls for five demographic differences and overall weight of viewing television, youngsters who frequently watched family shows in general tended to believe more strongly than less frequent viewers of these shows that families in real life typically show support and concern for each other. There were no strong tendencies for children's viewing of these programmes to be related to the belief that real-life families today are frequently characterised by intra-family conflict and strife.

The strength with which children's viewing of family shows was related to their beliefs about how mutually supportive family members are in real life was mediated to some extent by the perceived realism of television portrayals. The more like real-life television's family portrayals were seen to be the stronger the latter relationship became. Relationships between children's viewing of family shows and their beliefs about affiliative family behaviour were strongest also when children believed they could learn a lot from television.

Parental mediation also influenced the relationships between children's viewing of television family shows and their beliefs about family behaviours in real life. Thus the relationship between viewing family shows and the belief that real-life families tend to be affiliative rather than non-affiliative was enhanced considerably amongst children whose parents exhibited a certain degree of control over what they were permitted or encouraged to view, and who often viewed and discussed programmes with their children.

Another factor influencing what children think about television families is how like their own family experiences the ones seen on television appear to be. How well children are able to comprehend the plots of television programmes featuring families may be mediated by the degree of similarity between their own social class and that of the television family.

Newcomb and Collins (1979) investigated children's comprehension of two television situation comedies that portrayed either a white middle-class family or a black working-class family in similar conflict-resolution situations. Participants in this study were boys and girls aged 7, 10 and 13 years. They were fairly evenly divided between whites and blacks, middle-class and working-class. After viewing one of the programmes in their school, all participants were tested for their understanding of the story in each case. The researchers found that following the programme featuring the middle-class family, comprehension was better among middle-class children than working-class children, while after the programme with the working-class family, higher comprehension scores occurred among working-class children. These differences were significant among the youngest children only, and indicate that comprehension difficulties of young children may reside partly in their lack of familiarity with types of roles, characters and settings portrayed in many adult entertainment programmes. When the social class settings of television family portrayals are similar to their own, young children's comprehension of programme content may be enhanced. Among older children, plot comprehension appears to depend less on the degree of match between their own social class and that of characters in television programmes.

This study suggests that young viewers' comprehension of fictional television is not the same across all programmes, even of the same genre (in this study, situation comedy). Difficulties in understanding may be less pronounced when there is some congruence between the information to be comprehended and the children's own social experiences.

Effects among adults

Buerkel–Rothfuss and Mayes (1981), in a study on adult subjects, investigated relationships between amount of viewing of television soap operas and subjective estimates of real-life occurrences of divorce, infidelity, illegitimacy, abortions and happy marriages. Heavy viewing of soap operas was positively associated with higher estimates of the number of males and females out of ten who have had affairs, been divorced, had illegitimate children, and with higher estimates of women who have had abortions. Soap opera viewing was unrelated to perceptions of how many women or men are happily married however.

A number of writers have suggested that television's portrayal of marital relations may serve as a set of examples for unmarried individuals or may offer lessons of value to those who are already married and having problems. Two studies have recently investigated these claims. Fallis, Friedsted and Fitzpatrick (1985) in the USA conducted a study of 51 couples to determine if television viewing was related to discussion of their relationship between spouses. The results showed that the degree of television's influence seems to depend upon the nature of the relationship between the couples.

Fitzpatrick and her colleagues had in earlier papers developed a typology of relational difficulties, derived from the responses of individuals to a 77-item Marital Dimensions Instrument (Fitzpatrick, 1977; Fitzpatrick and Best, 1979; Fitzpatrick and Indvik, 1982). From this test, each individual was now classified as either 'traditional', 'independent' or 'separate' depending on the marital information he or she gave.

'Traditionals' are characterised by a high degree of sharing and the corresponding tendency to engage in, rather than avoid, conflict when it arises. Couples in this type of marriage are usually highly interdependent. 'Independents' reject a belief system that stresses traditional values; they are most committed to an ideology of uncertainty and change. This type of marriage is defined by a moderate amount of sharing between partners and little conflict avoidance. Partners appear to negotiate autonomy in this type of relationship. 'Separates' have been labelled the emotionally divorced (Fitzpatrick, 1977) and report that they are more dissatisfied in their marital relationships than do the other two types (Fitzpatrick and Best, 1979). The separates avoid conflict, are not very expressive, and despite their apparent independence, such individuals do not feel particularly free or autonomous.

In a review of relationships as portrayed on television, Fallis *et al.* found a preponderance of traditional sex-role portrayals and conventional value systems depicted by television families. Female deference and dependence rather than autonomy mark relationships that are harmonious while conflict is prevalent when partners deviate from traditionalism. Television couples are extremely affiliative and partners tend to express intimate thoughts readily and with positive outcomes.

Television portrayals of relationships present the most striking discrepancy from real-life experience for those defining their own marriages as separate. On television, traditionalism rather than autonomy breeds harmony, independence is associated with conflict, and couples are both affiliative and expressive in their interactions. Separates, who vacillate between conventional and non-conventional values, appear extremely reluctant to engage in conflict, and those who are neither expressive nor compassionate with their partners rarely appear on television.

To examine the impact of television viewing, Fallis *et al.* asked participants about their television viewing behaviour and topics they say they discuss with their spouse as a result of seeing something on television. Television viewing was measured in terms of numbers of hours usually viewed per day and the amount of time they normally view with their spouse. General frequency of discussion with spouse prompted by television content was assessed on a five-point scale ranging from 'never' to 'very often'. An attempt was also made to ascertain specific topics of discussion between partners by providing respondents with a list of issues: political and social issues, subjects related to the family, subjects related to your job, subjects related to your relationship with your spouse, subjects related to your children and subjects related to your physical or mental health. High and low-viewing television groups were compared among traditionals, independents and separates.

High and low-viewing 'separates' differed in the extent to which they discussed three of the four relationship-relevant issues, as a result of watching television. Only among 'separates' was amount of viewing related to amount of conversation about subjects relating to the family, to relationship with spouse, and to physical or mental health. High-viewing 'separates' engaged in more television-prompted conversations about marital and family issues than did low-viewing 'separates'. Relationships were also examined between amount of television watching with spouse and frequencies of discussion of something seen on television. Once again, significant relationships emerged only among 'separates' and only with respect to issues concerning their marriage. Television viewing with spouse did not appear to promote conversations about social, political or job-related issues.

Fallis *et al.* concluded that television content can provide an avenue for discussion in a relationship where partners typically do not share, are not affiliative or expressive, and avoid arguments or any sort of conflict. The authors could not say whether this kind of discussion is functional or dysfunctional for those couples classified as 'separates'. It may be, however, that such talk is directed at airing problems and issues that would not otherwise be brought out into the open. On the other hand, if such essentially dispassionate couples begin to compare themselves with harmonious television marriages, relational distance between them may turn to dissatisfaction.

Perceptions of marital unhappiness on television and in real life

In a recent British study the distinctions made by adults between television and real-life families were related to viewing habits (Gunter, 1984). A questionnaire was distributed with the regular appreciation diary on which ten propositions were listed about the possible causes of marital unhappiness. On one side respondents were asked to say how important they thought each of these reasons was for marital unhappiness as portrayed on television. On the other side, the same propositions were presented and respondents were asked to say how important they believed each reason to be for marital unhappiness in real life. The propositions were designed to reflect rules of marital unhappiness discovered in recent research by Argyle and his colleagues (Argyle and Henderson, 1985).

Table 8.1 shows the percentages of respondents who said that each cause was 'nearly always' or 'fairly often' important for marital unhappiness either on television or in real life. Three items were endorsed in this way by eight out of ten or more respondents. Top of the list was unfaithfulness between partners. This was followed by loss of shared personal feelings between marriage partners and one partner becoming bored with the other. In each case these reasons for marital unhappiness were seen as being more pertinent to real life than to television by a margin of between 5 and 9 per cent.

Over half of the respondents also thought that the husband being away at work for long periods and couples being unable to afford a decent home were important causes of marital discord, both in real life and on television.

Further down the list, failure to share household chores, conflict

Table 8.1 Opinions about causes of marital unhappiness on television and in real life among single and married respondents.

Respondents: Location observed:	Single		Married		All (563)	
	TV %	Real Life %	TV %	Real Life %	TV %	Real Life %

Those who say the following causes are nearly always or fairly often important sources of marital unhappiness

Subset (i)

When husband and wife no longer share personal feelings with each other	70	81	85	93	82	91
When one partner simply becomes bored with the other	69	84	78	84	77	85
Average:	69.5	82.5	81.5	88.5	79.5	88.0

Subset (ii)

When one partner is unfaithful to the other	87	89	90	94	88	93
When the husband is away for long periods	54	57	63	64	62	64
When married couples cannot afford a decent home of their own	37	39	51	53	51	53
When married couples are unable to have any children of their own	35	39	39	38	41	41
When husband and wife cannot agree on when to start a family	26	25	34	39	33	38
When husband and wife do not share household chores	21	25	30	31	30	31
Average:	43.3	45.7	51.1	53.3	50.8	68.7

Subset (iii)

When one partner does not get on with his/her in-laws	29	17	39	29	38	28
When the husband is against his wife having a job	27	19	32	32	34	31
Average:	28.0	18.0	35.5	30.5	36.0	29.5

over whether the wife should work, and problems with in-laws were the least often endorsed causes of marital unhappiness. Whilst there was a high degree of consistency between television percepts and real life percepts among these items, one exception was the finding that respondents thought that problems with in-laws were more often an important cause of marital unhappiness as depicted on television than in real life.

Comparisons were made between the opinions of males and females in the sample and between those who were single and those who were married. Male and female respondents were in agreement about the three principal causes of marital discord as shown on television and as occurring in everyday life. Males, however, found loss of shared personal feelings as an important determinant of marital unhappiness in real life more often than they noted this to occur on television. Female respondents were more likely than males to say that marital unhappiness in real life often occurs when couples cannot have children of their own. The difference between sexes on this item in the context of television marriages, however, was much smaller, as males saw this as a problem more often on television than in reality. Table 8.1 shows the extent to which various opinions about marital unhappiness were held by respondents who were themselves married or single. What emerged from this comparison was that there were substantial differences of opinion between these two groups. Married respondents generally endorsed more potential sources of marital discord than did single respondents, especially in the context of marriage in real life. Let us examine some specific examples of this.

It is possible to group the potential sources of marital breakdown into three subsets. In the first subset labelled (i) observers agree that television under-represents real life; here we have affective and cognitive disjunctions which can be seen as fundamental rather than as remediable conditions. Single observers are more likely than married ones to consider that television under-represents this pair of items in comparison with real life.

Next comes a set of six situations (subset (ii)) which are seen as equally often presented on television as they occur in real life. These difficulties can conceivably be surmounted by forgiveness, negotiation, patience or an appreciation of the two attributes referred to in the first set of breakdown conditions. Here, both married and single respondents consider that television portrayals match events in real life.

Finally, two items (subset (iii)) remain which both married and single respondents think are represented on television as reasons for marital breakdown more often than happens in real life. In short, British viewers think that television largely reflects real life in showing a range of causes of marital discord; it slightly underplays the two most important difficulties (more so in the view of those who may know less about marriage from personal experience) and it slightly over-represents the two least important problems (again, more so in the opinion of those who are not actually married themselves).

As well as comparing respondents' perceptions of the causes of unhappiness in marriage on television and in reality, this study also investigated whether these two sets of perceptions were differentially related to television viewing. Measures of viewing behaviour were obtained from completed diaries. These provided information about how much television respondents watched in total during the survey week and about how much they watched different types of programmes.

Multiple-classification analysis was used to find out the degree to which viewing patterns were significantly related to perceptions of the reasons for unhappiness in marriage on television or in real life. This technique permitted an assessment of the strength of the relationships between amount or type of television viewing and beliefs about marital discord whilst important factors such as sex, age, social class and education of respondents were held in control.

An initial series of analyses was computed for all respondents which revealed no significant relationships between total amount of viewing and any perceptions of the principal causes of marital unhappiness either as depicted in television or as thought to occur in real life. Further analyses over all respondents failed to show any significant relationships either between viewing of particular types of programming, such as action-adventure, soap opera or news, and perceptions of marital unhappiness. We have seen, however, that the extent to which different possible reasons for marital unhappiness were endorsed did vary between married and single respondents. Therefore multiple classification analyses were next computed separately for married and for single respondents. A number of significant results emerged from these analyses (see Gunter, 1985).

Among married respondents the perception of one possible cause of marital discord, as portrayed on television, related to the amount of viewing they did of action-adventure material. No longer sharing the same feelings was more often noted by heavy than by medium and light viewers of this genre. Two less important reasons for discord – not being able to afford a decent home or protracted absence of the husband – were more often noted by heavy viewers of soap opera, who were themselves married, both in television portrayals and in real life.

Married viewers were uniform in the direction of associations they revealed – more viewing was linked with greater considerations of importance attributed to various reasons for marital discord. However, there was no item for which a relationship between amount of viewing of a given genre and perception of that item on that segment of television was matched by a similarly significant relationship between viewing and perception of that phenomenon in real life.

For single respondents, a number of links between viewing and perceptions of reasons for marital discord exist. Viewing of action-adventure programming were found to be significantly related to perceptions of marital unhappiness on television being caused importantly by failure of one partner to get on with his or her in-laws and when husband and wife cannot agree on when to start a family.

Here, both relationships were non-linear and in all of them it is the heaviest viewers who saw less importance in the items tabulated. Medium viewers tended to be more likely to accord importance to these items, but light viewers returned again to perceptions of lesser importance. Perceptions of the causes of marital unhappiness in real life were significantly related to television viewing scores on four items. The relationships again were, with one exception, non-linear. Heavier single viewers of action-adventure believed that failure to share the household chores was more important to marital discord than did lighter single viewers of these programmes. Weight of soap opera viewing was significantly related to the other three beliefs – in a U-shaped fashion. In each case, heavy single viewers of soaps believed that the husband being away for long periods, failure of marriage partners to share household chores and failure of one partner to get on with his or her in-laws were more important to marital unhappiness than did either light or medium viewers. However, medium viewers were least likely of all to perceive these factors as important causes of real life marital disorder. Overall, there are no items for which a relationship between its perceived portrayal in a given television genre and amount of viewing of that genre is matched by a relationship between viewing that genre and perceptions of that item in real life.

The outcomes both for single and for married respondents make it impossible to argue convincingly that watching more television has brought about alterations in the way that people perceive the real world, in this case, as it concerns the operation of marital relationships in British society. Nor is it possible to argue a 'mainstreaming' case in which heavy and light viewers develop perceptions more like those of medium viewers; for more of the differences were found to move in the direction of polarisation rather than of centralisation.

The present results indicate, in line with those reported in earlier chapters, that viewers' perceptions, beliefs and attitudes often relate more closely to viewing of particular kinds of programmes than to television viewing in total. Whilst heavy viewers of television in general are likely to be heavy viewers of many specific kinds of programming, amounts of viewing of particular programme types are not related in the same way or to the same extent to conceptions of social reality. Furthermore, relationships may vary according to the types of people among whom they are being considered. Opinions about marital discord varied among respondents depending on whether or not they were married.

The perceived causes of marital unhappiness that were most closely related to television viewing differed between single and married respondents. And even on the one item that was commonly related to television viewing among both groups, the direction of the relationship was different among married people from what it was among the single. Thus heavy soap opera viewers who were married thought that the husband being away for long periods was more important as a cause of marital unhappiness in real life than did light soap opera viewers. The reverse was the case among single viewers.

The notion of mainstreaming as advanced by the Annenberg groups is based on an assumption about a long-term effect of television in total. At no stage are any statements made about the differential impact on social perceptions of viewing different kinds of television content. The evidence presented above, however, indicates quite clearly that amounts of viewing of particular categories of programming may operate in different ways from total television viewing in relation to conceptions of particular aspects of social reality. The fact that viewing measures of just one programme type among married respondents (soap operas) and of two types (soap operas and action-adventure) among single respondents were related to real-world perceptions of the causes of marital unhappiness suggests that any cultivation effects of television at all may depend in an important way on viewing preferences, rather than on total viewing volume.

The particular reasons for marital unhappiness that were related to viewing behaviour among married respondents were mostly different from those found among single respondents. This suggests that, if cultivation effects are occurring they vary according to the characteristics or background of respondents.

There is a distinct indication from the present evidence that the real-life experiences and associated beliefs of respondents may influence the kinds of 'messages' they associate with television. Married respondents, for example, tended to believe quite strongly that two principal causes of marital unhappiness in real life are when the husband is away from home for long periods of time and when husband and wife no longer share personal feelings with each other. Both of these beliefs were stronger still among married respondents who were heavy viewers of soap operas, even though they did not consider this to be a particular feature of soap opera content. This finding could indicate that married respondents who, as a group already tended to perceive the above factors as important sources of marital discord had these beliefs further reinforced by watching soap operas. Alternatively, the fact that soap opera viewing was the only aspect of married respondents' television viewing that was related to their real world beliefs about marriage, may indicate a selective viewing syndrome on the part of those among married respondents who hold such beliefs about marital unhappiness particularly strongly.

A third possibility is that of 'false consciousness', in which viewers do not notice a feature of their particular diet of heavy viewing, which nevertheless operates so as to cause them more often or more strongly to notice that feature in real life. The difficulty with arguments about false consciousness is that they may apply to social scientists just as well as to their subject respondents; and only extremely compelling evidence, of a kind that does not exist here, could support such an interpretation. The survey reported here has examined 140 multiple classification analyses (ten possible causes of discord, for each of seven programme types, among two sub-groups of respondents), out of which only one is significant at a 1:100 level of chance, while nine others are significant at a level of 5:100. These significant relationships did not occur evenly spread across all seven programme types but were concentrated in the two types involving serial narrative material. Among married observers, heavy viewers showed some increased awareness of two causes of marital discord in real life; but singles who were heavy viewers showed some lowered awareness of four sources of real-life marital discord, none of which came at the top of the list of the most widely recognised causes of disruption.

The important comparisons of this chapter are between the American study of Buerkel–Rothfuss and Greenberg, in which broadly positive outcomes were reported among children, for their perceptions of family life as a result of heavy viewing of television drama, the studies among American adults by Fitzpatrick and Fallis which provide cautious optimism over the contribution of television viewing for certain married couples, and the British evidence which does not suggest any harm either. As far as perceptions of family life are concerned, neither American television nor British television appears to show harmful effects.

9   Conclusion: Two methods of control –
by the self or through delegated
institutions

It is not a cliché but of its essence that research must end as it
began, with questions. Those at the end should be sharper than
the ones at the onset, and we believe that in this book this is so.
We are dealing with a field in which some workers have stood ortho-
dox scientific methodology on its head. In science one should ideally
observe an array of 'facts', develop a theory about how they are
related, make up hypotheses predicting these and 'new' facts and
links as yet unnoticed and then, when these have been found (or
not), accept (or reject) the hypotheses as genuine explanations, perhaps with a few adjustments built in. Instead, what we have frequently discussed in this book is a trial-and-error process in which
explanations have been the starting-point for confirmatory pattern
hunts. In some cases if contradictory evidence has been found, it
has been neglected. When a challenge had been levelled at a part
of this process there has been some acrimony but after an intellectual
convulsion new and more useful positions have been taken, some
of which actually resemble older fruits of wisdom. There has thus
been an advance and refinement in our understanding of how television may or may not affect human society.

A historian of science, Thomas Kuhn (1960), referred to 'para-
digms' which had a life of a decade or two, during which the scientific
community would see an idea proposed, much work done and then
through exhaustion, fulfilment or inability to accommodate newly-
discovered phenomena, the scene would change. One such paradigm
was the simple 'effects' model of television's supposed influence
on individuals and through them, on society. As early as 1960 Joseph
Klapper demurred from this; it was not so much what television
did to viewers that mattered, he said; it was what they took to
their viewing that did most to affect any outcome of the experience.
While many writers quoted and noted Klapper, it did not seem
to do much to blunt the momentum of the 'effects' paradigm which
was in full swing, propelled mainly by an interest in the potential
imitative effects of screened violence.

As part of the larger caravan the Annenberg researchers, led by George Gerbner, embarked on thoroughgoing content analyses of American television programmes. A revolutionary idea from the Gerbner group was that the content patterns they were chronicling might act in a direction opposite to that of mere imitation. To get this idea across, and it is a luminous one, it had to be and it was stated with force – so much so, that when studying the texts about 'cultivation effects' and later about 'mainstreaming' and 'resonance', the reader might have expected to see evidence of major effects and phenomena sustaining these claims. But usually the differences being discussed were only of the order of 10 or 12 percentage points between two extreme groups (see Chapters 2 and 6). Correlations, albeit significant, seldom exceed 0.15. So, for all the rhetoric, the cultivation effects even in America are modest.

The Gerbnerian theory is a 'grand' one embracing a wide range of phenomena from the production to the consumption of information, and this book recognises the major scope of his work. It also sets out to go a step further, to discuss and place it in a wider cross-national format and to test it more rigorously and empirically.

As the energy blew out of the progress of the imitation research paradigm, it was to some extent replaced by Gerbner's new reaction model, which was at first preoccupied with violence. And what was the outcome of the previous intellectual crusade? Seen from outside America it appears, paradoxically, that it was all in vain. Violence is still common on the American screen. It may take new forms now; three decades ago it was horses which would bite the dust while their cowboy heroes found new mounts. Now the automobile steeds roll over and burst into flames, or helicopters crash in ravines while A-teams and their parallels walk away unscathed. In the face of the demonstration (see Cook, Kendzierski and Thomas, 1983) that violence on screen probably increases aggression in real life, the mechanism of social response in America appears to be inadequate to bring about changes in television content.

The prospect of legal restraint on screened violence is countered in America with recourse to the First Amendment designed to safeguard *political* freedom of expression. Fictional violence and news violence are treated as of one piece, ironically complementing Gerbner's research view of television uses and content as homogeneous rather than as differentiated. A view in Europe, on the other hand, looks for conceptual discriminations, and employs them in the service of legal measures prohibiting discrimination. In America this happened in one instance where the derogatory figures of Amos, Andy and Beulah were banished from the screens; the call is now made there to cut down on violence, either across the board, or in particular cases where research may have indicated some kind of social problem or harm may be caused.

Accordingly, in Sweden there is very little televised violence allowed; in Britain there are restraints on the amount, kind and positioning in the schedule of programmes containing violence. There is still controversy between those who wish for more control to ensure less violence, and those who disbelieve the imitation or the reaction effects research (and in Britain, at any rate, there is good reason to disbelive some of the latter), or who focus on a desire to allow freedom of expression and consumption; but the principle is recognised that there is a need for caution about televised violence, and that society, through certain delegated institutional mechanisms, will restrain its availability.

In assessing the reaction effects paradigm we have to examine not only the evidence that has been collected, but also the concepts which market it and give it some form. The Gerbnerian grand theory, which exceeds in scope anything else on offer from other communications researchers, virtually amounts to a doctrine. This doctrine says that television, as it is run in America, is bad for humanity there. Gerbner calls television a religion and a 'pulpit in the home', though this perhaps says more about his notion of religion than about his portrait of television as a malign social force. Its harm is said to extend beyond the realm of violence to causing fear and political conservatism, to a division of ethnic minorities from the majority, and to derision of the weakest age and sex groups – in all cases leaving one segment of society at a clear and unfair disadvantage. When data or analyses are brought forward that do not substantiate the original form of the doctrine that more of a harmful phenomenon is more harmful, the overarching doctrine is still maintained, while readjustments are made in the arguments designed to sustain it.

Thus 'mainstreaming' was advanced as a new label for what looks like a phenomenon termed by other researchers as 'agenda-setting'. Agenda-setting is a process aimed at producing a widespread recognition in society of the existence of some phenomenon, topic or problem and is usually concerned with a relatively superficial level of public awareness of events, whereas mainstreaming goes further and assumes that such an awareness will also result in a consensus of understanding about social phenomena, and in a broad agreement about how people or society should deal with the matter. Meanwhile, 'resonance' is used as a new label for what resembles the Klapperian formulation of a selective process of reinforcement between viewers' predispositions and messages they take from the screen.

We remain unconvinced that the American evidence sustains the particular form of the case being made; but that is to be resolved in America. Apart from the area of violence, however, in the worlds of political attitudes and possibly also sexism and ageism there may be a case for quite ordinary 'forward' modelling effects on adults but more especially on children, in which the Gerbner theory and evidence does not depart much from previous views, but merely demonstrates that there are grounds for social concern.

Factors limiting television cultivation
One important factor that may control the cultivation effects of television is the degree of viewers' involvement in programmes and the way they interpret what they see in programmes. The cultural indicators model assumes that certain patterns of social reality-construction automatically follow from exposure to particular patterns of programme content. Implicit in the notion of enculturation by television is the assumption that the messages identified in television drama programming by an *a priori* system of content analysis are also the messages that are salient to and absorbed by viewers. At no stage in their research do the cultural indicators group put this assumption to empirical test. There is no assessment of the nature of audience perceptions and their interpretations of programme content. However, research conducted elsewhere has indicated that the interpretations viewers place on television content may not only differ from those that derive from content analysis, but may also function as important mediators or controllers of the cultivation effects of television.

The perceived reality of television may be a powerful mediator of television cultivation inflence. Hawkins and Pingree (1980), for example, found that, among Australian students taking a media studies course, stronger cultivation effects occurred with lower level of perceived reality of television content. The degree of thought people put into their viewing may also affect the extent or strength of television's cultivation effects. Pingree, Starrett and Hawkins (1979) compared the social reality effects of soap opera viewing among soap opera fans who were attending a soap opera convention and luncheon with the stars, and a random sample of women from the same city. Results showed that the relationship between amount of soap opera viewing and soap opera-biased ideas of social reality was greater among the random sample of women. The fans' more active and often more critical processing of the soap operas seen, it is argued by the authors, may have limited the programmes' cultivation effects.

Hawkins and Pingree (1982) offer the term 'critical consumer' to cover this active viewing process which they describe as an 'evaluation of information during reception, greater retention of the bits and pieces of information provided by television, awareness of exceptions to patterns, more active search (not simply exposure) for confirming or disconfirming information, a more rational weighing of evidence in constructing social reality ... ' (p. 241).

In our own research reported in this book, comparisons of viewers' 'television percepts' and 'real-world percepts' of the same categories of social events or groups indicated that there were often differences between the two. Not only did viewers' opinions about, for instance, women and men or about marital unhappiness differ on certain items with respect to television and the real world, but television and real-world opinions exhibited different patterns of relationships with television viewing behaviours.

It is very important when considering the influence of television viewing to place the television experience in the broader context of social experiences generally. Patterns of television viewing and interpretations of and reactions to television content are all influenced, for example, by family and peer groups to which individuals belong. One study has indicated that young viewers' peer groups can have a particularly significant delimiting effect on the relationships between television viewing and various social beliefs.

Rothschild (1979) categorised eight- and ten-year-old children according to the peer groups to which they belonged. Some children belonged to what were termed 'cohesive' peer groups in which there was a great deal of mutual liking. Other children were found to belong to less cohesive groups, and others to no groups at all. Rothschild found that group cohesiveness may inhibit the cultivation effects of television. The more children were involved with their peers at school, as against being outsiders, the weaker were any relationships between television viewing and predicted television-biased responses for gender-related qualities, occupational aspirations and interpersonal mistrust. Gross and Morgan, members of the cultural indicators team, also found that the kind of relationship children had with their parents at home in the context of television watching (such as degree of parental control and of conflict between parents and children over viewing) had some influence on the strength of relationships between television viewing and social perceptions. High parental protectiveness, selective use of television and low conflict over what to watch were associated with weakened correlations between viewing and interpersonal mistrust beliefs (Gross and Morgan, 1982).

While the Gerbner group pay little or no attention to what viewers say they make of screen contents, atmosphere and reality, we do pay attention to these matters. As Buerkel–Rothfuss *et al.* (1982)

have shown, and as we have also reasoned and shown in matters of ethnic minority and sex-role concepts, how viewers perceive the screen contents is related to how they perceive reality and also ideals. It is not merely the 'objective' screen contents which, covertly, may exert an effect on perceptions of and feelings about the real world.

Validating the mainstream

Although different population sub-groups may hold divergent beliefs about the world around them, Gerbner and his co-workers have hypothesised that heavy viewing of television can lead to a convergence of social opinions towards a 'mainstream' point of view that is more consistent with the way things are depicted in the fictional world of television drama. On the other hand, some population sub-groups may already hold opinions that are consistent with the way things are shown on television. When the television world and real world 'resonate' in this way, the social perceptions in question are reinforced. The notions of mainstreaming and resonance are only hypotheses that have been applied in a post hoc fashion to account for certain population sub-group differences or convergences, in social beliefs. There is more than one reason, however, for calling the validity of these hypotheses into question.

If mutually consistent or 'resonating' television and real-life experiences function to produce strengthening of social perceptions, then women, blacks and the poor ought to be *most* affected by portrayals of television crime and violence since they are the sub-groups most at risk in the real world and the most victimized on television. Yet, as Hirsch (1980; 1981) points out, relationships between violence-related beliefs and television viewing are often weakest in these groups.

There does in fact appear to be a circularity to the mainstreaming hypothesis whereby it is argued, on the one hand, that television *produces* a convergence of beliefs among heavy viewers in different population sub-groups towards its own 'mainstream'. On the other hand, the television 'mainstream' is often defined as that point *towards* which the beliefs of divergent groups converge. An additional external validation of the television mainstream is needed in order to identify where that point of view actually lies.

The question then is whether this validity of the mainstream can best be achieved via traditional content analysis procedures in which event occurrences are catalogued in an objective fashion, or whether a subjective element is also required whereby viewers are invited to give opinions about programme materials. For example, with respect to perceptions of the occurrence of violence in society, it may be pertinent to derive 'television answers' from objective counts of violent incidents in television drama programmes. However, with respect to violence-related *feelings*, such as fear of crime or personal victimisation, it may be less meaningful to base television-biased responses on purely objective incident counts. Whilst people may be aware of the incidence of crime, either on television or in their own neighbourhood, it does not necessarily follow that they are also fearful. With beliefs such as those of interpersonal mistrust, it may be more appropriate to find out from viewers whether they perceive a lack of trust or trustworthiness among characters on television drama, or whether they perceive social anxiety or anomic reactions among individuals who populate the world of television.

Selective viewing and cultivation effects
One of the fundamental assumptions made by the Annenberg group is that television is used non-selectively. Viewing is done by the clock rather than by the programme. Furthermore, it is argued that, in comparison with the use of other mass media, television consumption tends to be non-selective. Neither of these notions about television usage is entirely true. It we deal with the second point first, there is growing evidence that television as a medium is used in a selective fashion these days. With the emergence of multiple-channel communities and video recorders, television viewing behaviour has become increasingly selective. Research done in Britain on the use of video recorders, for example, has illustrated that users tend to record certain types of programmes much more often than others, and tend to play back and watch what they have recorded more often at certain times and on certain days than others. Action adventure series, soap operas and comedy shows tend to be the ones most often recorded off-air and Sunday afternoon tends to be the most popular time for playing back programmes that have been recorded (Harlech Television, 1983). Possession of a video recorder means having the freedom and opportunity to reschedule programmes or even to determine one's own schedule for that day's or evening's viewing.

On the question of selective viewing by programme type and consequently selective cultivation effects associated with different kinds of content, ample evidence is now available that both phenomena occur. Hawkins and Pingree (1982) point out that different categories of programmes may present different patterns of events and characterisations. Yet, content analyses have tended to de-emphasise or ignore programme types. In a study with a Perth, Australia, sample, Hawkins and Pingree (1981) examined correlations between viewing of different programme types and social reality beliefs and found considerable variations in the nature of these relationships across different content types. By controlling for all other viewing, partial correlations indicated the relationship of each programme type independently with social beliefs. Hawkins and Pingree (1981) found that different types of fictional programming such as crime-adventure, situation comedies and cartoons were not equally related to social reality perceptions. Viewing of crime-adventure shows, cartoons, game shows and children's shows was in each case related to perceptions of the amount of violence in society, while only viewing of crime-adventure shows was significantly related to levels of interpersonal mistrust. In Chapter 2, we reported findings from a British survey which showed that only viewing of action-adventure programmes was related significantly with beliefs in a just world (Gunter and Wober, 1983). Neither overall amount of television viewing nor viewing of any other programme types were related to any social reality perceptions.

There are many studies in the 'uses and gratifications' field which point to a widespread need for escape, and for removal from reality amongst viewers. Thus many viewers for much of their time take television knowingly as unreal. Particularly in the realm of action adventure and series dramas (not to be confused with soap opera) events portrayed with exaggerated opulence, danger and depravity are pointedly out of the realm of the everyday. Viewers are not so naive (dare one say, as some researchers) as to take television as a plane window on reality, but acknowledge that its surface is curved like a lens and that it refracts and distorts reality. On the other hand, these are not their expectations of television news, which tries its hardest to display its wares as real and which repeated polls have shown is accorded a very high degree of credence.

Likewise, both soap opera and even situation comedy, for all the latter's particular kind of exaggeration, do set out to portray real life with its problems and pitfalls. These considerations suggest, as indeed much of our evidence confirms, that attention has to be paid to different programme types and genres when attempting to account for their significance in the eyes and the experience of the viewers.

An issue which we have not seen explicitly discussed, but which is certainly implicit in much of Gerbner's work, is that of 'false consciousness'. The notion of false consciousness goes against the grain of much that is fine and direct rather than devious in American ideology, which perhaps accounts for its unpopularity. Thus a view derived from Thomas Paine, Jefferson, de Tocqueville, Thoreau, and a long and sturdy pedigree of others sees the citizen as a competent, resilient, basically trustworthy and righteous creature who, with access to valid information about society, can and must be trusted to act as he or she sees fit in his or her own interest. The notion of false consciousness implies a quite different concept of the person. It holds that what people say about their thoughts and experience can be self- and other deluding and false. Thus if people say they are happy this is insufficient if people who think they know better show that such happiness is bought at the expense of penalties the witness does not notice or explicitly attribute. If women disclose (as has copiously been shown that they do, in Britain) that they appreciate television more than men do, the direct model accepts this as satisfactory and an answer to those who consider that the content is sexist or degrading to women. The concept of false consciousness holds that in the very act of disclosing their appreciation some women fail to realise how they have been duped: this seemingly satisfying viewing has been reinforcing a world view which is fundamentally not in their best interests.

In short, the false consciousness concept implicit in the Annenberg work holds that many people often do not know fully what is happening to them through television. It follows that it is for the expert to detect and display such harm making processes. What is more, it follows that expert advice should be socially harnessed through suitable institutions to control and ameliorate such a potent medium. European philosophies are either already less direct and more cynical than the American, and explicitly acknowledge the operation of false consciousness, or at least implicitly act as if they do. Thus European broadcasting is in various ways in different countries brought under a control that tries to be social rather than political in emphasis. Its critics accuse it of erring in the latter direction partly as an outcome of its efforts in the former; but usually they do not advocate less central control in the American way. Rather, they wish for more control but in a fashion of their particular choosing. In practice, the controls usually work to promote variety of programme type availability in schedules, to avoid political partiality in information programming and to minimise offensiveness of an aesthetic or cultural kind.

Two further links between Gerbner's and other theories have been pointed out. One sees the resemblance between 'resonance' and agenda-setting, and adds something that others have hardly explicitly described. This is agenda-cutting, the reverse process whereby problems or issues have attention directed away from them by receiving little or no media coverage. This is related to the 'symbolic annihilation' reportedly detected by some feminists. Another process complementary to resonance is known as 'media dependency theory'. This, as our examples about Northern Ireland and from Israel suggest, point out that when viewers have no independent knowledge of some matter then they do depend on mass media such as television for their information, more than do viewers who had direct experience of the issue. So if television exaggerates or underplays an issue the non-involved viewers can only develop their impressions and knowledge on the basis of the information given to them by TV and other media.

In the realm of foreign policy and events home viewers have no ready source of corroboration. Thus, while many believe that Ethiopia is especially hit by famine, fewer may have realised that drought has blighted the whole Sahelian belt, but that nations such as Mali are simply not on the main agenda. Likewise, if politicians and television repeat that Saudi Arabia is in some sense a 'moderate' country because its rulers oppose terrorism, then viewers may come to see it as an ideologically flexible nation in spite of it being a rigorous guardian and defender of the ideals of Islam.

Protecting children
On some matters many adults do lack independent corroboration of televised messages, leaving them in an 'unresonant' or 'muffled' and vulnerable position. Children are in a similar position over a much wider array of topics. The research heading of 'socialisation' is not always seen as a particularly important version of the 'cultivation effects' that have been explored amongst adults, but we make this connection and underline it. Hedinsson's research from Sweden is a particularly important example in this regard, as also is much of the American work in the realm of sex role identification. In a study contrasting the provision of viewing for children in Japan, England and Sweden, with what occurs in the United States, the American Ed Palmer (1983) considers that 'these three industrialised countries excel the US in important respects in the quality of their children's televisions offerings'.

Without regarding the methods of regulation practised in Europe as perfect, and being aware of the economic pressures that would make them more like the American model, we observe that children cannot fit that American model of the adult viewer for whom accountability rests in his or her own hands. Children are more in the position of the adult whose competence does not extend to a full understanding of the processes entailed in viewing television. The way in which society handles the screen fare available for its children is therefore a priority for research. In a similar way, and we have tried to set an example in this respect, the use of a personality discriminator such as the locus of control scale which indicates which people are more and which are less effective as critically aware arbiters of their own fates, helps to point to where unseen effects may impinge on unsuspecting viewers.

The merit of the Annenberg approach is that it has sought to integrate detailed analysis of content with an exploration of effects contingent on the meanings viewers absorb from the screen. These two major fields of enquiry that Gerbner has brought together constitute an important contribution that gives his work a scope greater than the piecemeal results of most other researchers. Our contribution in turn is to have said that this is not enough; we ask for, provide in some modest extent and point the way to more.

References

Adoni, H., Cohen A.A. and Mane, S. (1984), 'Social reality and television news, perceptual dimensions of social conflicts in selected life areas', *Journal of Broadcasting*, **23**, 33–49.

Airey, C. (1984), 'Social and moral values', in R. Jowell and C. Airey (eds), *British Social Attitudes: The 1984 Report*, Aldershot: Gower.

Allen, R.L. and Bielby, W.T. (1979), 'Blacks, attitudes and behaviours towards television', *Communication Research*, **6**, 437–62.

Anwar, M. (1983), *Ethnic Minority Broadcasting*, London: Commission for Racial Equality.

Anwar, M. and Shang, A. (1982), *Television in a Multi-racial Society*, London: Commission for Racial Equality.

Argyle, M., Clarke, D. and Collett, P. (1984), *The Social Psychology of Long-term Relationships*, Fourth Annual Report to ESRC, Department of Experimental Psychology, Oxford University, Oxford.

Argyle, M. and Henderson, M. (1985), *The Anatomy of Relationships*, London: Heinemann.

Aronoff, C. (1974), 'Old age in prime-time', *Journal of Communication*, **24**, 86–7.

Atkin, C. and Miller, M.M. (1975), *Experimental Effects of Television Advertising on Children*, Paper presented at the International Communication Association convention, Chicago, April.

Atkin, C., Greenberg, B. and McDermott, S. (1977) *Race and Social Role of Learning from Television*, Paper presented at ACT Research Workshop, Television Role Models and Young Adolescents, Harvard Graduate School of Education, November.

Atkin, C.K., Greenberg, B.S., and McDermott, S. (1978), *Television and Racial Socialisation*, Paper presented at meeting of the Association for Education in Journalism, Seattle.

Atkin, C., Hocking, J. and Block, M. (1984) 'Teenage drinking: Does advertising make a difference?', *Journal of Communication*, **34**, 157–67.

Balon, R.E. (1978), 'The impact of *Roots* on a racially heterogeneous southern community: An exploratory study', *Journal of Broadcasting*, **22**, 299–307.

Baptista–Fernandez, P. and Greenberg, B.S. (1980) 'The context, characteristics, and communication behaviours of blacks on television', in B.S. Greenberg (ed.), *Life on Television: Content analysis of U.S. TV drama*, Norwood, N.J.: Ablex.

Baran, S.J., Chase, L.J. and Cartwright, J.A. (1979), 'Tele-drama as a facilitator of prosocial behaviour: 'The Waltons', *Journal of Broadcasting*, **23**, 277–84.

Barcus, F.E. (1971), *Saturday Children's Television: A report on TV programming and advertising on British commercial television*, Newtonville, Mass.: Action for Children's Television.

Barcus, F.E. (1983), *Images of Life on Children's Television: Sex roles, minorities and families*, New York: Praeger.

Barwise, P. and Ehrenberg, A.S. (1982), 'Glued to the box? Patterns of TV repeat-viewing', *Journal of Communication*, **32**, 22–9.

BBC (1973), *'Till Death Us Do Part' as Anti-prejudice Propaganda*, London: British Broadcasting Corporation, Audience Research Report.

BBC (1978), *Annual Review of BBC Audience Research Findings*, No. 5, London: British Broadcasting Corporation.

BBC (1979), *Annual Review of BBC Audience Research Findings*, No. 6, London: British Broadcasting Corporation.

Becker, L.B., McCombs, M.E. and McLeod, J.M. (1975) 'The development of political cognitions,' in S.H. Chaffee (ed.), *Political Communication: Issues and Strategies for Research*, London: Sage, pp. 21–64.

Becker, L., and Whitney, D.C. (1980), 'Effects of media dependencies', *Communication Research*, **7**, 95–120.

Behr, R.C. and Iyengar, S. (1982) 'Television news, real world cues and changes in the public agenda', Paper given at the 37th Annual Meeting of the American Association for Public Opinion Research, Hunt Valley, Maryland, 20–23, May.

Belson, W.A. (1978) *Television Violence and the Adolescent Boy*, Aldershot: Gower.

Bem, S. (1974), 'The measurement of psychological androgyny', *Journal of Consulting and Clinical Psychology*, **52**, 155–62.

Bem, S. (1975) 'Sex role adaptability. One consequence of psychological androgyny', *Journal of Personality and Social Psychology*, **31**, 634–43.

Bem, S. (1976), 'Probing the promise of androgyny', in A. Kaplan and J. Bean (eds.), *Beyond Sex-role Stereotypes: Readings towards a psychology of androgyny*, Boston: Little, Brown.

Berry, C. (1983), 'A duel effect of pictoral enrichment in learning from television news: Gunter's data revisited', *Journal of Educational Television*, **9**, 171–174.

Berry, C., and Clifford, B. (1987), *Learning from television news:*

Effects of presentation and knowledge on comprehension and memory, London: Independent Broadcasting Authority and North East London Polytechnic, Research Report.

Berry, C., Gunter, B., and Clifford, B. (1982) 'Research on television news', *Bulletin of the British Psychology Society*. **35**, 301–4.

Berry, G.L. (1980), 'Television and Afro-Americans: Past legacy and present proposals' in S.B. Withey and R.P. Abeles (eds), *Television and social behaviour: Beyond violence and children.* Hillsdale: N.J. Lawrence Erlbaum Associates.

Beuf, F.A. (1974), 'Doctor, lawyer, household judge', *Journal of Communication*, **24**, 110–18.

Blumler, J.G., (1983a), *Communicating to Voters: Television in the first European Parliamentary elections*, London: Sage.

Blumler, J.G. (1983b), 'Communication and turnout', in J.G. Blumler (ed.) *Communicating to Voters: Television in the first European Parliamentary elections*, London: Sage.

Blumler, J.G., Gurevitch M. and Ives, J. (1978), *The Challenge of Election Broadcasting*, Leeds: Leeds University Press.

Borke, H. (1967), 'The communication of intent. A systematic approach to the observation of family interaction', *Human Relations*, **20**, 13–23.

Bouwman, H. (1984), 'Cultivation analysis: The Dutch case', in G. Melischek, K.E. Rosengren and J. Stappers (eds.), *Cultural Indicators: An International Symposium*, Vienna: Austrian Academy of Sciences.

Bouwman, H. and Stappers, J. (1984), 'The Dutch Violence Profile: A replication of Gerbner's message system analysis', in G. Melischek, K.E. Rosengren and J. Stappers, (eds.), *Cultural Indicators: An International Symposium*, Vienna: Austrian Academy of Sciences.

Bower, R.T. (1973), *Television and the Public*, New York: Holt, Rinehart and Winston.

Boyanowsky, E. O. (1977), 'Film preferences under conditions of threat: whetting the appetite for violence, information or excitement?' *Communication Rsearch*, **4**, 33–45.

Boyanowsky, E.O., Newtson, D. and Walster, E. (1974), 'Film preferences following a murder, *Communication Research*, **1**, 32–43.

Breed, W., and DeFoe, J.R. (1981), 'The portrayal of the drinking process on prime-time television, *Journal of Communication*, **31**, 58–67.

Briggs, A. (1979), *Governing the BBC*, London: British Broadcasting Corporation.

Bronson, C.W. (1969), 'Sex differences in the development of fearfulness. A replication', *Psychonomic Science*, **17**, 367–8.

Bryant, J., Carveth, R. and Brown, D. (1981), 'Television viewing and anxiety: An experimental examination', *Journal of Communication*, **31**, 106–19.

Budge, I. and Farlie, O. (1983), 'Explaining and predicting the 1979 result', in M. Harrop and R. Worcester (eds), *Political Communication: The General Election Campaign of 1979*, London: Allen and Unwin.

Buerkel–Rothfuss, N.L. and Mayes, S. (1981), 'Soap opera viewing: The cultivation effect', *Journal of Communication*, **31**, 108–115.

Buerkel–Rothfuss, N.L., Greenberg, B., Atkin, C. and Nuendorf, K.A. (1982), 'Learning about the family from television', *Journal of Communication*, **32**, 191–201.

Busby, L.J. (1975), 'Sex role research on the mass media', *Journal of Communication*, **25**, 107–31.

Bush, R.F., Soloman, P.J. and Hair, J.F., (1977), 'There are more blacks on TV commercials', *Journal of Advertising Research*, **17**, 21–5.

Butler, M. and Paisley, W. (1980), *Women and the Mass Media*, New York: Human Sciences Press.

Cairns, E., Hunter, D. and Herring, L. (1980), 'Young children's awareness of violence in Northern Ireland: The influence of Northern Irish television in Scotland and Northern Ireland', *British Journal of Social and Clinical Psychology*, **19**, 3–6.

Cantor, M. (1979), 'Our days and nights on TV', *Journal of Communication*, **29**, 66–74.

Carey, J.W. (1965), 'Variations in Negro–White television preferences' *Journal of Broadcasting*, **10**, 199–212.

Cassata, M.B., Anderson, P.A. and Skill, T.D. (1980), 'The older adult in daytime serial drama', *Journal of Communication*, **30**, 48–9.

Cassata, M.B., Skill, T.D. and Boadu, S.O. (1979), 'In sickness and in health', *Journal of Communication*, **29**, 73–80.

Central Statistics Office (1980), *Social Trends 10*, London: HMSO.

Chaffee, S.H. (1977), 'Mass communication in political socialization,' in S. Renshon (ed.), *Handbook of political socializations*, New York: Free Press.

Chaffee, S.H., McLeod, J.M. and Atkin, C.K. (1971), 'Parental influences on adolescent media use,' *American Behavioural Scientist*, **14**, 323–40.

Chaffee, S.H., Ward, L.S. and Tipton, L.P. (1970), 'Mass communication and political socialization', *Journalism Quarterly*, **47**, 647–59.

Choate, R.B., (1976), *Testimony before the Federal Trade Commission in the Matter of a Trade Regulation Rule on Food Nutrition Advertising* Washington: Council on Children, Media and Merchandising.

Clark, C. (1969), 'Television and social control: some observations on the portrayal of ethnic minorities', *Television Quarterly*, **8**, 18–22.

Clark, C. (1972), 'Race, identification and television violence', in G.A. Comstock, E.A. Rubinstein, and J.P. Murray (eds.), *Television and Social Behaviour. Vol. 5, Further Explorations*, Washington, D.C.: US Government Printing Office.

Cobb, N.J., Stevens-Long, J. and Goldstein, S. (1982), 'The influence of televised models on toy preference in children, *Sex Roles*, **5**, 1075–80.

Coleman, J.S. (1961), *The Adolescent Society*, Glencoe: Free Press.

Comstock, G.A., Chaffee, S., Katzman, N., McCombs, M. and Roberts, D., (1978), *Television and Human Behaviour* New York: Columbia University Press.

Conway, M.M., Stevens, A.J. and Smith, R.G. (1975), 'The relations between media use and children's awareness', *Journalism Quarterly*, **8**, 240–7.

Cook, T.D., Kendzierski, D.A. and Thomas, S.V. (1983), 'The Implicit Assumptions of Television Research: An Analysis of the 1982 NIMH Report on Television and Behaviours', *Public Opinion Quarterly* **47**, 161–261.

Courtney, A.E. and Whipple, T.W. (1974), 'Women in TV commercials', *Journal of Communication*, **24**, 110–18.

Critcher, C. *et al.* (1977), 'Race in the provincial press: A case study of five West Midlands newspapers', in *Ethnicity and the Media*, Unesco Press.

Culley, T.D. and Bennett, R. (1976), 'Selling women, Selling blacks', *Journal of Communication*, **26**, 160–74.

Curran, J., and Seaton, J. (1981), *Power Without Responsibility. The Press and Broadcasting in Britain*. London: Fontana.

Dans, R.H. (1980), *Television and the Ageing Audience*, Los Angeles Andrus Gerontology Centre, University of Southern California.

Dates, H. (1980), 'Race, racial attitudes and adolescent perceptions of black television characters', *Journal of Broadcasting*, **24**, 549–60.

Davidson, E.S., Yasina, A. and Towers, A. (1979), 'The effects of television cartoons on sex role stereotyping in young girls', *Child Development*, **50**, 597–600.

Davies, M.M., Berry, C., and Clifford, B. (1985), 'Unkindest cuts? Some effects of picture editing on recall of television news information', *Journal of Educational Television*, **11**, 85–98.

Davis, R.H. and Kubey, R.W. (1982), 'Growing old on television and with television', in D. Pearl, L. Bouthilet and J. Lazar (eds.), *Television and Behaviour: Ten years of scientific progress and implications for the eighties*, Rockville, Maryland: National Institute of Mental Health.

De Fleur, M. (1964), 'Occupational roles as portrayed on television', *Public Opinion Quarterly*, **28**, 57–74.

'De Fleur, M. and De Fleur, L. (1967), 'The relative contribution of television as a learning source for children's occupational knowledge', *American Sociological Review*, 32, 777–89.

De Grazia, S. (1961), 'The uses of time', in R.E. Kleemeier (ed.), *Ageing and Leisure*, New York: Oxford University Press.

De Vito, A.J., Bogdowicz, J. and Reznikoff, M. (1982), 'Actual and intended health-related information seeking and health locus of control', *Journal of Personality Assessment*, 46, 63–9.

Dervin, B. (1980), 'Communication gaps and inequities: moving toward a reconceptualisation', in B. Dervin and M.J. Voigt (eds.), *Progress in Communication Sciences*, Vol. II, Norwood, N.J.: Ablex.

Dimas, C. (1970), *The Effects of Motion Pictures Portraying Black Models on the Self-concept of Black Elementary School Children*, Unpublished doctoral dissertation, Syracuse University, NY.

Dominick, J.R. (1972), 'Television and political socialisation: Are the media teaching today's child to be tomorrow's voter?', *Educational Broadcasting Review*, 6, 48–56.

Dominick, J. and Greenberg, B.S. (1970), 'Three seasons of blacks on television', *Journal of Advertising Research*, 10, 21–7.

Dominick, J. and Rauch, G. (1971), 'The image of women in network TV commercials', *Journal of Broadcasting*, 15, 41–7.

Donohue, T. (1975), 'Effects of commercials on black children,' *Journal of Advertising Research*, 15, 41–6.

Donohue, W.A. and Donohue, T.R. (1977), 'Black, white, gifted and emotionally disturbed children's perceptions of the reality in television programming', *Human Relations*, 30, 609–21.

Doob, A.N. and MacDonald, C.E. (1979), 'Television viewing and fear of victimization: Is the relationship causal?' *Journal of Personality and Social Psychology*, 37, 170–9.

Downing, M. (1974), 'Heroine of the daytime serial', *Journal of Communication*, 24, 130–9.

Drabman, R.S. and Thomas, M.H. (1974), 'Does media violence increase children's toleration of real life aggression?', *Development Psychology*, 10, 418–42.

Drabman, R.S., Robertson, S.J., Patterson, J.N., Jarvie, G.J., Hanover, D. and Cordun, G. (1981), 'Children's perception of media-portrayed sex roles', *Sex Roles*, 7.

Dunn, G. (1977), *The Box in the Corner*, London: Macmillan.

Durkin, K. (1983), *Sex Roles and Children's Television*, A report to the Independent Broadcasting Authority, Social Psychology Research Unit, University of Kent, Canterbury.

Eiser, J.R., Sutton, S.R. and Wober, J.M. (1978), 'Can television influence smoking? Further evidence', *British Journal of Addiction*, 73, 291–8.

Fallis, S.F., Fitzpatrick, M.A. and Friedsted, M.S. (1985), 'Spouses' discussion of television portrayals of close relationships', *Communication Research*, **12**, 59–81.

Farquhar, J., Maccoby, N., Wood, P., Alexander, J., Breitrode, H., Brown, B., Haskell, W., McAlister, A., Meyer, A., Nash, J. and Stern, M. (1977), 'Community education for cardiovascular health', *Lancet*, **1**, 1192–5.

Feshbach, S. (1961), 'The stimulating versus cathartic effects of a vicarious aggressive activity', *Journal of Abnormal and Social Psychology*, **63**, 381–5.

Feshbach, S. and Singer, R.D. (1971), *Television and Aggression: An experimental field study*, San Francisco: Jossey-Bass.

Fife, M.D. (1981), 'The minority in mass communication research', in H.A. Myrick and C. Keegan (eds.), *In Search of Diversity*, Washington: Corporation For Public Broadcasting.

Filep, R., Miller, G. and Gillette, P. (1971), *The Sesame Mother Project: Final report*, Institute for Educational Development, El Segundo, California.

Fisher, C.D. (1974), 'A typological approach to communication in relationships', in B. Rubin (ed.), *Communication Yearbook I*, New Brunswick, N.J.: Transaction Press.

Fitzpatrick, M.A. (1977), 'A typological approach to communication in relationships', in B.D. Rubin (ed.), *Communication Yearbook I*, New Brunswick, N.Y. Transition Books.

Fitzpatrick, M.A. and Best, P. (1979), 'Dyadic adjustment in relational types: Consensus, cohesion, affectional expression and satisfaction in enduring relationships', *Communication Monographs*, **46**, 167–78.

Fitzpatrick, M.A. and Indvick, J. (1982), 'The instrumental and expressive domains of marital communication', *Human Communication Research*, **8**, 195–213.

Flerx, V., Fidler, D. and Rogers, R. (1976), 'Sex role stereotypes: Developmental aspects and early intervention', *Child Development*, **47**, 998–1007.

Fletcher, A. (1969), 'Negro and white children's television preferences', *Journal of Broadcasting*, **13**, 359–66.

Fox, W. and Philliber, W. (1978), 'Television viewing and the perception of affluence', *Sociological Quarterly*, **19**, 103–12.

Francher, J.S. (1973), 'It's the Pepsi generation. Accelerated ageing and the television commercial', *International Journal of Ageing and Human Development*, **4**, 245–55.

Frank, R. and Greenberg, M. (1979), 'Zooming in on TV audiences', *Psychology Today*, **73**, 94–114.

Freeman, J. (1983), 'Environment and High IQ – a consideration of fluid and crystalised intelligence', *Personality and Individual Differences*, **4**, 307–13

Frueh, T. and McGhee, P.E. (1975), 'Traditional sex-role development and amount of time spent watching television', *Development Psychology*, **11**, 109.

Frieze I.H., Parson, J.E., Johnson, P.B., Ruble, D.N. and Zellman, G.L. (1978), *Women and Sex Roles: A Social Psychological Perspective*, New York: Norton.

Furnham, A., and Gunter, B. (1983), 'Political knowledge and awareness in adolescents', *Journal of Adolescence*, **6**, 373–85.

Gandy, O. (1981), 'Toward the production of minority audience characteristics', in H.A. Myrick and C. Keegan (eds.) *In Search of Diversity*, Washington: Corporation For Public Broadcasting.

Garlington, W.K. (1977), 'Drinking on television: A preliminary study with emphasis on method', *Journal of Studies on Alcohol*, **38**, 2199–205.

Gaziano, C. (1983), 'The knowledge gap: An analytical review of media effects', *Communication Research*, **10**, 447–86.

Gerbner, G. (1961), 'Regulation on mental illness content in motion pictures and television', *Gazette*, **6**, 365–85.

Gerbner, G. (1972), 'Violence in television drama: Trends and symbolic functions', in G.A. Comstock and E.A. Rubinstein (eds.), *Television and Social Behaviour. Vol. I, Media content and control*, Washington, D.C.: US Government Printing Office.

Gerbner, G. and Gross, L. (1976), 'Living with television: The violence profile', *Journal of Communication*, **26**, 173–99.

Gerbner, G., and Signorielli, N. (1979), *Women and Minorities in Television Drama: 1969–1978: Research report*, Annenberg School of Communications, Philadelphia, in collaboration with the Screen Actors Guild, AFL–CIO, October 29.

Gerbner, G. and Tannenbaum, P. (1962), 'Mass media censorship and the portrayal of mental illness: Some effects of industry-wide controls in motion pictures and television', in W. Schramm (ed.), *Studies of Innovation of Communication to the Public*, Stanford: Stanford University Press.

Gerbner, G., Gross, L., Eleey, M.F., Jackson-Beeck, M., Jeffries-Fox, S. and Signorielli, N. (1977), 'Television violence profile No. 8: The highlights, *Journal of Communication*, **27**, 171–80.

Gerbner, G., Gross, L., Jackson-Beeck, M., Jeffries-Fox, S. and Signorielli, N. (1978), 'Cultural indicators: Violence profile No. 8' *Journal of Communication*, **28**, 176–207.

Gerbner, G., Gross, L., Signorielli, N., Morgan, M. and Jackson-Beeck, M. (1979), 'The Demonstration of power: Violence profile No. 10', *Journal of Communication*, **29**, 177–96.

Gerbner, G., Gross, L., Morgan, M. and Signorielli, N. (1980a), 'The 'mainstreaming' of America; Violence profile No. 11', *Journal of Communication*, 30, 10–29.

Gerbner, G., Gross, L., Morgan, M. and Signorielli, N. (1980b), 'Some additional comments on cultivation analysis', *Public Opinion Quarterly*, 44, 408–10.

Gerbner, G., Gross, L., Signorielli, N. and Morgan, M. (1980), 'Ageing with television: images on television drama and conceptions of social reality', *Journal of Communication*, 30, 37–47.

Gerbner, G., Gross, L., Morgan, M. and Signorielli, N. (1981a), 'A curious journey into the scary old world of Paul Hirsch', *Communication Research*, 8, 39–72.

Gerbner, G., Gross, L., Morgan, M. and Signorielli, N. (1981b), 'Final reply to Hirsch', *Communication Research*, 8, 259–80.

Gerbner, G., Gross, L., Morgan, M. and Signorielli, N. (1982a), 'Charting the mainstream: Television's contribution to political orientations', *Journal of Communication*, 32, 100–127.

Gerbner, G., Morgan, M. and Signorielli, N. (1982b), 'Programming health portrayals: What viewers see, say and do', in D. Pearl, L. Bouthilet and J. Lazar (eds.), *Television and Behaviour: Ten years of scientific progress and implications for the eighties*, Rockville, Maryland: National Institute for Mental Health.

Gerson, W.M. (1966), 'Mass Media socialisation behaviour: Negro-white differences', *Social Forces*, 45, 40–50.

Glasgow University Media Group (1976), *Bad News*, London: Routledge and Kegan Paul.

Glennon, L.M. (1979), *Women and Dualism: A sociology of knowledge analysis*, New York: Longman.

Glennon, L.M., and Butsch, R. (1977), *The Devaluation of Working-class Lifestyle in Television Family Series, 1947–1977*, Paper presented at meeting of the Popular Culture Association, Baltimore.

Glennon, L.M. and Butsch, R. (1982), 'The family as portrayed on television, 1946–1978', in D. Pearl, L. Bouthilet and J. Lazar (eds.), *Television and Behaviour: Ten years of scientific progress and implications for the eighties*, Rockville, Maryland: National Institute of Mental Health.

Goldsen, R.K. (1975), 'Throwaway husbands, wives, lovers (soap opera relationships)', *Human Behaviour*, 4, 64–9.

Greenberg, B.S. (1980), *Life on Television*, Norwood, N.J.: Ablex.

Greenberg, B.S. and Atkin, C. (1978), *Learning about Minorities from Television*, Paper presented at the UCLA Centre for Afro-American Studies conference, Los Angeles.

Greenberg, B.S., Buerkel-Rothfuss, N., Neuendorf, K. and Atkin, C. (1980), 'Three seasons of television family role interactions, in B.S.

Greenberg, (ed.), *Life on Television*, Norwood, N.J.: Ablex Press.

Greenberg, B.S., Fernandez-Collado, C., Graef, D., Korzenny, F. and Atkin, C. (1980), 'Trends in the use of alcohol and other substances on television', in B.S. Greenberg (ed.), *Life on Television*, Norwood, N.J.: Ablex.

Greenberg, B.S. and Hanneman, G.J. (1970), 'Racial attitudes and the impact of TV blacks', *Educational Broadcasting Review*, **6**, 27–34.

Greenberg, B.S., Korzenny, F. and Atkin, C. (1979), 'The portrayal of the ageing trends on commercial television', *Research on Ageing*, **1**, 319–34.

Greenberg, B.S., Richards, M. and Henderson, L. (1980), 'Trends in sex role portrayals on television', in B.S. Greenberg (ed.) *Life on Television*, Norwood, N.J.: Ablex Press.

Gross, L. (1984), 'The Cultivation of Intolerance: Television, Blacks and Gays', in Melischek, G., Rosengren, H.E. and Stappers, J. (eds) *Cultural Indicators. An International Symposium*, Vienna: Austrian Academy of Science.

Gross, L. and Jeffries-Fox, S. (1978), 'What do you want to be when you grow up, little girl?', in. G. Tuchman, A. Daniels, and J. Benet (eds.), *Hearth and Home: Images of women in the mass media*, New York: Oxford University Press

Gross, L. and Morgan, M. (1982) 'Television and Enculturation' in J.R. Dominick and J. Fletcher (eds), *Broadcasting Research Methods*, Boston: Allyn & Bacon.

Grusec, J.E. and Brinker, D.B. (1972), 'Reinforcement for imitation as a social learning determinant with implications for sex role development', *Journal of Personality and Social Psychology*, **21**, 149–58.

Gunter, B. (1984a), *TV Viewing and Perceptions of Men and Women on TV and in Real Life*, London: Independent Broadcasting Authority Research Paper, September.

Gunter, B. (1984b), *TV viewing and Perceptions of Marital Happiness*, London: Independent Broadcasting Authority Research Paper.

Gunter, B. (1984c), *News Awareness: A British survey*. London: Independent Broadcasting Authority Research Paper, August.

Gunter, B. (1985a), *Television Viewing and Perceptions of the Sexes*, London: Independent Broadcasting Authority Research Monograph.

Gunter, B. (1985b), *Dimensions of Television Violence*, Aldershot: Gower.

Gunter, B. and Wober, M. (1982), 'Television viewing and perceptions of women in TV and in real life', *Current Psychological Research*, **2**, 277–88.

Gunter, B. and Wober, M. (1983), 'Television viewing and public trust', *British Journal of Social Psychology*, 22, 174–6.

Gunter, B., Svennevig, M. and Wober, M. (1984), 'Viewers' experience of television coverage of the 1983 General Election', *Parliamentary Affairs*. 37, 271–82.

Hanneman, G. and McEwan, V. (1976), 'The use and abuse of drugs: An analysis of mass media content', in R. Ostman (ed.), *Communication Research and Drug Education*, Beverly Hills: Sage.

Harris, A. and Feinberg, J. (1977), 'Television and ageing: Is what you see what you get?', *Gerontologist*, 17, 464–8.

Hartmann, P. and Husband, C. (1974), *Racism and the Mass Media*, London: Davis-Poynter.

Hawkins, R. and Pingree, S. (1980), 'Some processes in the cultivation effect', *Communication Research*, 7, 193–226.

Hawkins, R. and Pingree, S. (1982), 'Television's influence on social reality', in D. Pearl, L. Bouthilet, and J. Lazar (eds.), *Television and Behaviour: Ten years of scientific progress and implications for the eighties*, Rockville, Maryland: Institute of Mental Health.

Head, K. (1954), 'Content analysis of television drama programmes', *Quarterly of Film, Radio and Television*, 9, 175–94.

Hedinsson, E. (1981), *TV, Family and Society: The social origins and effects of adolescents' TV use*, Stockholm: Almquist and Wiksell International.

Hennessee, J. and Nicholson, J. (1972), 'NOW says: TV commercials insult women', *New York Times Magazine*, 28, May, 13, 48–51.

Himmelweit, H.T. and Bell, N. (1980), 'Television as a sphere of influence on the child's learning about sexuality', in E.J. Roberts (ed.), *Childhood Sexual Learning: The unwritten curriculum*, Cambridge Mass.: Ballinger.

Himmelweit, H.T. and Swift, B. (1976), 'Continuities and discontinuities in media usage and taste: A longitudinal study', *Journal of Social Issues*, 32, 133–56.

Hines, M., Greenberg, B.S. and Buerkel, N. (1979), *An Analysis of Family Structures and Interactions in Commercial Television. Project CASTLE* (Report No. 6), Department of Communication, Michigan State University, East Lansing.

Hinton, J., Seggar, J., Northcott, H. and Fowles, B. (1973), 'Tokenism and improving imagery of blacks in TV drama and comedy', *Journal of Broadcasting*, 18, 423–32.

Hirsch, P. (1980), 'The "scary" world of the non-viewer and other anomalies: A reanalysis of Gerbner *et al*'s finding on cultivation analysis: Part I', *Communication Research*, 7, 403–56.

Hirsch, P. (1981a), 'On not learning from one's own mistakes: A reanalysis of Gerbner *et al*'s findings on cultivation analysis: Part II', *Communication Research*, **8**, 3–37.

Hirsch, P. (1981b), 'Distinguishing good speculation from bad theory: Rejoinder to Gerbner *et al.*', *Communication Research*, **8**, 73–96.

Hobson, D. (1982), *'Crossroads' – The drama of a soap opera*, London: Methuen.

Horney, K. (1945), *Our Inner Conflicts*, New York: Norton.

Howard, J.A., Rothbart, G. and Sloan, L. (1978), 'The response to 'Roots'': A national survey', *Journal of Broadcasting*, **22**, 229–88.

Hughes, M. (1980), 'The fruits of cultivation analysis: A re-examination of the effects of television in fear of victimization, alienation and approval of violence', *Public Opinion Quarterly*, **44**, 287–302.

Hur, K. (1978), 'Impact of "Roots" on black and white teenagers', *Journal of Broadcasting*, **22**, 289–98.

Hur, K. (1981), 'Asian-American audience research and public broadcasting programmes', in H.A. Myrick and C. Keegan (eds.), *In Search of Diversity*, Washington: Corporate Free Public Broadcasting.

IBA (1974), *Children and Television: A Survey of the role of TV in children's experience and of parents' attitude towards TV for their children*, London: Independent Broadcasting Authority Research Report, July.

IBA (1979a), *Children's Viewing of Television*. London: Independent Broadcasting Authority Research Department Weekly Summary, 2 March.

IBA (1979b), *Channels and Children's Appreciation*, London: Independent Broadcasting Authority Research Department Weekly Summary, 2 November.

Jennings, J., Geis, F.L. and Brown, V. (1980, 'Influence of television commercials on women's self-confidence and independent judgement', *Journal of personality and Social psychology*, **39**, 203–10.

Johnson, E. (1984), 'Credibility of black and white newscasters to a black audience', *Journal of Broadcasting*, **28**, 315–64.

Johnson, J. and Ettema, J.S. (1982), *Positive Images*, Beverly Hills: Sage.

Katzman, N. (1972), 'Television soap operas. What's been going on anyway?', *Public Opinion Quarterly*, **36**, 200–12.

Kaufman, L. (1980), 'Prime-time nutrition', *Journal of Communication*, **30**, 37–46.

Kelly, M. and Siune, K. (1983), 'Television campaign structures', in J. Blumler (ed.), *Communicating to Voters*, London: Sage.

Kimball, M.M. (1977), *Television and Children's Sex Role Attitudes*,

Paper presented at the Canadian Psychological Association convention, Vancouver, June.

King, J. (1982), 'The patient's dilemma', *New Society*, March, 388–9.

Klapper, J. (1960), *The Effects of Mass Communication*, New York: Free Press.

Kline, F.G., Miller, P.V., and Morrison, A.J. (1974), 'Adolescents and family planning information: An exploration of audience needs and media effects', in J.G. Blumler and E. Katz (eds) *The uses of mass communications: current perspectives in gratification research*, Beverley Hills, CA: Sage.

Knill, B.J., Pesch, M., Pursey, G., Gilpin, P. and Perloff, R.M. (1981), 'Still typecast after all these years: Sex role portrayals in television advertising', *International Journal of Women's Studies*, 4, 497–506.

Kohlberg, L.A. (1966), 'A cognitive-developmental analysis of children's sex-role concepts and attitudes, in E. Maccoby (ed.), *The Development of Sex Differences*. Stanford: Stanford University Press.

Korzenny, F. and Neuendorf, K. (1980), 'Television viewing and self-concept of the elderly', *Journal of Communication*, 30, 71–80.

Krattenmaker, T.G. and Powe, L.A. (1978), 'Televised violence: First amendment principles and social science theory', *Virginia Law Review*, 64, 1123–74.

Kubey, R.W. (1980), 'Television and ageing: Past, present, future', *Gerontologist*, 20, 16–35.

Kuhn, T. (1960) *The Structure of Scientific Knowledge*. Chicago: University of Chicago Press.

Larsen, S.F. (1981), *Knowledge updating: Three papers on news memory, background knowledge and text processing*. (Psychological Reports, 6(4). Aarhus: University of Aarhus, Institute of Psychology.

Larson, R. and Kubey, R (1983), 'Television and music: Contrasting media in adolescent life', *Youth and Society*, 15, 13–31.

Lau, R.R. (1982), 'Origins of health locus of control beliefs', *Journal of Personality and Social Psychology*, 42, 322–34.

Leckenby, J. and Surlin, S. (1976), 'Incidental social learning and viewer race: All in the family and Sanford and Son', *Journal of Broadcasting*, 20, 481–94.

Lee, D (1979), 'The media habits of Korean-Americans in the Los Angeles area', Unpublished MA thesis, California State University at Northridge.

Lefkowitz, M.M., Eron, L.D., Walder, L.O. and Huesmann, L.R. (1972), 'Television violence and child aggression: A follow-up study', in G. Comstock and E. Rubinstein (eds.), *Television and*

Social Behaviour. Vol. 3, Television and adolescent aggressiveness, Washington, D.C.: US Government Printing Office.

Lemon, J. (1977), 'Women and blacks on prime-time television', *Journal of Communication,* **27**, 70–4.

Lemon, R. (1968), 'Black is the colour of TV's newest stars', *Saturday Evening Post,* 30 November, 42–4, 82–4.

Levinson, R. (1975), 'From Olive Oyl and Sweet Polly Purebread: Sex role stereotypes and televised cartoons', *Journal of Popular Culture,* **9**, 561–72.

Leyens, J.P., Camino, L., Parke, R.D. and Berkowitz, L. (1975), 'Effects of movie violence on aggression in a field setting as a function of group dominance and cohesion', *Journal of Personality and Social Psychology,* **32**, 346–60.

Liebert, R.M. and Baron, R.A. (1972), 'Some immediate effects of televised violence on children's behaviour', *Developmental psychology,* **6**, 469–75.

Liebmann-Smith, J. and Rosen, S.C. (1978) 'The presentation of illness on television', in C. Winnick (ed.), *Deviance and Mass Media,* Beverly Hills: Sage.

Livingstone, S. and Green, G. (1986), 'Television advertisement and the portrayal of gender', *British Journal of Social Psychology,* **25**, 149–54.

Long, M. and Simon, R. (1974), 'The roles and statuses of women and children on family TV programmes', *Journalism Quarterly,* **51**, 107–10.

McAlister, A. (1976) *Television as a medium for delivering behavior therapy. A pilot study of a televised smoking cessation program.* Paper presented at the Association for the Advancement of Behavior Therapy, 10th Annual Convention, New York.

McArthur, L.Z. and Eisen, S. (1976), 'Achievements of male and female storybook characters as determinants of achievement behaviour in boys and girls', *Journal of Personality and Social Psychology,* **33**, 467–73.

McArthur, L.Z. and Resko, B.G. (1975), 'The portrayal of men and women in American television commercials', *Journal of Social Psychology,* **97**, 209–20.

McCombs, M.E. (1968), 'Negro use of television and newspapers for political information, 1952–1964', *Journal of Broadcasting,* **12**, 261–6.

McEwan, W. and Hanneman, G. (1974), 'The depiction of drug use in television programming', *Journal of Drug Education,* **4**, 281–93.

McLaughlin, J. (1975), 'The doctor shows', *Journal of Communication,* **25**, 182–4.

McNeil, J. (1975), 'Feminism, femininity and the television shows: A content analysis', *Journal of Broadcasting*, **19**, 259–69.

McWhirter, L., Young, V. and Majury, J. (1983), 'Belfast children's awareness of violent death', *British Journal of Social Psychology*, **22**, 81–92.

Maccoby, E.E. and Jacklin, C.N. (1973), *The Psychology of Sex Differences*, Stanford, CA.: Stanford University Press.

Manes, A.I. and Melnyk, P. (1974), 'Televised models of female achievement', *Journal of Applied Social Psychology*, **4**, 365–74.

Manstead, A.R.S. and McCulloch, C. (1981), 'Sex role stereotyping in British television advertisements', *British Journal of Social Psychology*, **20**, 171–80.

Maracek, J., Piliavin, J.A., Fitzsimmons, E., Krogh, E.C., Leader, E. and Trudell, B. (1978), 'Women as TV experts: The voice of authority?', *Journal of Communication*, **28**, 159–68.

Mauro, F.J. and Feins, R.P. (1977), *Kids, Food, and Television: The compelling case for state action*, Report for the Office of Research and Analysis Program and Committee Staff, New York State Assembly, March.

Mayes, S.L. and Valentine, K.B. (1979), 'Sex role stereotyping in Saturday morning cartoon shows', *Journal of Broadcasting*, **23**, 41–50.

Mendelsohn, H. (1983), *Using the Mass Media for Crime Prevention*, Paper presented at the annual convention of the American Association for Public Opinion Research, Buck Hill Falls, May.

Merton, R.K. (1957), *Social Theory and Social Structure*, Glencoe, Ill.: Free Press.

Mertz, R.J. (1970), *Analysis of the Portrayal of Older Americans in Commercial Television Programming*. Paper presented at the International Communication Association, Minneapolis.

Milavsky, R.J., Pekowsky, B. and Stipp, H. (1975), 'TV drug advertising and proprietary and illicit drug use among teenage boys' *Public Opinion Quarterly*, **39**, 457–81.

Milavsky, J.R., Stipp, H., Kessler, R.C. and Rubens, W.S. (1982), *Television and Aggression: A panel study*, New York: Academic Press.

Miles, B. (1975), *Channelling Children; Sex stereotyping as prime-time TV*, P.N.J.: Women on Works and Images.

Milgram, S. and Shotland, L. (1974), *Television and Antisocial Behaviour; Field experiments*, New York and London: Academic Press.

Miller, M. and Reeves, B. (1976), 'Dramatic TV content and children's sex-role stereotypes', *Journal of Broadcasting*, **20**, 35–50.

Miller, P.V., Morrison, A.J. and Kline, F.G. (1974), *Approaches* to *Characterising Information Environments*, Paper presented at the meeting of the International Communication Association, New Orleans.

Mischel, W. (1970), 'A social learning view of sex differences in behaviour', in P.H. Mussen, (ed.), *Carmichael's Manual of Child Psychology*, New York: Wiley.

Moody, K. (1978), *Growing up on Television*, New York: Times Books.

Morgan, M. (1982), 'Television and adolescents sex role stereotypes; 'A longitudinal study', *Journal of Personality and Social Psychology*, **43**, 947–55.

Morgan, M. (1984), 'Symbolic interaction and real world fear', in G. Melischek, K.E. Rosengren and J. Stappers (eds.), *Cultural Indicators: An international symposium*, Vienna: Austrian Academy of Sciences.

Murphy, C. (1983), *Talking about Television: Opportunities for language development in young children*, London: Independent Broadcasting Authority, Fellowship Report.

Ndumbu, A. (1975), *'Love Thy Neighbour'*, London: Independent Broadcasting Authority, Special Report.

Neville, T. (1980), *Television Viewing and the Expression of Interpersonal Mistrust*, unpublished doctoral dissertation. Princeton University, Princeton, N.J.

Newcomb, A.F. and Collins, W.A. (1979), 'Children's comprehension of family role portrayals in televised dramas: Effects of socio-economic status, ethnicity and age', *Developmental Psychology*, **15**, 417–23.

Newcomb, H.M. and Hirsch, P. (1984), 'Television as a cultural forum: Implications for research', in W.D. Roland, Jr and B. Watkins (eds.), *Interpreting Television: Current Research Perspectives*, Beverly Hills: Sage.

Noble, G. (1975), *Children in Front of the Small Screen*, London: Constable.

Nolen, W.A. (1976), 'Examining the TV doctor shows', *McCalls*, January, **54**, 56–8.

Northcott, H.C. (1975), 'Too young, too old – age in the world of television', *Gerontologist*, **15**, 184–6.

Northcott, H.C., Seggar, J. and Hinton, J. (1975), 'Trends in TV portrayals of blacks and women', *Journalism Quarterly*, **52**, 741–4.

Nunally, J.C. Jr (1961), *Public Conceptions of Mental Health*, New York: Holt, Rinehart and Winston.

O'Donnell, W.J. and O'Donnell, K.J. (1978), 'Update: sex-role messages in TV commercials', *Journal of Communication*, **28**, 156–8.

O'Kelly, C. (1974), 'Sexism in children's television', *Journalism Quarterly*, **51**, 722–4.

O'Kelly, C.G. and Bloomquist, L.E. (1976), 'Women and blacks on TV', *Journal of Communication*, **26**, 179–92.

Ostman, R.E. and Scheibe, C.L. (1984), *Characters in American Network Television Commercials as indicators of Ageism and Sexism*, Paper presented at the meeting of the International Communication Association, San Francisco, May.

Parke, R.D., Berkowitz, L., Leyens, J.P., West, S.G. and Sebastian, R.J. (1977), 'Some effects of violent and non-violent movies on the behaviour of juvenile delinquents', in L. Berkowitz (ed.), *Advances in Experimental Social Psychology*, Vol. 10, New York: Academic Press.

Patterson, T. (1980), *The mass media election*, New York: Praeger.

Pearl, D. Bouthilet, L. and Lazar, J. (1982), *Television and behaviour: Ten years of scientific progress and implications for the eighties*, Rockville, Maryland: National Institute of Mental Health.

Peevers, B.H. (1979), 'Androgyny on the TV screen? An analysis of sex role portrayal,' *Sex Roles*, **5**, 797–809.

Peterson, M. (1973), 'The visibility and image of old people on television', *Journalism Quarterly*, **50**, 569–73.

Phelps, E. (1976), *Comparison of Programmes with and without Close Male–Female Relationships*, Unpublished paper based on analysis of Cultural Indicators Project. Annenberg School of Communications, University of Pennsylvania, Philadelphia, May.

Piepe, A., Charlton, P., Morey, J. White, G. and Yarrell, P. (1986), 'Smoke Opera? A content analysis of the presentation of smoking in TV soap' *Health Education Journal*, **45**, 199–203.

Piepe, A., Crouch, J. and Emerson, M. (1977), 'Violence and television', *New Society*, **41**, 536–8.

Pierce, C.M., Carew, J.V., Pierce-Gonzales, D. and Wills, D. (1977), 'An experiment in racism: TV commercials', *Education and Urban Society*, **10**, 61–87.

Pingree, S. (1978), 'The effects of nonsexist television commercials and perceptions of reality on children's attitudes and women', *Psychology of Women Quarterly*, **2**, 262–76.

Pingree, S. and Hawkins, R.P. (1981), 'US programs on Australian television: The cultivation effect', *Journal of Communication*, **33**, 97–105.

Pingree, S., Starrett, S. and Hawkins, R.P. (1979), *Soap Opera Viewers and Social Reality*, Unpublished manuscript, Women's Studies Program, University of Wisconsin-Madison.

Poindexter, P.M. and Stroman, C.A. (1981), 'Blacks and television:

A review of the research literature', *Journal of Broadcasting*, 25, 103–22.

Porter, P. (1977), *Television with Slow Learning Children*. London: Independent Broadcasting Authority, Fellowship Report.

Postman, N. (1982), *The Disappearance of Childhood*. London: W.H. Allen.

Potter, W.J. (1986), 'Perceived reality and the cultivation hypothesis', *Journal of Broadcasting and Electronic Media*. 30, 159–73.

Rainville, R.E., and McCormick, (1977), 'Extent of covert racial prejudice in pro-football announcers' speech', *Journalism Quarterly*, 54, 20–6.

Ranney, A. (1983), *Channels of Power*, New York: Basic Books.

Rawcliffe-King, A. and Dyer, N. (1983), 'The knowledge-gap reconsidered. Learning from "Ireland; A Television History by Robert Kee",' London: BBC Annual Review of Research.

Reeves, B. and Greenberg, B.S. (1976), 'Children's perceptions of television characters', *Human Communication Research*, 3, 113–27.

Reid, P.T. (1979), 'Racial stereotyping on television', *Journal of Applied Psychology*, 64, 465–71.

Roberts, E. (1982), 'Television and sexual learning in childhood', in D. Pearl, L. Bouthilet and J. Lazar (eds.), *Television and Behaviour; Ten years of scientific progress and implications for the eighties*, Rockville, Maryland: National Institute of Mental Health.

Roberts, L. (1975), 'The presentation of blacks in television network newscasts', *Journalism Quarterly*, 52, 50–5.

Robertson, T., Rossiter, J. and Gleason, T. (1979), 'Children's receptivity to proprietary medicine advertising', *Journal of Consumer Research*, 6, 247–55.

Robinson, M.J. (1981), 'Reflections on the nightly news, in R.P. Alder (ed.), *Understanding television. Essays on television as a social and cultural force*, New York: Praeger 313–64.

Rosenberg, M. (1957), *Occupation and Values*. Glencoe: Free Press.

Rosencrantz, P., Vogel, S., Bee, H., Broverman, I. and Broverman, D. (1968), 'Sex-role stereotypes and self-concepts in college students', *Journal of Consulting and Clinical Psychology*, 32, 287–95.

Rosow, I. (1974), 'The social context of the ageing self'. *Gerontologist*, 3, 82–7.

Rothschild, N. (1979), *Group as a Mediating Factor in the Cultivation Process among Young Children*, Unpublished master's thesis, Annenberg School of Communication, University of Pennsylvania, Philadelphia.

Rotter, J.B. (1954), *Social Learning and Clinical Psychology*, Englewood Cliffs, N.J.: Prentice-Hall.

Rotter, J.B. (1965), 'Generalized expectancies for internal versus external control of reinforcement', *Psychological Monographs*, **80**, (1, Whole No. **609**).

Rubin, Z. and Peplau, L.A. (1975), 'Who believes in a just world?',. *Journal of Social Issues*, **31**, 65–89.

Russo, F.D. (1971), 'A study of bias in TV coverage of the Vietnam war: 1969 and 1970' *Public Opinion Quarterly*, **35**, 539–43.

Ryback, D. and Connell, R.M. (1978), 'Differential racial patterns of school discipline during the broadcasting of "Roots",' *Psychological Reports*, **42**, 514.

Ryu, J. (1978), *Mass Media's Role in the Assimilation Process: A study of Korean immigrants in the Los Angeles area*, Paper presented at the International Communication Association convention, Chicago.

Salomon, G. (1979), *The Interaction of Media, Cognition and Learning*, San Francisco: Jossey-Bass.

Schechtman, S.A. (1978), 'Occupational portrayal of men and women on the most frequently mentioned television shows of pre-school children', *Resources of Education* (ERIC Document Reproduction Service N. Ed. 174–356).

Schneider, K.C. (1979), 'Sex roles in television commercials: New diagnosis for comparison', *Akron Business and Economic Review*, Fall, 20–4.

Schoenbach, K. (1983), 'What and how voters learned', in J.G. Blumler (ed.) *Communication to Voters*, London: Sage.

Schramm, W. (1969), 'Ageing and mass Communication', in M.W. Riley, J.W. Riley and M.E. Johnston (eds.), *Ageing and Society*, Vol. 2, *Ageing and the professions*, New York: Sage Foundation.

Schreiber, B.S. (1979), 'The effects of sex and age on the perceptions of TV characters. An inter-age comparison', *Journal of Broadcasting*, **23**, 81–93.

Schreiber, E.M. (1982), 'News structure and people's awareness of political events', *Gazette*, 139–49.

Schulz, W. (1983), 'Conceptions of Europe', in J.G. Blumler (ed.), *Communicating to Voters: Television in the First European Parliamentary Elections*, London: Sage.

Schwartz, L. (1974), 'The image of women in novels of Mme. de Souza', *The University of Michigan Papers in Women's Studies*, **I**, 142–8.

Segall, M.H. (1983), 'Social psychological research pointing towards localised development projects', in F. Blackler (ed.), *Social psychology and Developing Countries*, Chichester: Wiley, pp. 105–9.

Seggar, J. and Wheeler, P. (1973), 'World of work on TV: Ethnic and sex representation in TV drama', *Journal of Broadcasting*, **17**, 201–14.

Seggar, J.F., Hafen, J.K. and Hannemen-Gladden, H. (1981) 'Television's portrayal of minorities and women in drama and comedy drama: 1971–1980', *Journal of Broadcasting*, **25**, 277–88.

Sharits, N. and Lammers, B.H. (1983), 'Perceived attributes of models in prime-time and daytime television commercials; A person perception approach', *Journal of Marketing Research*, **20**, 64–73.

Sherman, J.A. (1971), *On the Psychology of Women*, Springfield, Ill.: Charles Thomas.

Shingi, P.M. and Moody, B. (1976), "The communication effects gap', *Communication Research*, **3**, 171–90.

Signorielli, N. (1981), 'Content analysis: More than just counting minorities', in H. Myrick and C. Keegan (eds.), *In Search of Diversity: Symposium on minority audiences and programming research*, Washington, D.C.: Corporation for Public Broadcasting.

Signorielli, N. (1984), 'The demography of the television world', in G. Melischek, K.E. Rosengren, and J. Stappers (eds.), *Cultural Indicators: An international symposium*, Vienna: Austrian Academy of Sciences.

Silverman, L., Sprafkin, J. and Rubinstein, E. (1978), *Sex on Television: A content analysis of the 1977–78 prime-time programs*, Stony Brook, New York: Brookdale International Institute, Inc.

Silverstein, A. and Silverstein, R. (1974), 'The portrayal of women in television advertising', *Federal Communications Bar Journal*, **27**, 71–98.'

Singer, D.G. and Singer, J.L. (1983), 'Learning how to be intelligent consumers of television', in M.J.A. Howe (ed.), *Learning from Television: Psychological and Educational Research*, London: Academic Press.

Smith, F.A., Truax, G., Zuehlke, D.A., Lowinger, P. and Nghiem, T.L. (1972), 'Health information during a week of television', *New England Journal of Medicine*, **286**, 518–20.

Smythe, D.W. (1954), 'Reality as presented by television', *Public Opinion Quarterly*, **18**, 143–56.

Spiegler, M.O. and Liebert, R.M., (1970), 'Some correlates of self-reported fear', *Psychological Reports*, **26**, 691–5.

Sprafkin, J. and Liebert, R.M. (1978), 'Sex-typing and children's television preferences' in G. Tucherman, A.K. Daniels and J. Benet (eds.) *Hearth and Home: Images of women in the mass media*, New York: Oxford University Press.

Sprafkin, J., Liebert, R.M. and Poulos, P. (1975), 'Effects of a prosocial televised example on children's helping', *Journal of Experimental Child Psychology*, **20**, 119–26.

Sprafkin, J. and Rubinstein, E. (1979), 'Children's television viewing habits and prosocial behaviour: A field-correlational study', *Journal of Broadcasting*, **23**, 265–76.

Srole, I. (1956), 'Social interpretation and certain corollaries', *American Sociological Review*, **21**, 709–16.

Stern, D.N. and Bender, E.P. (1974), 'An ethological study of children approaching a strange adult; Sex differences', in R.C. Friedman, R.M. Richards., R.L. Vandwick and L.D. Stern (eds), *Sex Differences in Children*, New York; Wiley.

Sternglanz, S. and Serbin, L. (1974), 'Sex role stereotyping on children's television programmes', *Developmental Psychology*, **10**, 710–15.

Stradling, R. (1977), *The Political Awareness of School Leavers*. London: Hansard Society.

Strickland, B.R. (1978), 'Internal–External expectancies and health-related behaviours; *Journal of Consulting and Clinical psychology*, **46**, 1192–211.

Suedfeld, P., Little, B.R., Rauch, A.D., Rawle, D.S. and Ballard, E.S. (1985), 'Television and adults: Thinking, personality and attitudes', in T.M. Williams (ed.), *The Impact of Television: A national experiment in three communities*. New York: Academic Press.

Surgeon General's Scientific Advisory Committee on Television and Social Behaviour (1972), *Television and Growing Up: The impact of televised violence. Report to the Surgeon General. United States Public Health Service*, Washington, D.C.: US Government Printing Office.

Surlin, S. (1978), '"Roots" research: A summary of findings'. *Journal of Broadcasting*, **22**, 309–20.

Tamborini, R., Zillmann, D. and Bryant, J. (1984), *Fear and Victimization: The short-lived effect of exposure to television on perception of crime and fear*, Paper presented at the annual convention of the International Communication Association, San Francisco, May.

Tan, A. (1979), 'TV beauty ads and role expectations of adolescent female viewers', *Journalism Quarterly*, **56**, 283–8.

Tan, A. and Tan, G. (1985), 'Television use and self-esteem of blacks', *Journal of Communication*, **29**, 129–35.

Tannenbaum, P.H. and Kostrich, L.J. (1983), *Turned-on TV, turned-off voters*, Beverly Hills, CA: Sage.

Tate, E.D. (1976), 'Viewer perceptions of selected television shows', The Royal Commission on Violence in the Communications Industry, Research Report, Ontario, Canada.

Tedesco, N. (1974), 'Patterns in prime-time', *Journal of Communication*, **24**, 119–24.

Thomas, S. and Callahan, B.P. (1982), 'Allocating happiness: TV females and social class', *Journal of Communication*, 32, 184–90.

Thoveron, G. (1983), 'How Europeans Received the Campaign: Similarities and Differences of National Response' in Blumler, J.G. (ed.), *Communicating To Voters. Television in the First European Parliamentary Elections.* London: Sage.

Tibbitts, C., Sauvy, A., Thomas, H., Cummings, E., Wedderbum, D., Rosemayr, L., Kockier, E., Townsend, P., Dumazedier, J. and Ripert, A. (1963), 'Old age', *International Social Science Journal*, 15, 339–48.

Tichenor, P.J., Donohue, G.A. and Olien, C.N. (1970), 'Mass media flow and differential growth in knowledge', *Public Opinion Quarterly*, 34, 159–70.

Troyna, B. (1981), *Public Awareness and Three Media: A study of reporting on race.* London: Commission for Racial Equality.

Tuchman, G. (1978), 'The symbolic annihilation of women by the mass media' in G. Tuchman, A. Daniels and J. Benet (eds.), *Hearth and Home: Images of women in the mass media*, New York: Oxford University Press.

Tuchman, G., Daniels, A. and Benet, J. (1978), *Hearth and Home: Images of women in the mass media*, New York: Oxford University Press.

Tuchman, S. and Coffin, T. (1971), 'The influence of election-night television broadcasts in a close election', *Public Opinion Quarterly*, 35, 315–26.

Tunstall, J. (1983), *The Media in Britain*, London: Constable.

Turner, M.E. (1974), 'Sex role attitudes and fear of success in relation to achievement behaviour in women', *Dissertation Abstracts International*, 35, (5–13), 2452–3.

Turow, J. (1974), 'Advising and ordering: Daytime prime-time', *Journal of Communication*, 24, 135–41.

Tyler, T.R. (1980), 'The impact of directly and indirectly experienced events; The origins of crime-related judgements and behaviours', *Journal of Personality and Social Psychology*, 39, 13–28.

Tyler, T.R. and Cook, F.L. (1984), 'The mass media and judgements of risk; Distinguishing impact on personal and societal level judgements', *Journal of Personality and Social Psychology*, 47, 693–708.

US Senate Select Committee on Nutrition and Human Needs (1977) *Dietary Goals for the United States*, Washington, D.C.: US Government Printing Office.

Valenzuela, N.A. (1981), 'Public Broadcasting: Developing a research agenda', in H.A. Myrick and C. Keegan (eds.), *In Search of Diversity*, Washington: Corporation for Public Broadcasting.

Van Wart, G. (1974), 'Evaluation of a Spanish/English educational television series with Region XIII', Final Report, Evaluation component, Education Service Centre, Region 13.

Volgy, J.J. and Schwartz, J.E. (1980), 'TV entertainment programming and socio-political attitudes', *Journalism Quarterly*, 57, 150–5.

Wakshlag, J., Vial, V. and Tamborini, R. (1983), 'Selectivity to fictional drama and apprehension about crime', *Human Communication Research*, 10, 227–42.

Wallston, B.S., Wallston, K.A., Kaplan, G.B. and Maides, S.A. (1976), 'Development and validation of health locus of control (HLC) scale', *Journal of Consulting and Clinical Psychology*, 44, 580–5

Ward, T. (1979), *The Media Monitoring Project: A study of the elderly on television*, London: Age Concern, Unpublished report.

Warner, C.I. (1979), 'The world of prime-time television doctors', Unpublished master's thesis, University of Pennsylvania, Philadelphia.

Weaver, J. and Wakshlag, J. (1986), 'Perceived vulnerability to crime, criminal victimisation experience, and television viewing', *Journal of Broadcasting and Electronic Media*, 30, 141–58.

Weigel, R., Loomins, J. and Soja, M. (1980), 'Race relations on prime-time television', *Journal of Personality and Social Psychology*, 39, 884–93.

White, M.A. and Sandberg, B. (1980) *The Television Prime-Time Diet*, Paper presented at the meeting of the American Psychological Association, Montreal, September.

Williams, F., La Rose, R. and Frost, F. (1981), *Children, Television and Sex Role Stereotyping*, New York: Praeger.

Williams, J.E., Benet, S.M. and Best, D.L. (1975), 'Awareness and expression of sex stereotyping in young children', *Developmental Psychology*, 6, 635–42.

Williams, T. (1982), *The Communication Revolution*, Beverly Hills, CA.: Sage.

Wilson, G.D. (1966), 'An electrodermal technique for the study of phobia', *New England Medical Journal*, 85, 696–8.

Wilson, G.D. (1967), 'Social desirability and sex differences in expressed fear', *Behaviour Research and Therapy*, 5, 136–51.

Wober, J.M. (1974), *Television coverage and the first 1974 General Election*. London: Independent Broadcasting Authority, Research Report, October.

Wober, J.M. (1978), 'Televised violence and paranoid perception: The view from Great Britain', *Public Opinion Quarterly*, 42, 315–21.

Wober, J.M. (1979a), *The May 1979 General Election: Viewers atti-*

tudes towards television coverage, London: Independent Broadcasting Authority, Special Report.

Wober, J.M. (1979b) *The Election of the European Parliament 1979*, London: Independent Broadcasting Authority, Research Paper.

Wober, J.M. (1979c), 'Public opinion and direct broadcasting of Parliament', *Political Quarterly*, 50, 316–25.

Wober, J.M. (1980a), *Television and Teenagers' Political Awareness*, London: Independent Broadcasting Authority, Special Report.

Wober, J.M. (1980b), *Teens and In-betweens*, London: Independent Broadcasting Authority, Research Summary.

Wober, J.M. (1980c), *Broadcasting and the Conflict in Northern Ireland*, London: Independent Broadcasting Authority, Special Report.

Wober, J.M. (1980d), *Television and Old People: Viewing TV and perceptions of old people in real life and on television*, London: Independent Broadcasting Authority, Special Report.

Wober, J.M. (1980e) *Attitudes Towards Advertisements On Television: Survey and Diary Evaluation*, London: Independent Broadcasting Authority, Special report.

Wober, J.M. (1981a), *Television And Women. Viewing patterns, and perceptions of ideal, actual and portrayed women's roles.* London: Independent Broadcasting Authority Research Report.

Wober, J.M. (1981b), 'British Attitudes Towards Europe: An Exploration of their Inner Structure'. *British Journal of Social Psychology*, 20, 181–8.

Wober, J.M. (1981c), *Teenagers' and Adult Viewers' Patterns of Viewing*, London: Independent Broadcasting Authority, Research Summary.

Wober, J.M. (1981d), *Situational Conflict in Comedy: Exploration of a research method, and some preliminary results on appealing or unappealing examples of conflict.* London: Independent Broadcasting Authority, Research Department Special Report.

Wober, J.M. (1982a), *The Falklands: Some systematic data on viewing behaviour and attitudes concerning television coverage of the conflict*, London: Independent Broadcasting Authority, Special Report.

Wober, J.M. (1982b), *The Falklands Conflict: Further analysis of viewers' behaviour and attitudes*, London: Independent Broadcasting Authority, Special Report.

Wober, J.M. (1982c), *Programme Type and Audience Size*, London: Independent Broadcasting Authority, Special Report.

Wober, J.M. (1982d), *Scenes from childhood*, London: Independent Broadcasting Authority, Research Summary.

Wober, J.M. (1983), *A Twisted Yarn. Some psychological aspects* of viewing soap operas. Paper given at the International Communication Association, Annual Convention, Dallas, May.

Wober, J.M. (1984a), *Television and The Ages of Man*, London: Independent Broadcasting Authority, Research Paper.

Wober, J.M. (1984b), *Sources of Sounds and Delight: Patterns of musical taste and radio and television use*, London: Independent Broadcasting Authority, Reference Paper.

Wober, J.M. (1985), *Television and Mental Ill-Health.* Viewers' Perception and Experience. London: Independent Broadcasting Authority, Research Department, Research paper, March.

Wober, M. and Dannheisser, P. (1977), 'Does televised violence provoke paranoid perception? Gerbner's theory explored', *Bulletin of the British Psychological Society*, **30**, 188–9.

Wober, J.M. and Fazal, S. (1984), *Citizens of Ethnic Minorities: Their prominence in real life and on television*, London: Independent Broadcasting Authority, Reference Paper.

Wober, J.M. and Gunter, B. (1982a), 'Television and personal threat: fact or artifact? A British survey', *British Journal of Social Psychology*, **21**, 43–51.

Wober, J.M. and Gunter, B. (1982b), 'Impressions of old people on TV and in real life', *British Journal of Social Psychology*, **21**, 335–6.

Wober, J.M. and Gunter, B. (1985), 'Television and Beliefs about Health Care and Medical Treatment', *Current Psychological Research and Reviews*, Winter, 291–304.

Wober, J.M. and Svennevig, M. (1980) *Party Political Broadcasts and their Use for the Viewing Public*, London: Independent Broadcasting Authority and British Broadcasting Corporation.

Yaffe, M. (1979), 'Pornography: An update review (1972–1977)', in B. Williams (ed.), *Report of the Commission on Obscenity and Film Censorship*, London: HMSO.

Zillmann, D. (1980), 'Anatomy of suspense', in P. Tannenbaum, (ed.), *Entertainment Functions of Television*, Hillsdale, N.J.: Lawrence Erlbaum Associates.

Zillman, D. and Wakshlag, J. (1984), 'Fear and victimization and appeal of crime data', in D Zillmann and J. Bryant (eds.), *Selective Exposure to Communication.* Hillsdale, N.J.: Lawrence Erlbaum Associates.

Zynda, T.H. (1984), 'Fantasy America. Television and the ideal of community', in Rowland, W.D. and Watkins, B. (eds.), *Interpreting Television: Current Research Perspectives*, Beverly Hills, Sage.

Subject index

action-adventure programmes 47,
49, 92, 219, 220, 229, 230
and authoritarian views 73
increased perceptions of
victimisation 47
action-drama 121–2
heavy viewers' perceptions of
women 124
under-representation of women
89, 90
women more independent 123
actuality programming 75
adolescents
contemporary music and politics
61
effect of violence viewing 1
and sex role portrayal 117–8
adulthood, and television 130–3
television and the aged 131–3
adults
effects of TV portrayals on
beliefs about marriage and the
family 214–16
perceptions of the sexes on TV
106
political socialisation among 65–
8, 86–7
affluence, perceptions of 11–13
affluent society, white, TV ideal
162
ageism 138–9, 226
agenda-cutting 81, 87, 231
agenda-setting 80–1, 85, 87, 225,
231
possible manipulation of public
opinion 80
aggression 45
imitative, among children 3
stimulated among young people
17
alcohol
attitudes towards merits of 181

consumption linked to exposure
to commercials 180
favourite prime-time drink
(American TV) 177–8
heavy and chronic drinkers 179
and mainstreaming 191–2
occurrence of consumption 178–
9
perceptions of portrayal on TV
181
variable usage 179
alienation 37
anomie 37, 40, 41, 42, 49
and education 41–2
anti-violence 29
anxiety
and action-adventure drama 46
fostering heavy viewing 46
and viewing study 47
apprehension, degree of (crime,
fear of victimisation 49–50
assimilation 171
attitudes, influence of programmes
not confirmed or denied 202–3
attitudes and perceptions viii
authoritarianism 55, 71–4, 170
and political attitudes 72–3

beliefs
determining viewing patterns 49
variation in 38
Bem's Sex Role Inventory 107

campaign exposure 83
campaign messages 80
career awareness, influence of TV
94
cartoons 28, 230
male-female interaction 103
causal analysis, rejected 37
childhood 204
a social product 126–7, 143–4

Author index

Yaffe, M. 18
Yasina, A. 115

Zillmann, D. 38, 46, 51
Zynda, T.H. 187